THE OUT SIDE

TRANS & NONBINARY COMICS

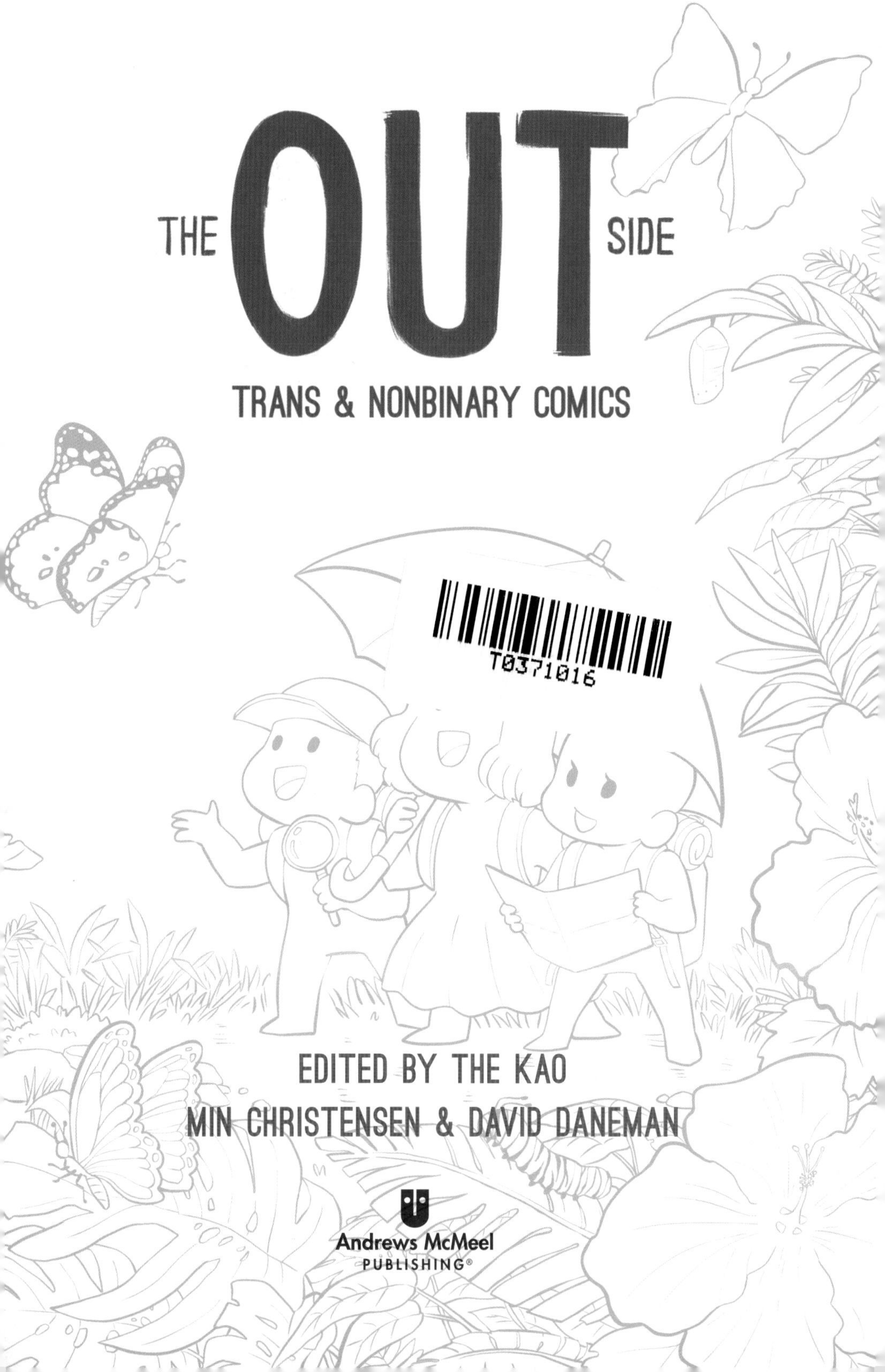

EDITED BY THE KAO

MIN CHRISTENSEN & DAVID DANEMAN

Andrews McMeel
PUBLISHING®

Edited by The Kao, Min Christensen, and David Daneman
Cover designed by The Kao and Min Christensen
Book designed by The Kao

Andrews McMeel Publishing
a division of Andrews McMeel Universal
1130 Walnut Street, Kansas City, Missouri 64106

www.andrewsmcmeel.com

24 25 26 27 28 IGO 10 9 8 7 6 5 4 3 2

ISBN: 978-1-5248-8012-5

Library of Congress Control Number: 2023932665

ATTENTION: SCHOOLS AND BUSINESSES
Andrews McMeel books are available at quantity discounts with bulk purchase for educational, business, or sales promotional use. For information, please e-mail the Andrews McMeel Publishing Special Sales Department: sales@amuniversal.com

CONTENTS

FOREWORD
BY JULIA KAYE

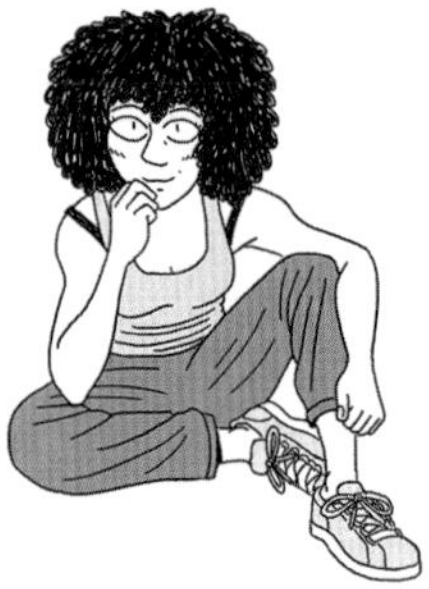

Back when I was growing up, positive trans representation in media simply didn't exist—there was a complete void in the culture. Any time media featured gender nonconformity it existed as something to either be laughed at, demonized, or often both. The messaging was clear: The discomfort I felt with the gender I was assigned at birth was something to be ashamed of, never vocalized or acted on. As a result, I grew up feeling entirely, impossibly alone. It wasn't until I was in my mid-20s that I learned about the existence of *actual* trans people, but even then, the lack of societal normalization of gender diversity held me back from finding self-acceptance for a few more years.

Even as recent as 2016, the year I came out as a trans woman, representation still felt scarce enough that I had to take to trawling internet forums in order to feel seen. I spent all my free time desperately sifting through years-old messages online for any glint of validation I could find. Everyone seemingly reaching out into the dark with the same burning questions: *Are my experiences valid? Valid enough to take those terrifying first steps toward embracing what I quietly know deep down to be true?* I found solace in those posts.

It was that sense of extreme isolation that drove me to create the comics that became my first memoir, *Super Late Bloomer*. It had felt imperative at the time to make them, not only to help me process my own experiences, but to create the type of accessible representation I had grown up without.

It's incredible how much progress there's already been since then.

This anthology is exactly the sort of book that I wish had existed when I was younger. Reading it feels like a warm embrace by a group of kindhearted friends who just want to let you know you're not alone. That it's okay to defy others' expectations of who you are and express yourself however you need or want to. And you know that they mean it because they live that truth every day.

It's incredible to see so many nuanced aspects of my own experiences in the stories to come—even when our relationships with gender differ greatly. I see myself in Min Christensen's reflection of feeling gender euphoria when being "misgendered" earlier in life. In managing to somehow hold on to the belief that you're cis despite struggling with dysphoria in Maddie Jacobus's comic. When Ashi touches on the horrors of not relating to your own reflection in the mirror. And on and on.

Each story is touchingly personal and unique—Jam Aden's narrative of finding comfort and happiness in embracing being a nonbinary trans man. Sage Coffey's exploration of the gender spectrum. TheNiftyFox's experiences with top surgery. They all have so much honesty and heart.

I'm so glad this book exists. It's a loud proclamation of our existence in the face of a culture that has for too long ignored our experiences. With each piece of media we create, we help to slowly shape and change society for the better. I hope you get as much out of it as I did.

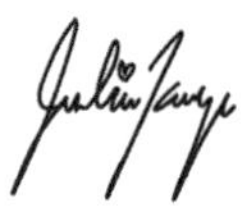

—Julia Kaye *(She/Her)*
Author of Super Late Bloomer *(2018)*
and My Life in Transition *(2021)*

INTRODUCTION
BY THE KAO

I've always been a huge fan of comic anthologies. They're truly a great way to discover multiple, talented artists all in the same place. As a member of the LGBT community, I am excited to see new trans-themed anthologies being made, but I couldn't help but feel that we needed more.

Personally, I'm a big fan of autobiographical stories of the authors' experiences, much like the memoirs of Julia Kaye that went on to receive critical acclaim. The reason is simple: Representation matters. It's one thing to relate to fictional characters, but something more powerful to see someone real going through struggles similar to your own. It gives you hope and comfort to know that change is possible and not just fantasy.

Therefore, in the pursuit of greater representation, I decided to organize this comics anthology. My goal was to feature a diverse group of proud trans and nonbinary artists and share their true stories of self-discovery and acceptance. My hope is that this collection will inspire anyone who may be struggling with their own identity and educate those who seek greater understanding.

Finally, I wish to give special thanks to my teammates David Daneman and Min Christensen for all of their hard work, to Julia Kaye for lending us her phenomenal voice, to the wonderful artists for sharing their lives with us, and of course, to you who personally made this book a reality. We couldn't have done it without you. Thank you so much!

Without further ado, please enjoy this journey to *The Out Side!*

—The Kao *(He/Him)*

SAM
(HE/HIM)

Sam is a comic artist from the New Jersey shore. He's best known as the creator of the webcomic *Man Time.* He's passionate about creating comics with LGBT characters— something he never saw growing up. When he's not at his desk scribbling away, you can find him out leading a trans-masc hiking club or laying around on the beach somewhere!

You can find him on Instagram:
@mantimecomic

OUTSIDER

WHEN YOU'RE TRANS, SOMETIMES IT'S EASY TO FEEL LIKE EVERYONE'S AGAINST YOU.

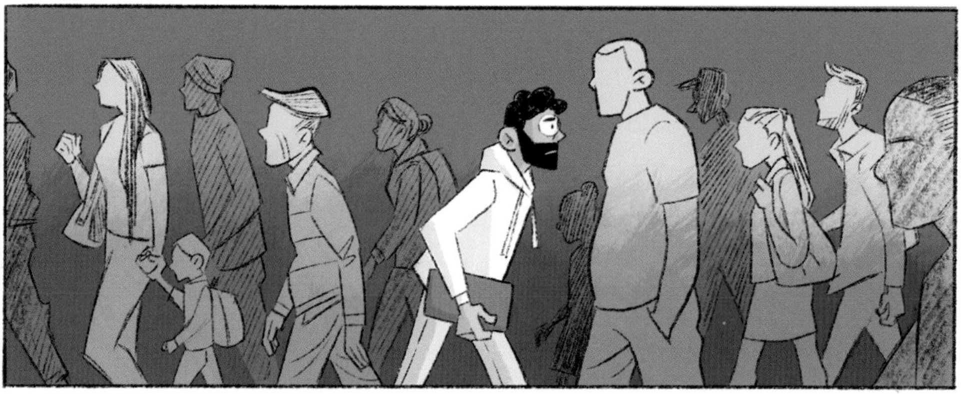

THAT CONVERSATIONS YOU HALF-OVERHEAR ARE ABOUT YOU.

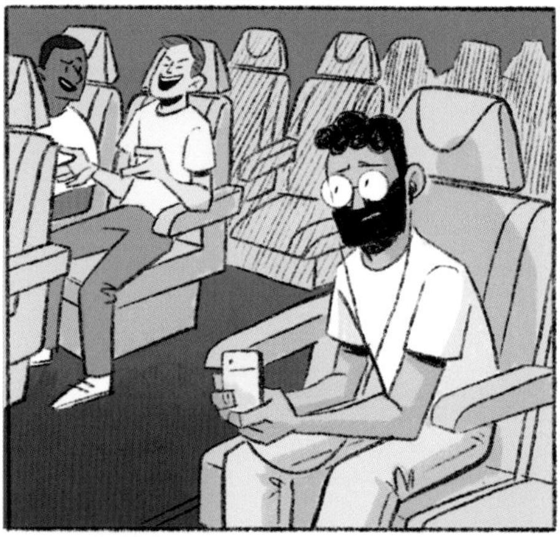

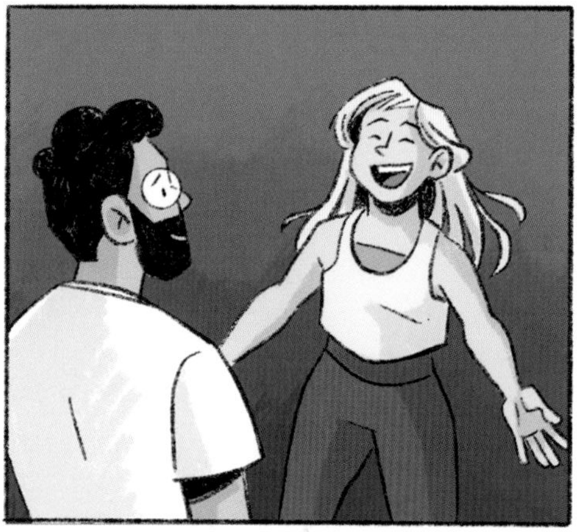

OR THAT PEOPLE ARE HIDING THEIR REAL THOUGHTS BEHIND FRIENDLY FACES.

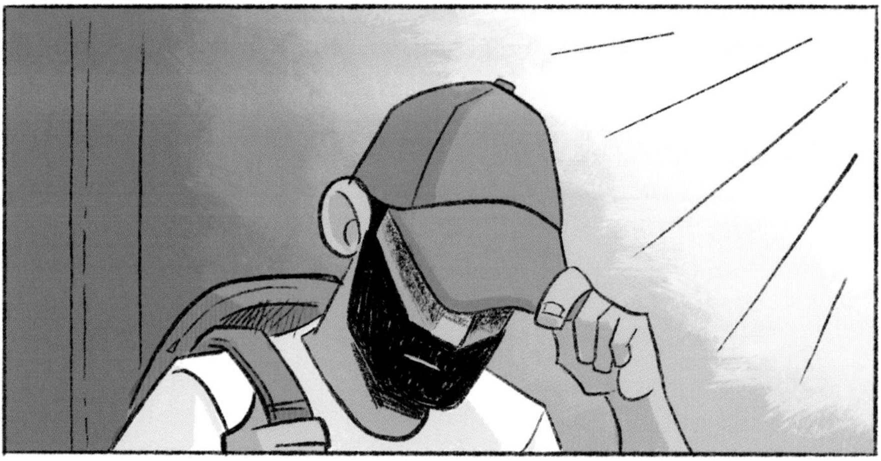

WHEN I FEEL LIKE THIS, THE BEST CURE IS TO GET OUTSIDE.

IT'S ONE OF THE BEST THINGS I CAN DO FOR MY MENTAL HEALTH.

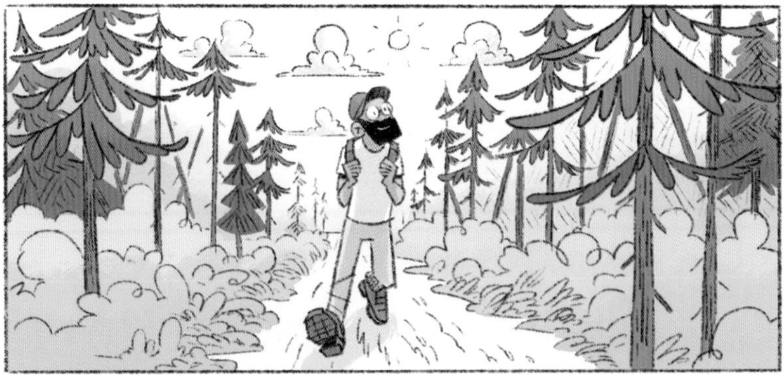

WHETHER IT'S A SMALL PARK,

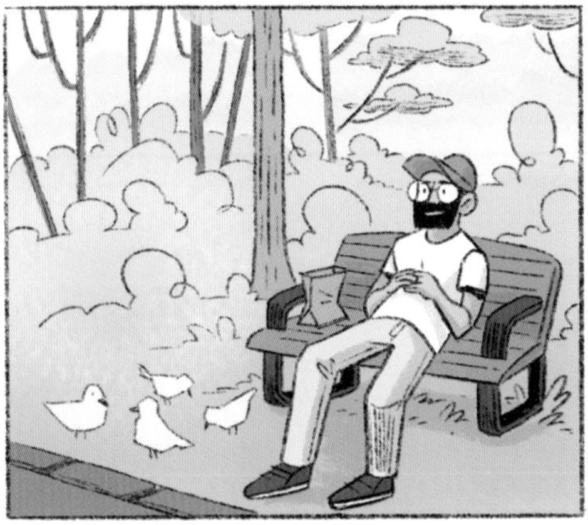

A DAY AT THE BEACH,

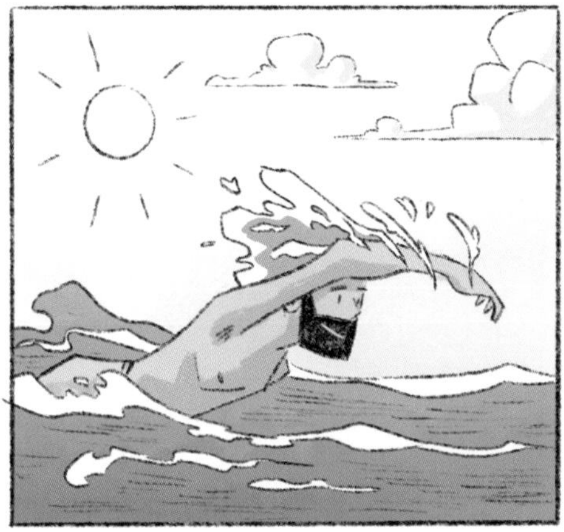

OR A BIG ADVENTURE...

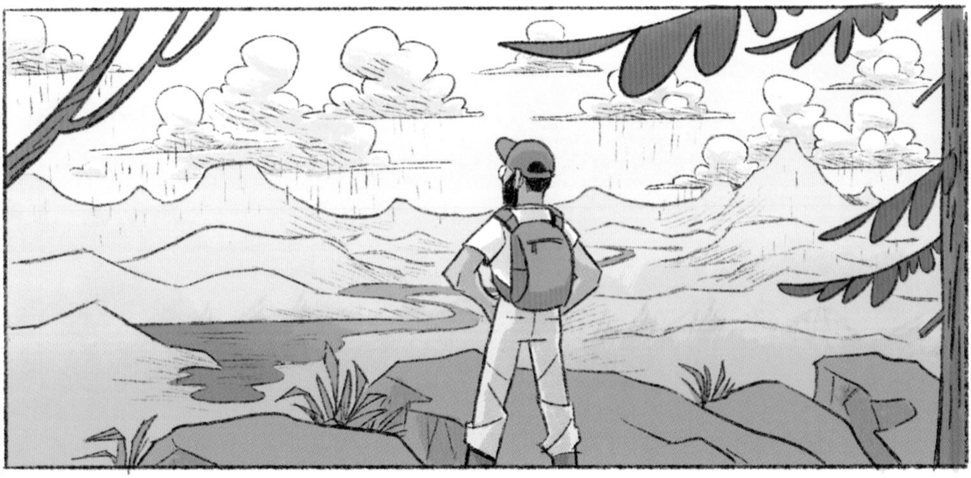

THERE'S A FEELING OF CALM I CAN ONLY GET OUT HERE.

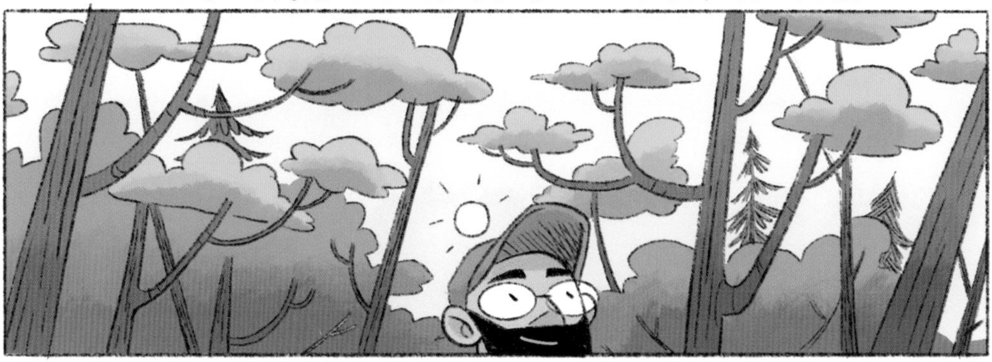

TREES DON'T CARE IF YOU'RE A GIRL OR A BOY.

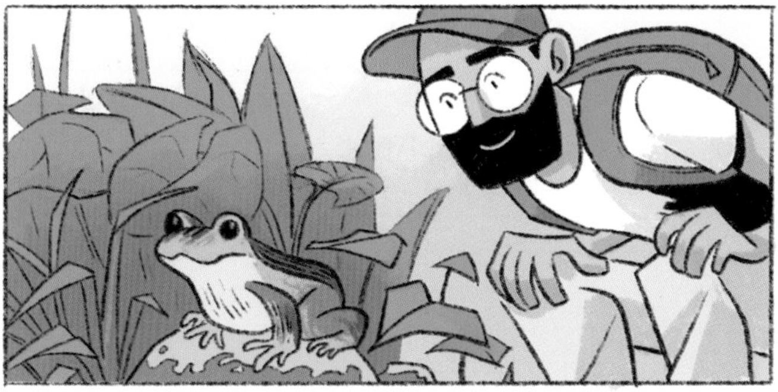

FROGS WON'T JUDGE YOUR APPEARANCE.

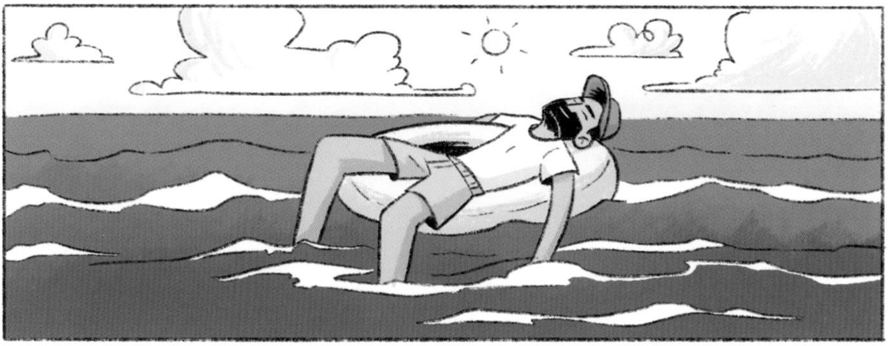

THE WATER DOESN'T WANT YOU TO CHANGE.

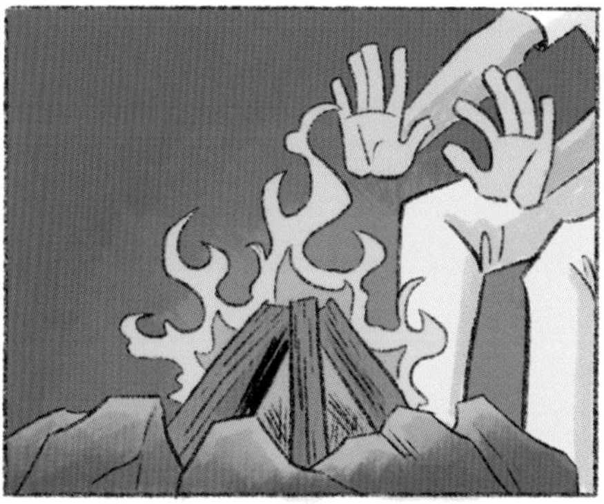

MY ANXIETY DIALS DOWN OUT HERE.

ALL I HAVE IS THE SOUND OF BIRDS CHATTERING...

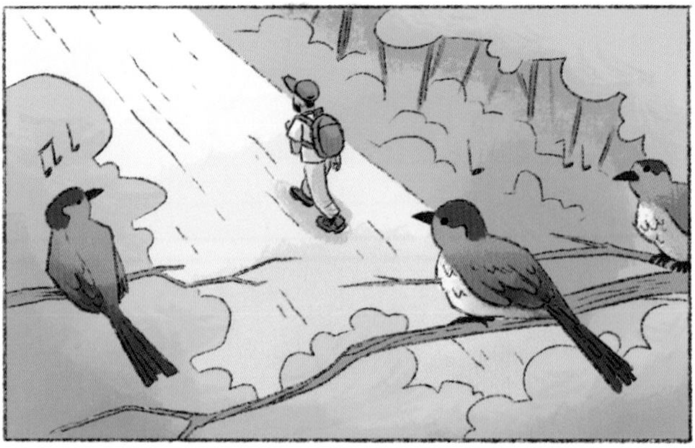

TREE FROGS CHIRPING...

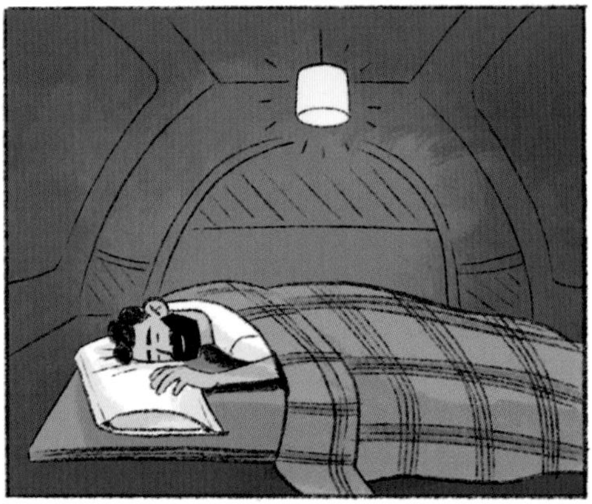

DEER RUSTLING...

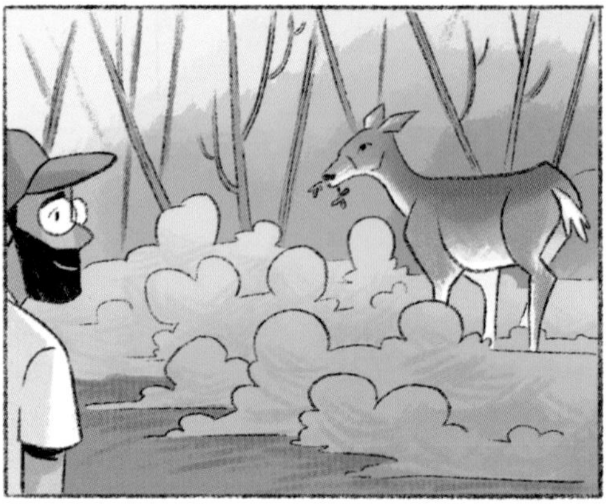

AND IN A WORLD THAT TRIES TO MAKE US FEEL UNNATURAL,

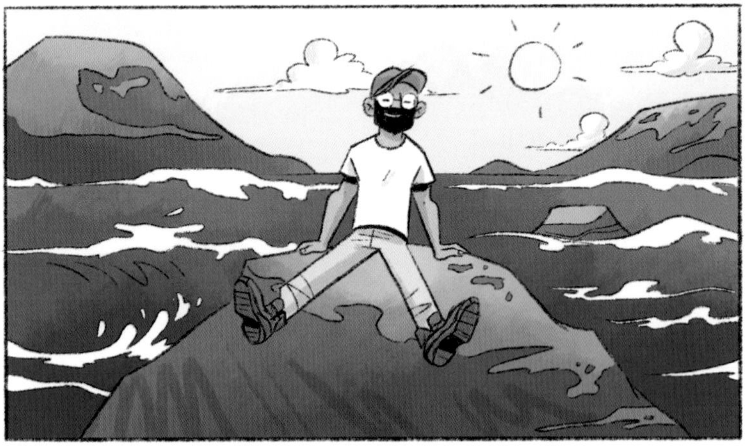

I FEEL LIKE JUST ANOTHER PART OF NATURE.

-SAM
@MANTIMECOMIC

WEY
(THEY/THEM)

Wey is an illustrator and comic artist currently based in Michigan. They hope that their stories are able to connect with people with themes of self-discovery, escapism, and a sense of nostalgia. Wey is a big fan of adventure stories and in their free time has spent too many hours on their Nintendo Switch.

You can find them online at:
sinameibo.com

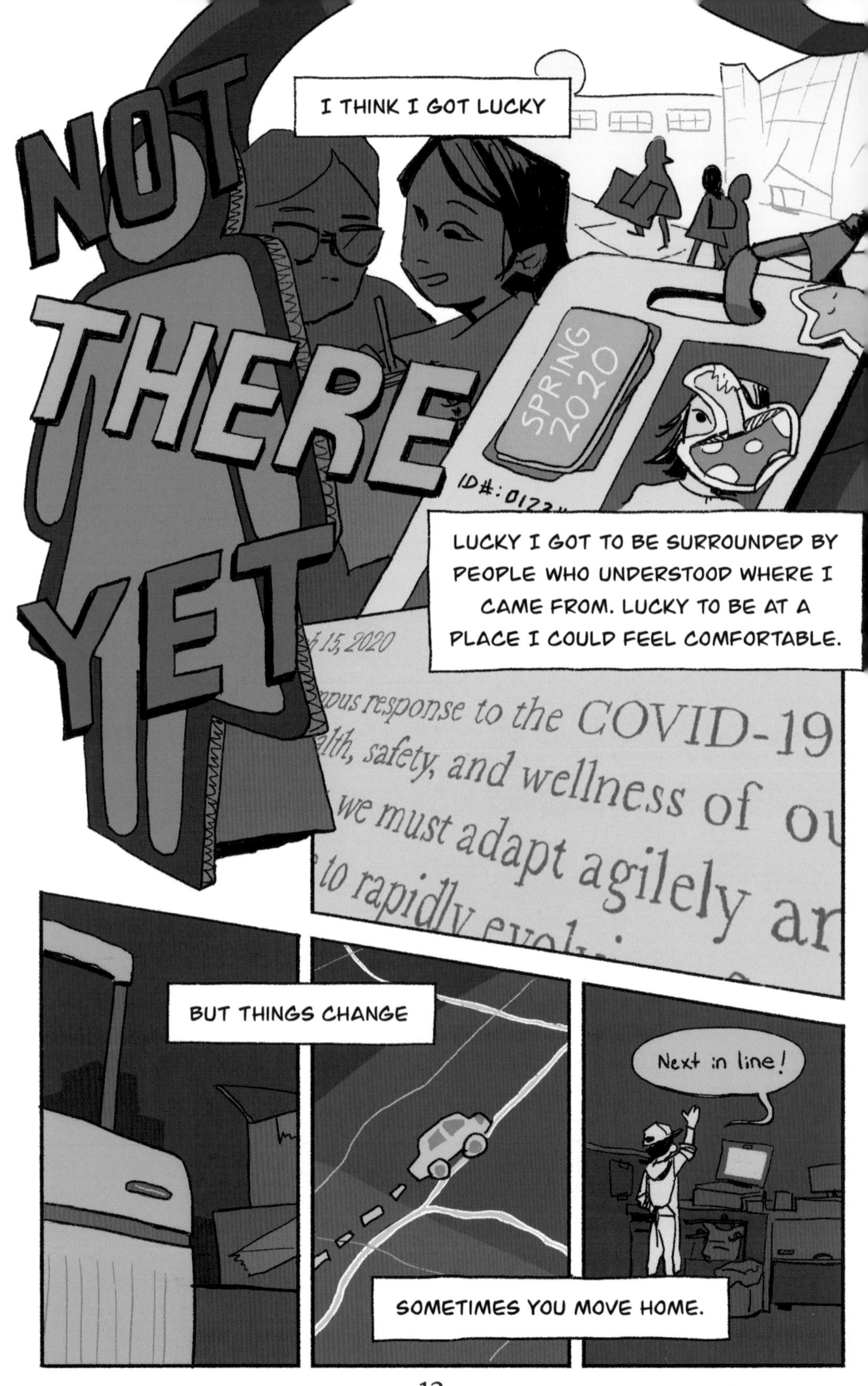
NOT THERE YET
I THINK I GOT LUCKY
SPRING 2020
LUCKY I GOT TO BE SURROUNDED BY PEOPLE WHO UNDERSTOOD WHERE I CAME FROM. LUCKY TO BE AT A PLACE I COULD FEEL COMFORTABLE.
15, 2020
response to the COVID-19
safety, and wellness of
we must adapt agilely
to rapidly
BUT THINGS CHANGE
SOMETIMES YOU MOVE HOME.
Next in line!

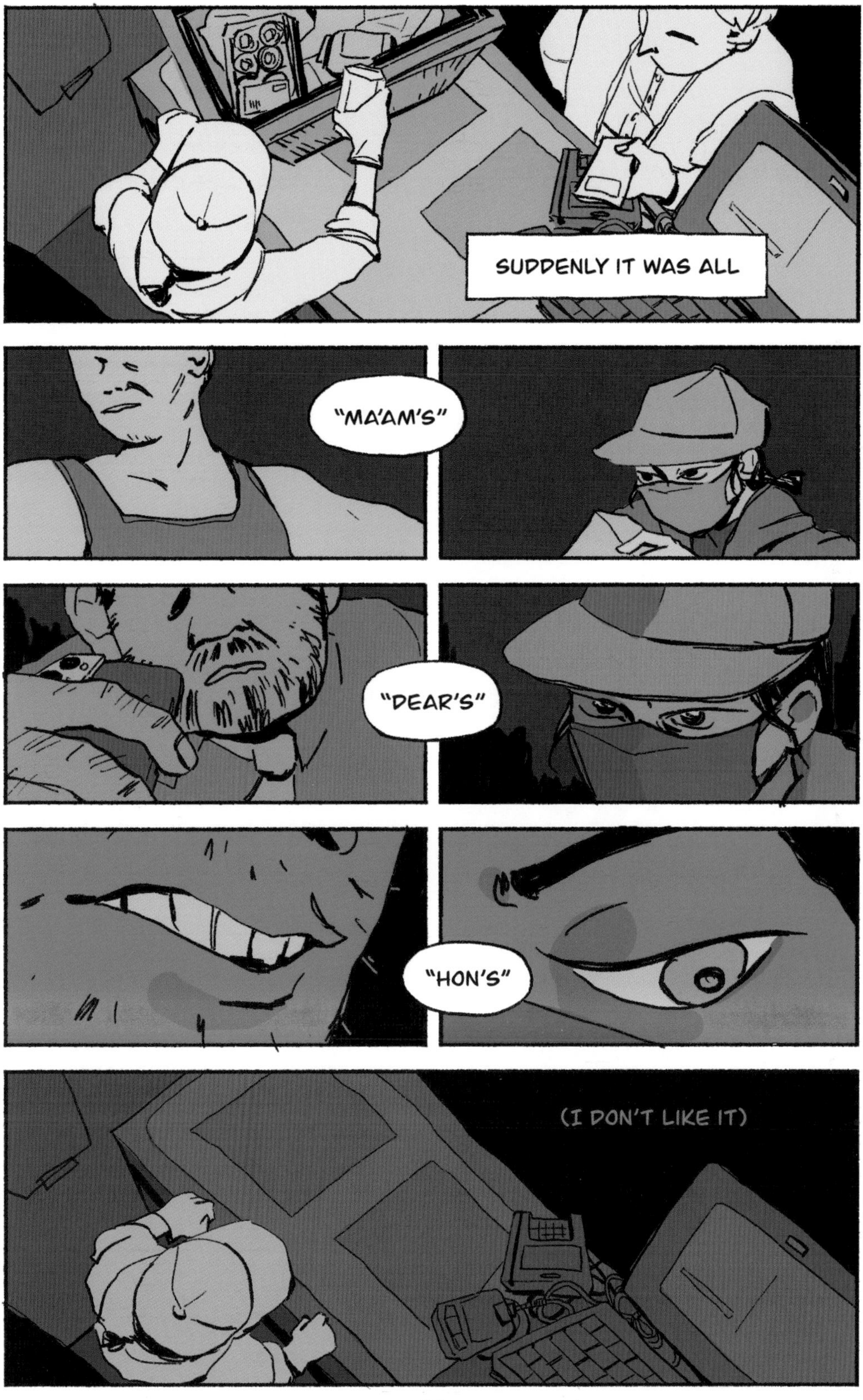
SUDDENLY IT WAS ALL
"MA'AM'S"
"DEAR'S"
"HON'S"
(I DON'T LIKE IT)

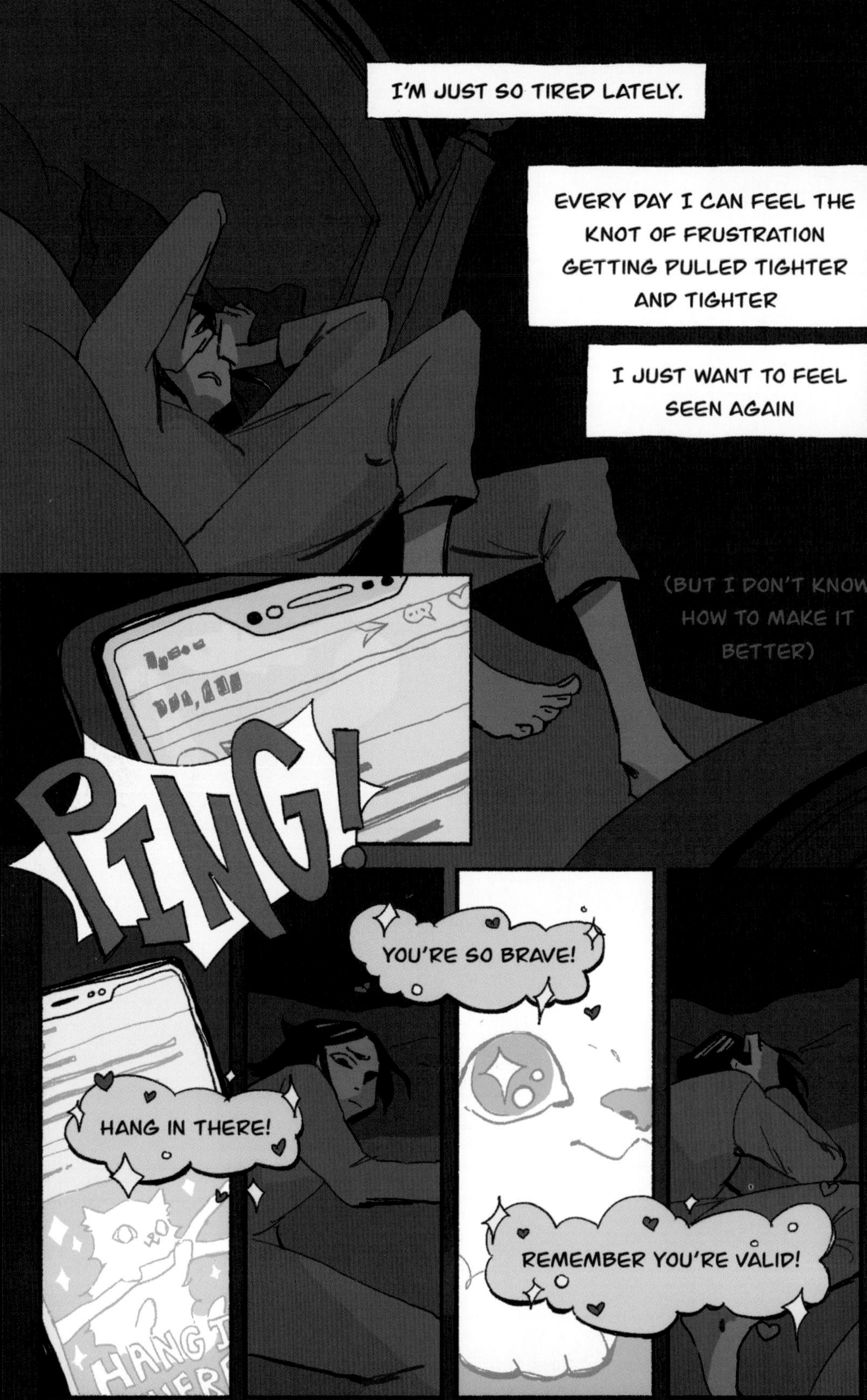
I'M JUST SO TIRED LATELY.
EVERY DAY I CAN FEEL THE KNOT OF FRUSTRATION GETTING PULLED TIGHTER AND TIGHTER
I JUST WANT TO FEEL SEEN AGAIN
(BUT I DON'T KNOW HOW TO MAKE IT BETTER)
PING!
HANG IN THERE!
YOU'RE SO BRAVE!
REMEMBER YOU'RE VALID!

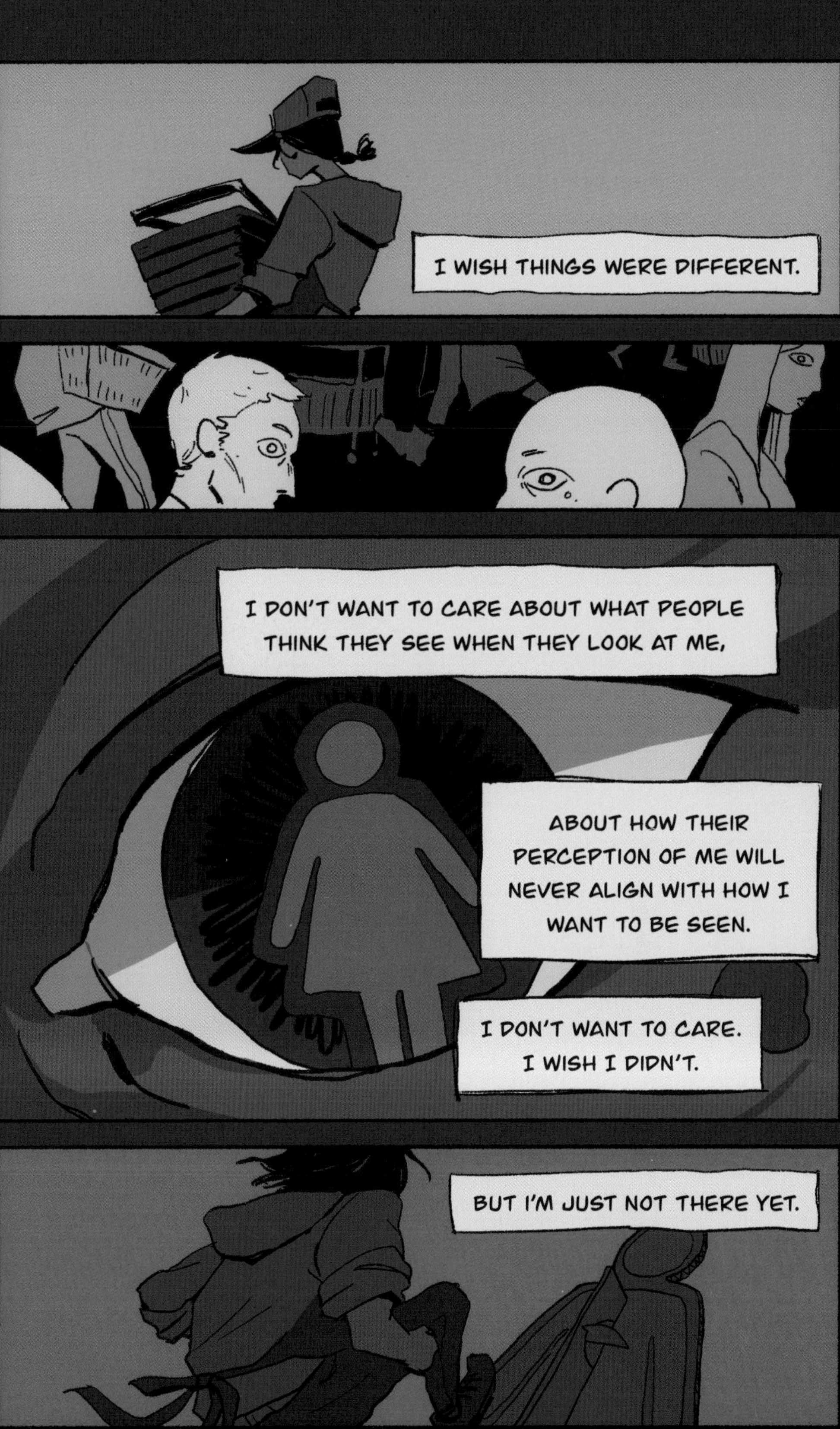
I WISH THINGS WERE DIFFERENT.
I DON'T WANT TO CARE ABOUT WHAT PEOPLE THINK THEY SEE WHEN THEY LOOK AT ME,
ABOUT HOW THEIR PERCEPTION OF ME WILL NEVER ALIGN WITH HOW I WANT TO BE SEEN.
I DON'T WANT TO CARE. I WISH I DIDN'T.
BUT I'M JUST NOT THERE YET.

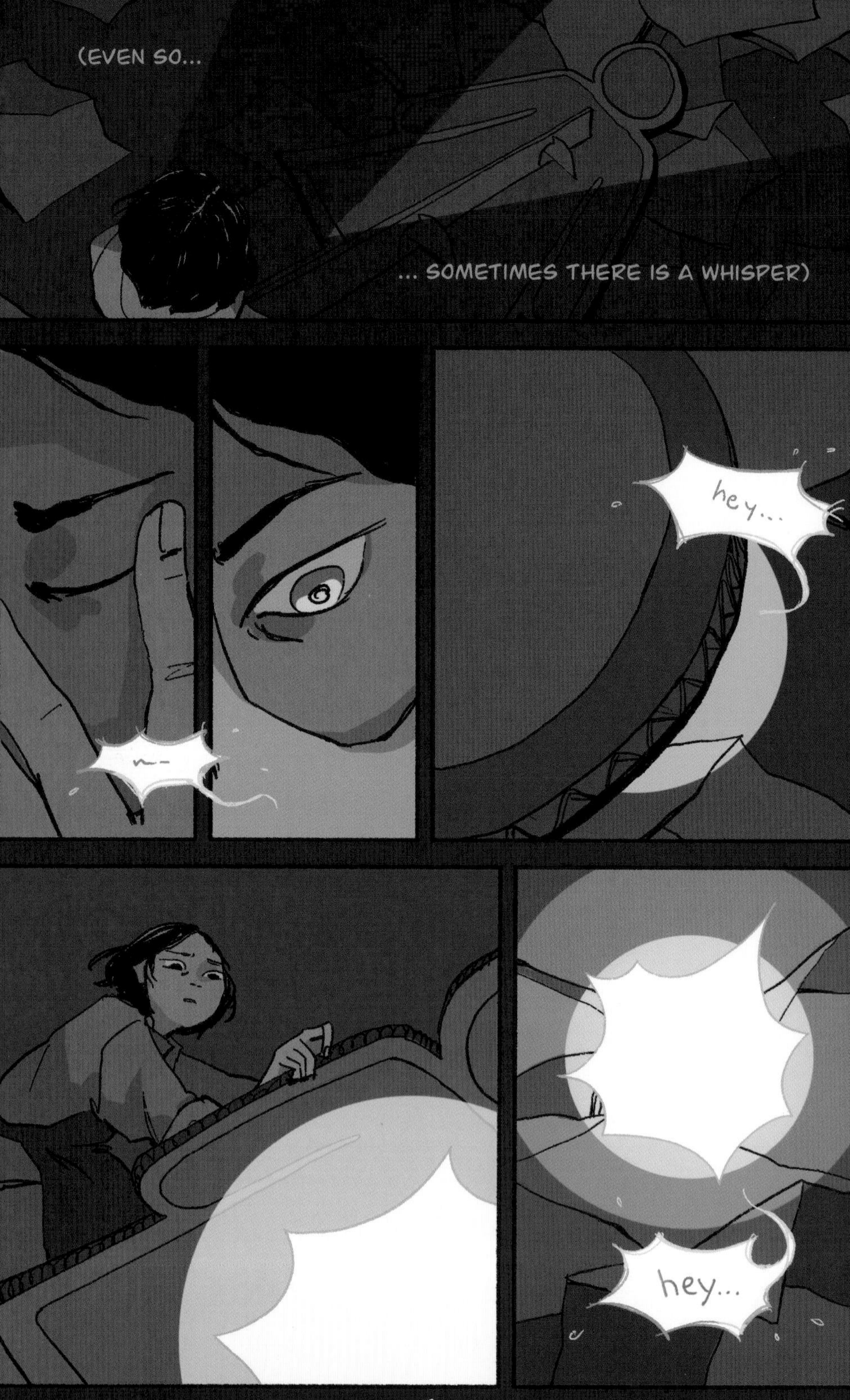

(EVEN SO...
... SOMETIMES THERE IS A WHISPER)
n-
hey...
hey...

I know you're trying.
I know you're working on it.
I'm sorry I can't get there sooner.
Please wait for me.

JAM ADEN
(HE/THEY)

I'm a swamp-dwelling creature who lives in a bog in Copenhagen. I make comics both for a living and for fun! I love mushrooms, funky plants, animals, and baking for my friends. You're all invited!

Find him on Instagram or Twitter:
@surmulefyr

"What's the point then?"

by Jam Aden

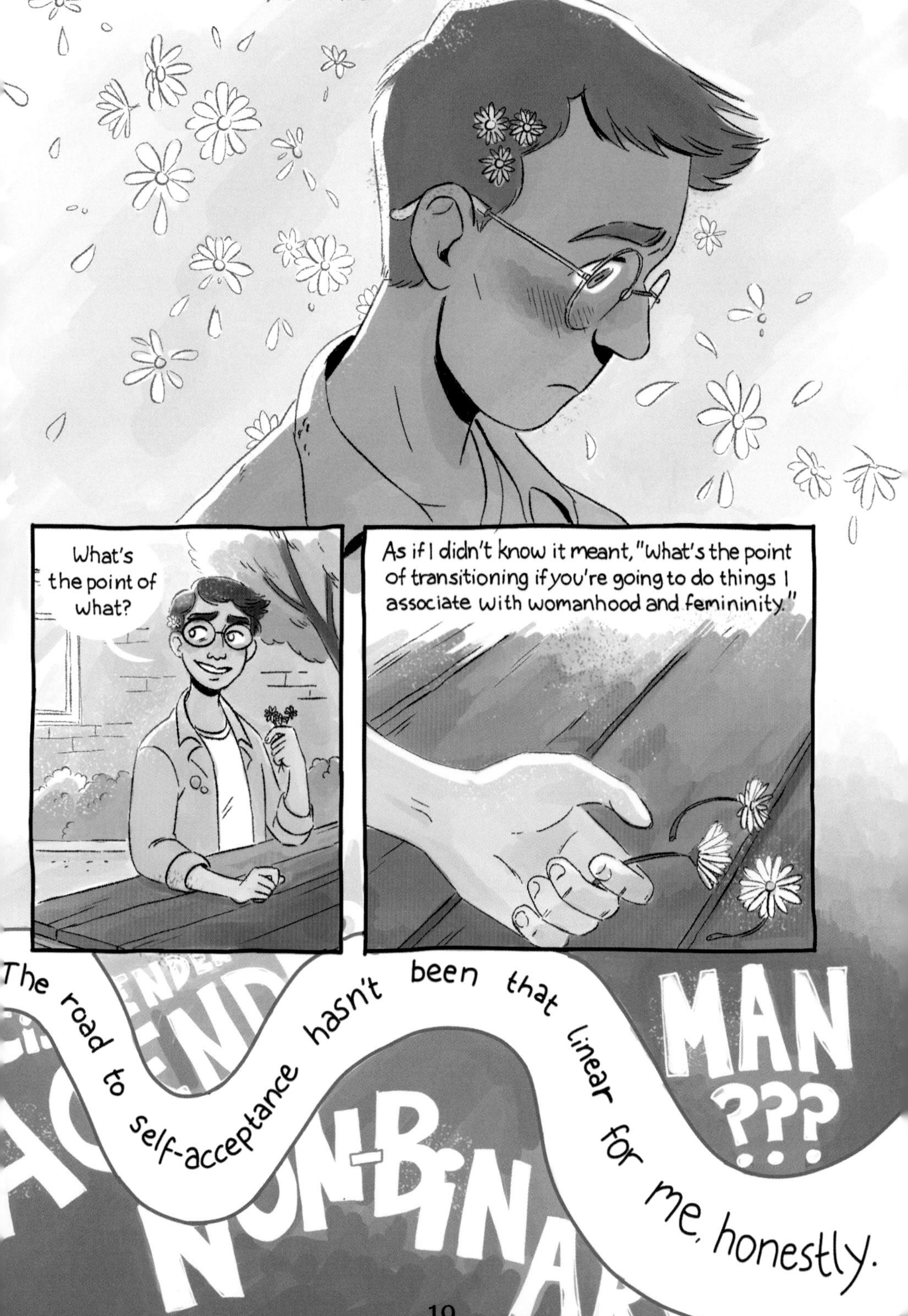
What's the point of what?
As if I didn't know it meant, "What's the point of transitioning if you're going to do things I associate with womanhood and femininity."
The road to self-acceptance hasn't been that linear for me, honestly.
MAN
???

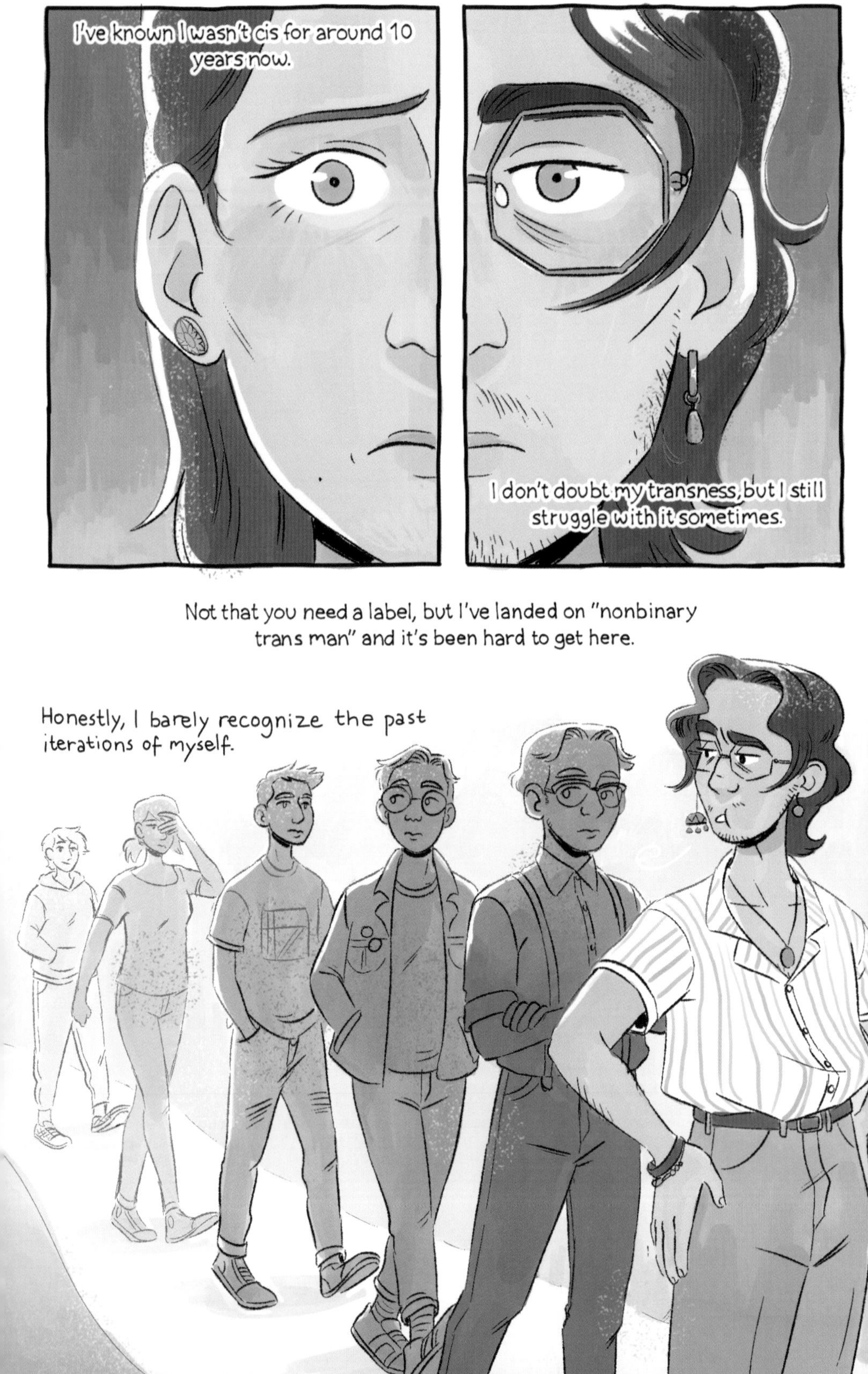
I've known I wasn't cis for around 10 years now.
I don't doubt my transness, but I still struggle with it sometimes.
Not that you need a label, but I've landed on "nonbinary trans man" and it's been hard to get here.
Honestly, I barely recognize the past iterations of myself.

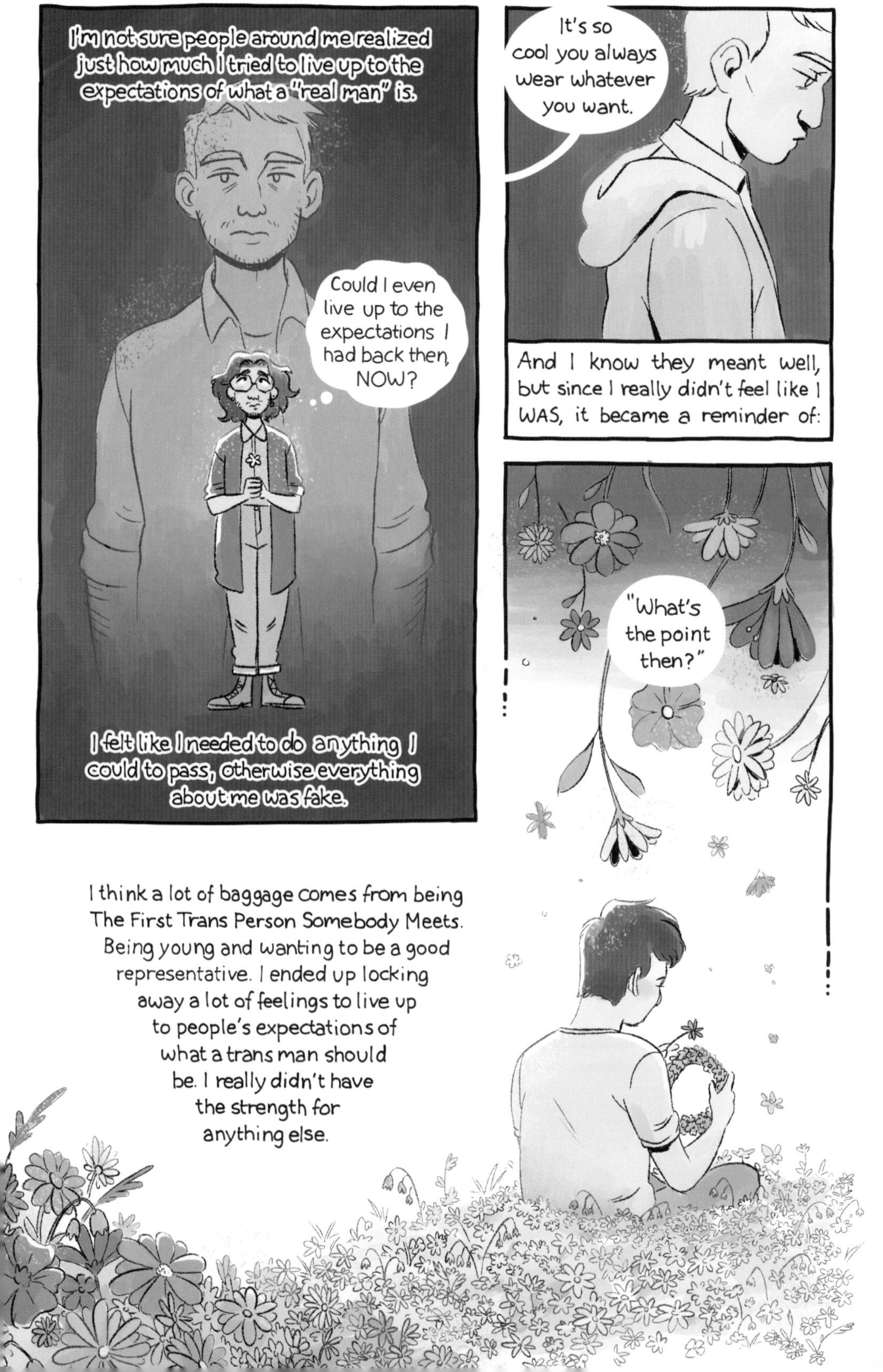

I'm not sure people around me realized just how much I tried to live up to the expectations of what a "real man" is.
Could I even live up to the expectations I had back then, NOW?
I felt like I needed to do anything I could to pass, otherwise everything about me was fake.
It's so cool you always wear whatever you want.
And I know they meant well, but since I really didn't feel like I WAS, it became a reminder of:
"What's the point then?"
I think a lot of baggage comes from being The First Trans Person Somebody Meets. Being young and wanting to be a good representative. I ended up locking away a lot of feelings to live up to people's expectations of what a trans man should be. I really didn't have the strength for anything else.

But over the past few years, I've come to realize that I'm not happy with the amount of femininity society allows me to express as a man.

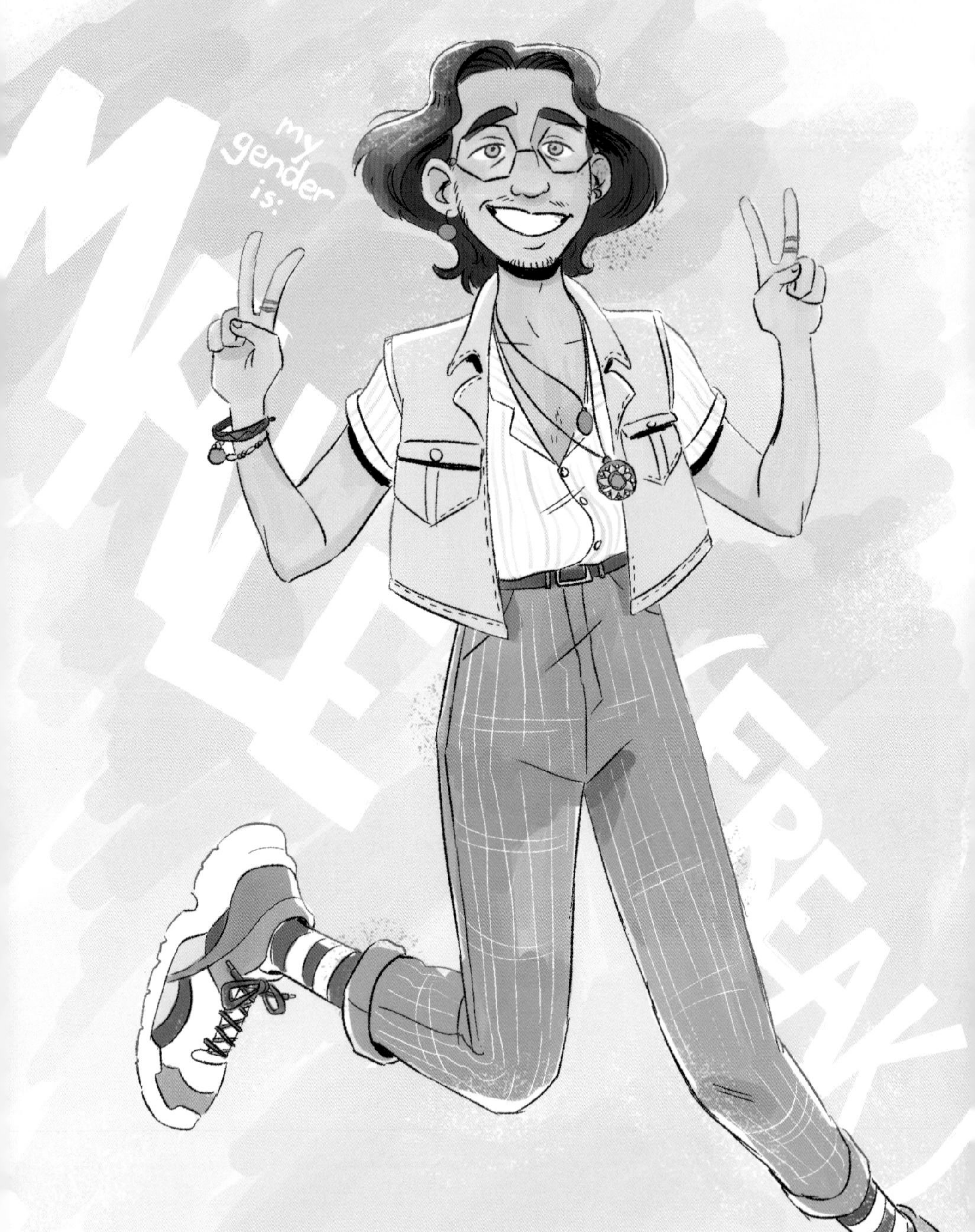
my gender is:
MALE
(FREAK)

I've accepted that I can transition to be a feminine man. Holding myself to the unwritten rules of society isn't helping anybody. I'd rather challenge the world head-on and be too much to swallow.

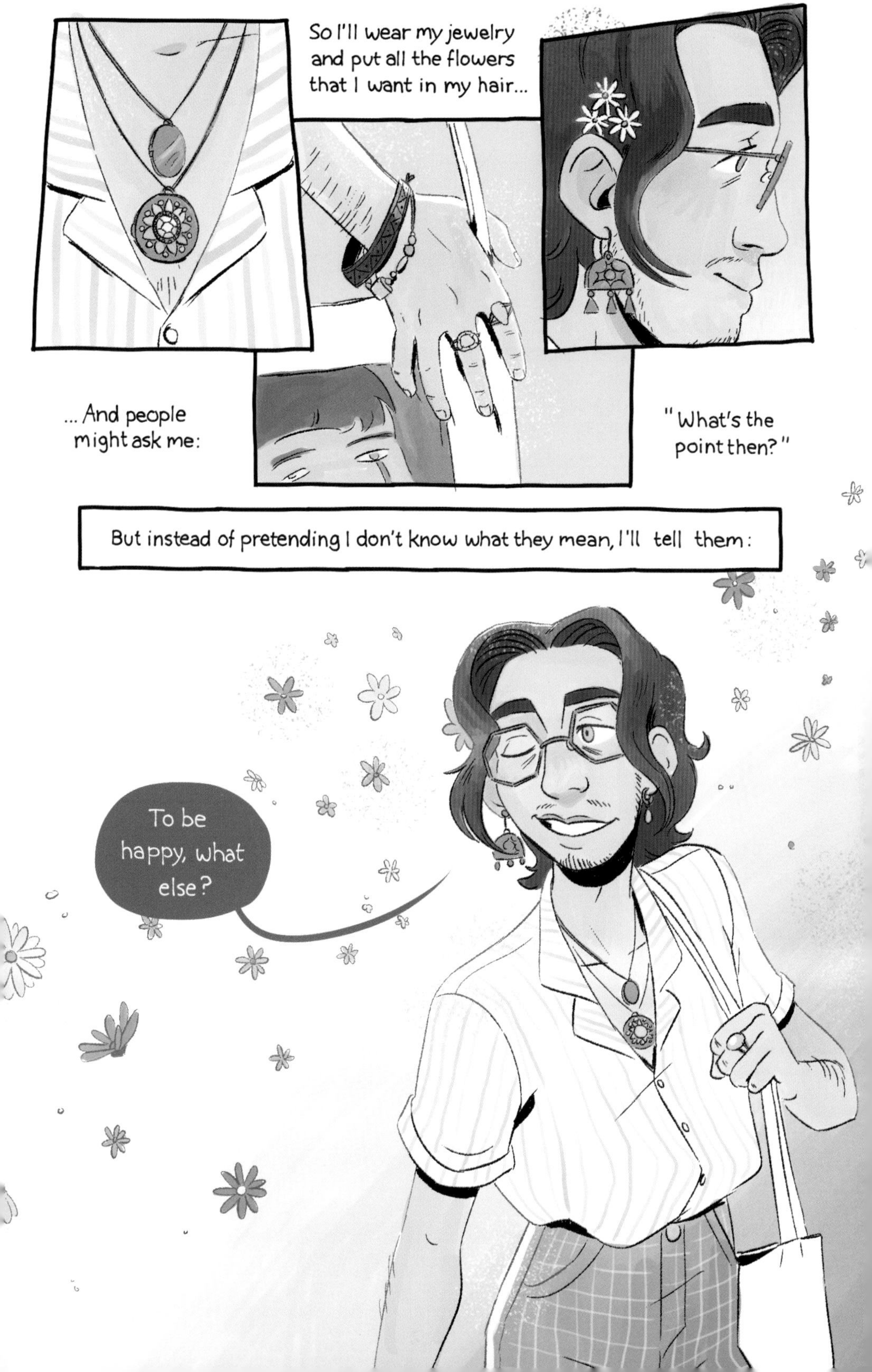

So I'll wear my jewelry and put all the flowers that I want in my hair...
... And people might ask me:
"What's the point then?"
But instead of pretending I don't know what they mean, I'll tell them:
To be happy, what else?

MADDIE JACOBUS
(SHE/HER)

Maddie is an illustrator and cartoonist from the California Bay Area, now living in Portland, Oregon. She's published a number of zines, as well as a collection of gag comics, *Bummer Corp: Sad Stories and Sexy Sharks.* When she's not drawing emotional comics, she's collecting action figures, chilling with her corgi, or eating hamburgers.

Find her on Instagram or Twitter:
@tacobusart

WELL-HIDDEN

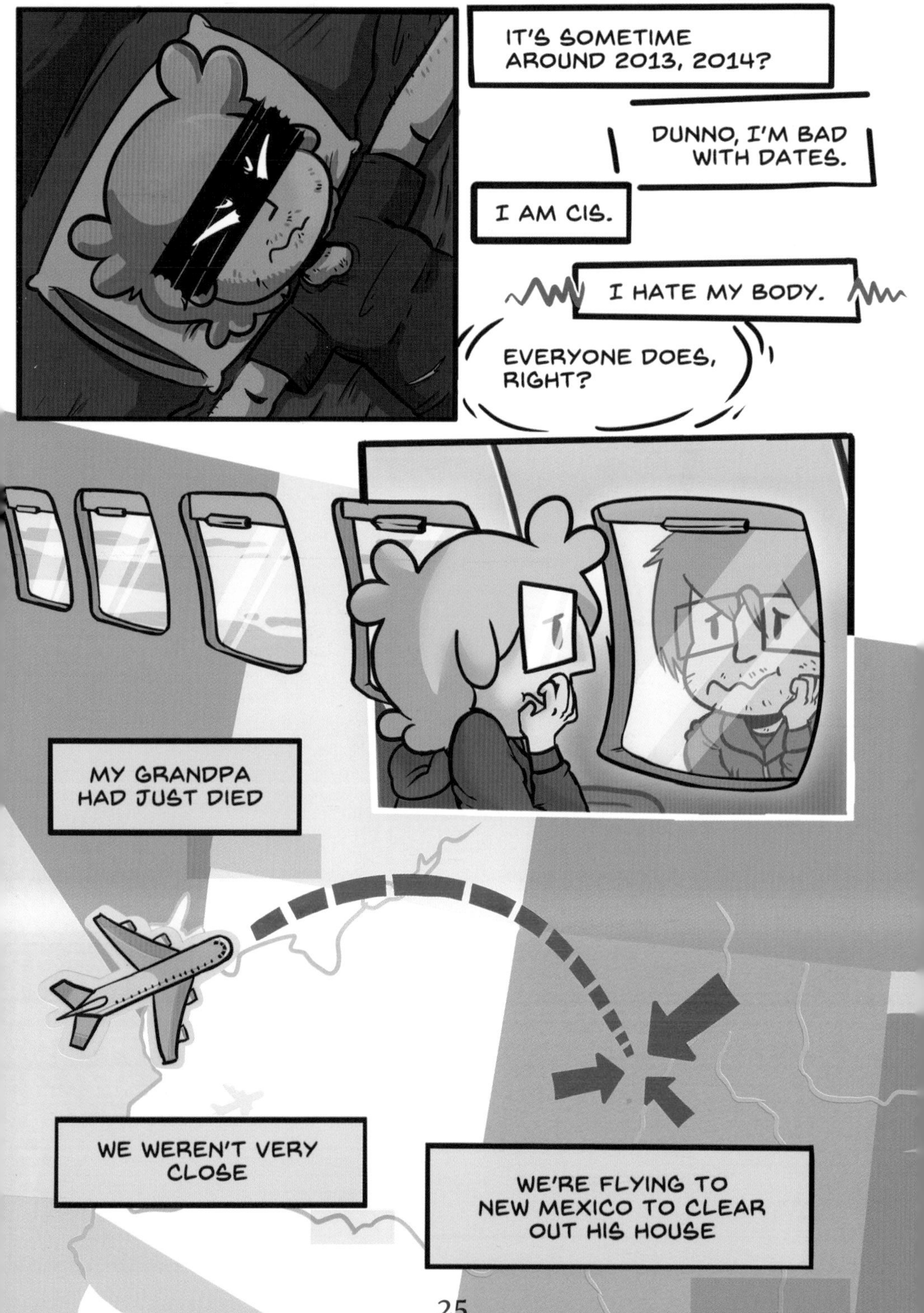

IT'S SOMETIME AROUND 2013, 2014?
DUNNO, I'M BAD WITH DATES.
I AM CIS.
I HATE MY BODY.
EVERYONE DOES, RIGHT?
MY GRANDPA HAD JUST DIED
WE WEREN'T VERY CLOSE
WE'RE FLYING TO NEW MEXICO TO CLEAR OUT HIS HOUSE

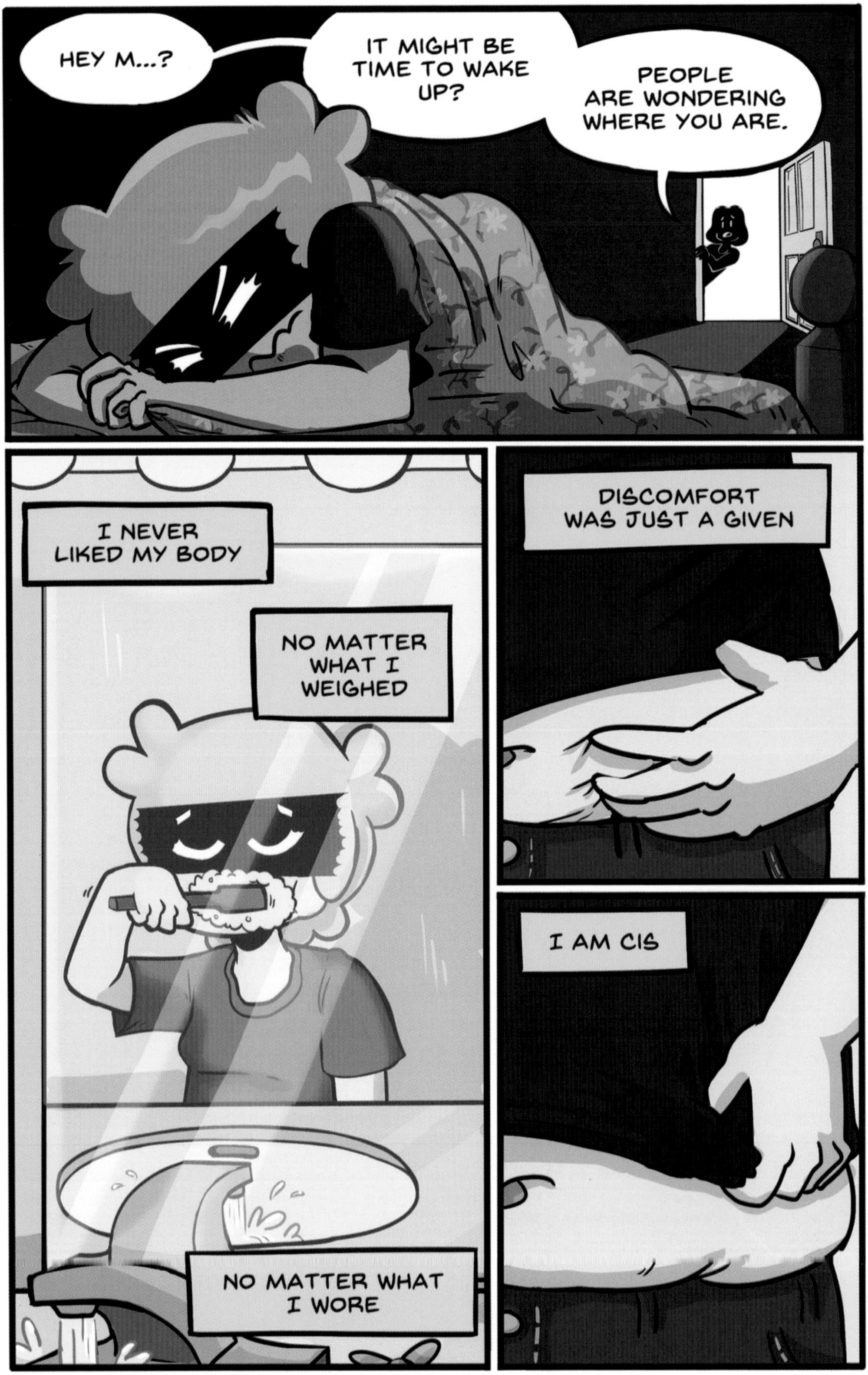
HEY M...?
IT MIGHT BE TIME TO WAKE UP?
PEOPLE ARE WONDERING WHERE YOU ARE.
I NEVER LIKED MY BODY
NO MATTER WHAT I WEIGHED
NO MATTER WHAT I WORE
DISCOMFORT WAS JUST A GIVEN
I AM CIS

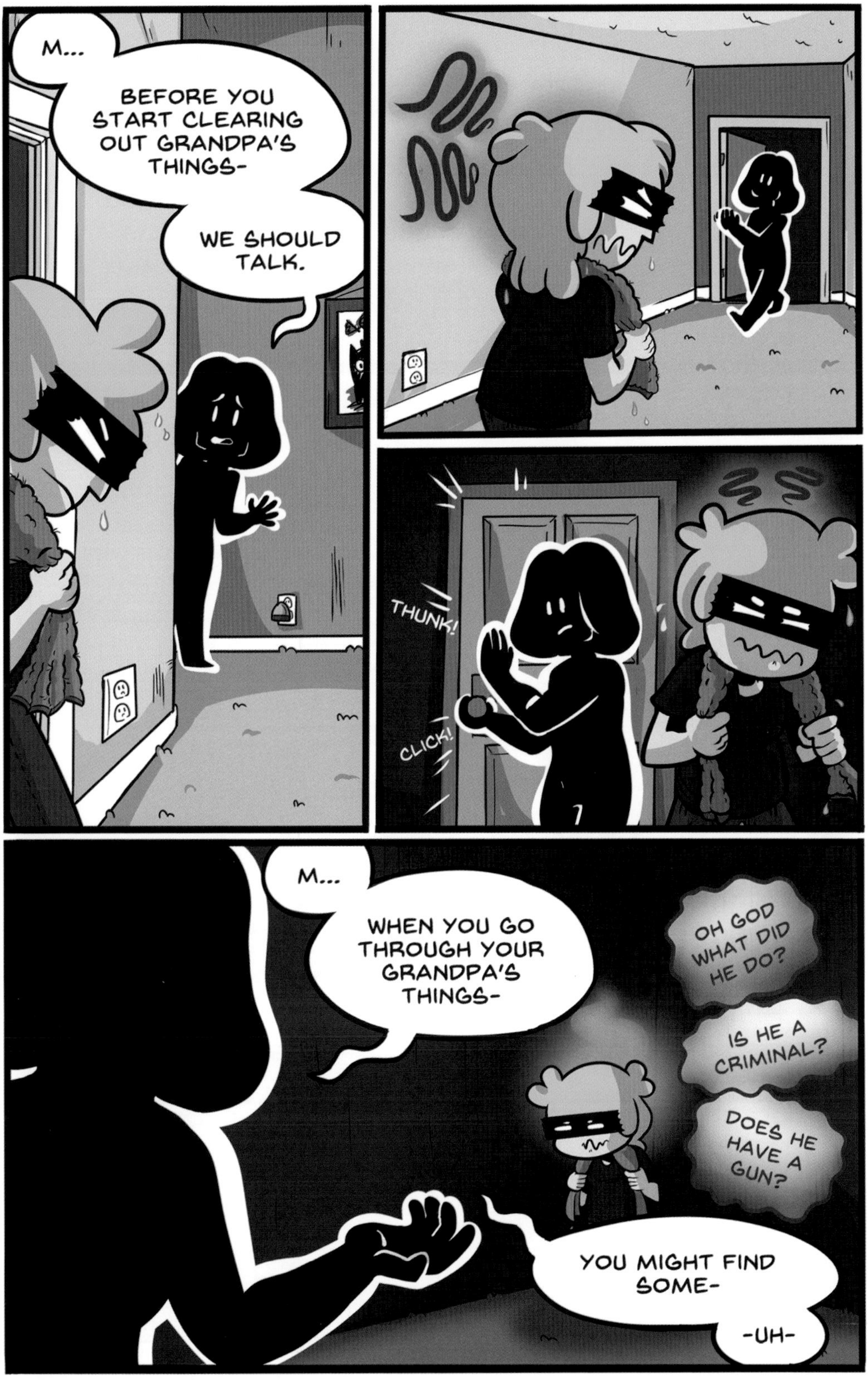
M...
BEFORE YOU START CLEARING OUT GRANDPA'S THINGS-
WE SHOULD TALK.
THUNK!
CLICK!
M...
WHEN YOU GO THROUGH YOUR GRANDPA'S THINGS-
OH GOD WHAT DID HE DO?
IS HE A CRIMINAL?
DOES HE HAVE A GUN?
YOU MIGHT FIND SOME-
-UH-

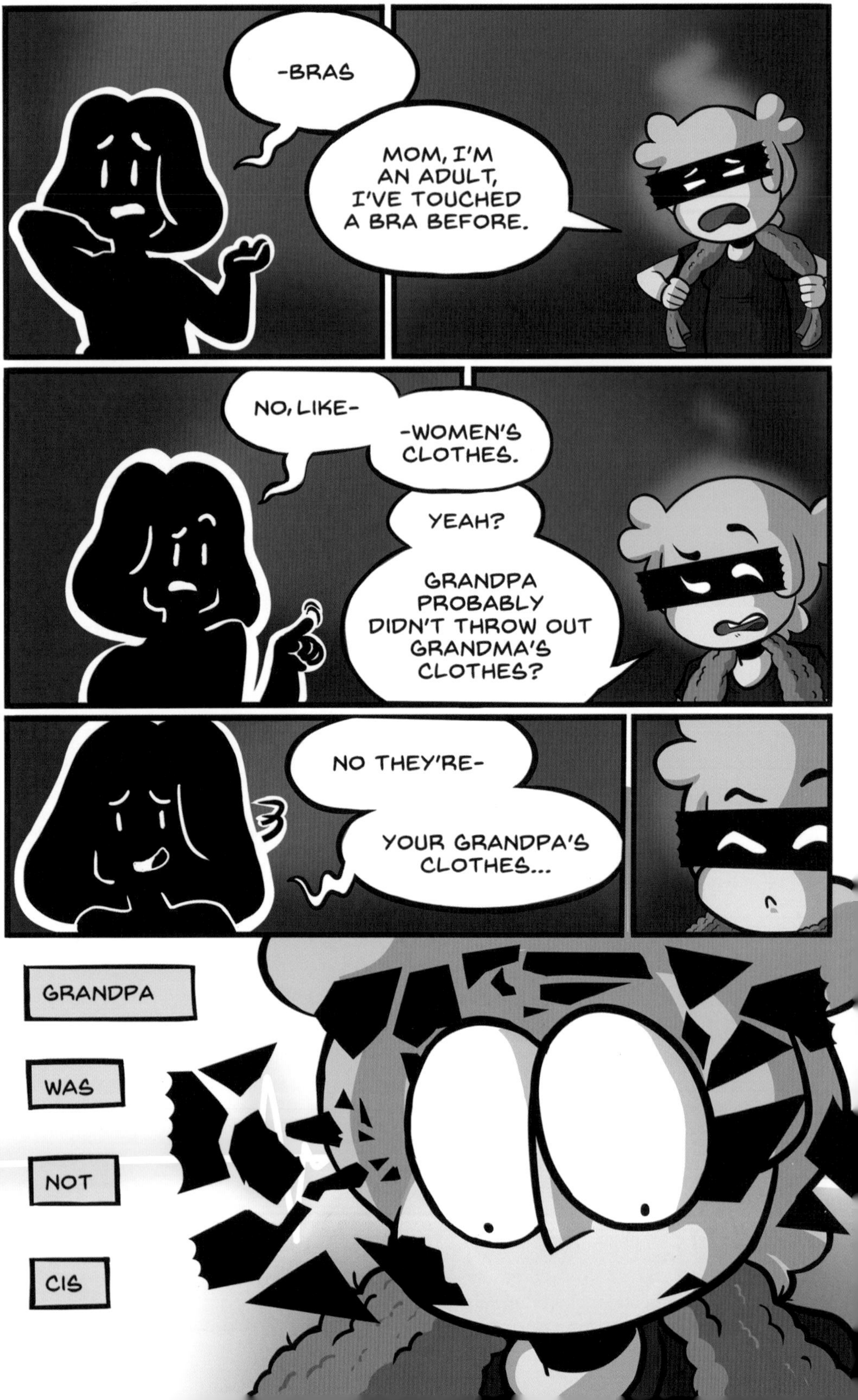
-BRAS
MOM, I'M AN ADULT, I'VE TOUCHED A BRA BEFORE.
NO, LIKE-
-WOMEN'S CLOTHES.
YEAH?
GRANDPA PROBABLY DIDN'T THROW OUT GRANDMA'S CLOTHES?
NO THEY'RE-
YOUR GRANDPA'S CLOTHES...
GRANDPA
WAS
NOT
CIS

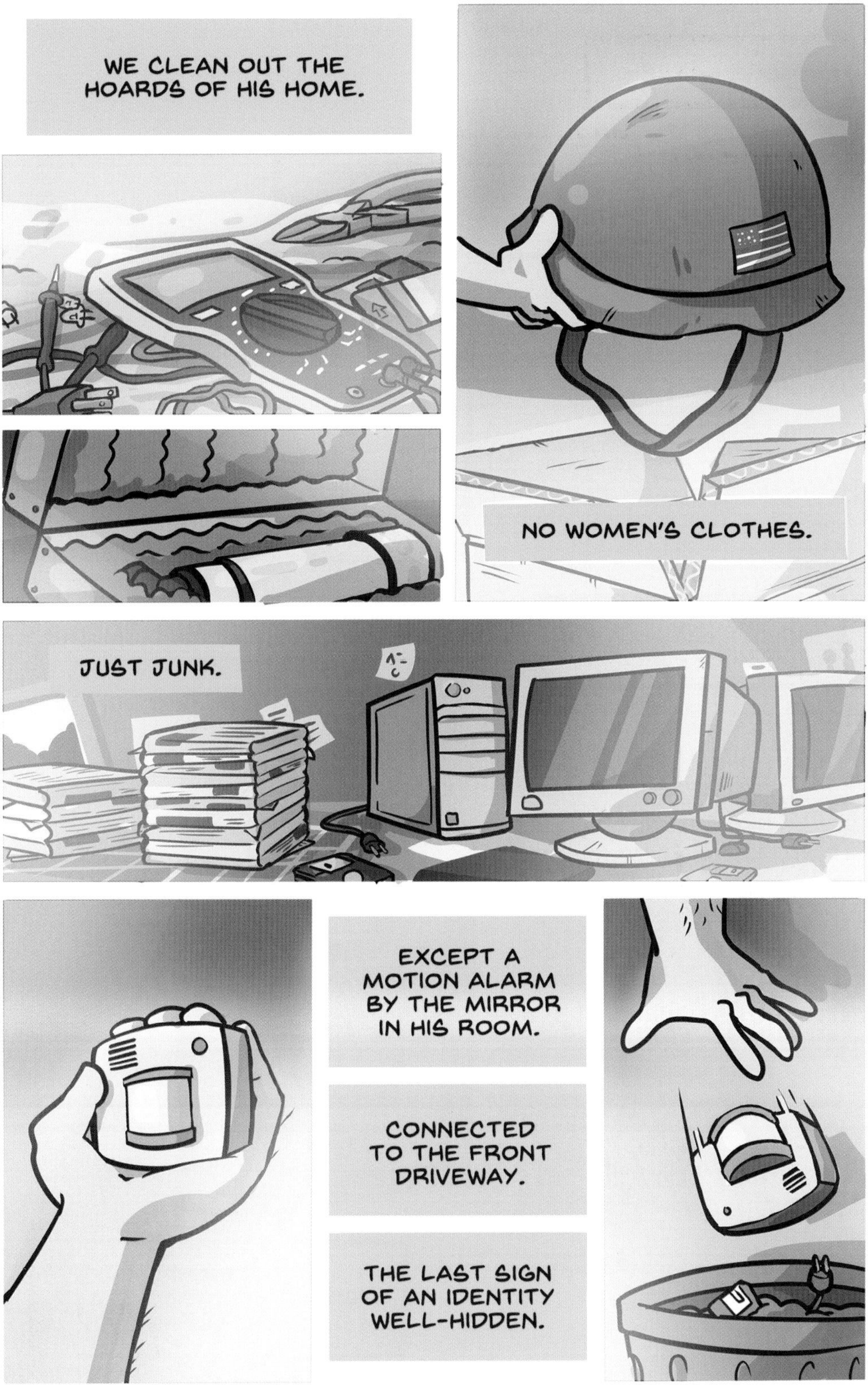
WE CLEAN OUT THE HOARDS OF HIS HOME.
NO WOMEN'S CLOTHES.
JUST JUNK.
EXCEPT A MOTION ALARM BY THE MIRROR IN HIS ROOM.
CONNECTED TO THE FRONT DRIVEWAY.
THE LAST SIGN OF AN IDENTITY WELL-HIDDEN.

YEARS LATER–

I STILL DON'T KNOW
WHO MY GRANDPA
REALLY WANTED TO BE.

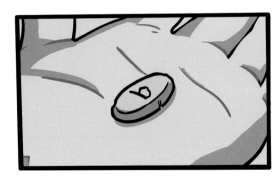

BUT I KNOW WHO I
WANT TO BE.

AND I WONDER IF HE
WOULD BE PROUD THAT
I REFUSE TO HIDE IT.

LAE LOUIE SCHÄFER
(HE/HIM)

Lae lives and works in Amsterdam with his two cat children. Even though figuring out his gender identity has taken quite a lot of time and effort, he has always been sure of his two main goals in life: making comics and becoming a cat parent. Both of these dreams have now been realized and have brought much joy into Lae's life. Besides comics or illustration, Lae regularly joins creative projects, such as live drawing at events, making sock puppets at music festivals, acting for music videos or photo comics, and dancing on stage dressed as a fuzzy skeleton at the KABOOM animation festival.

You can find him online at:
laeschafer.com

a transgender person who does not yet realise or admit that they are transgender is often referred to as an egg.

The following anecdotes feature me, Lae, when I was an egg.

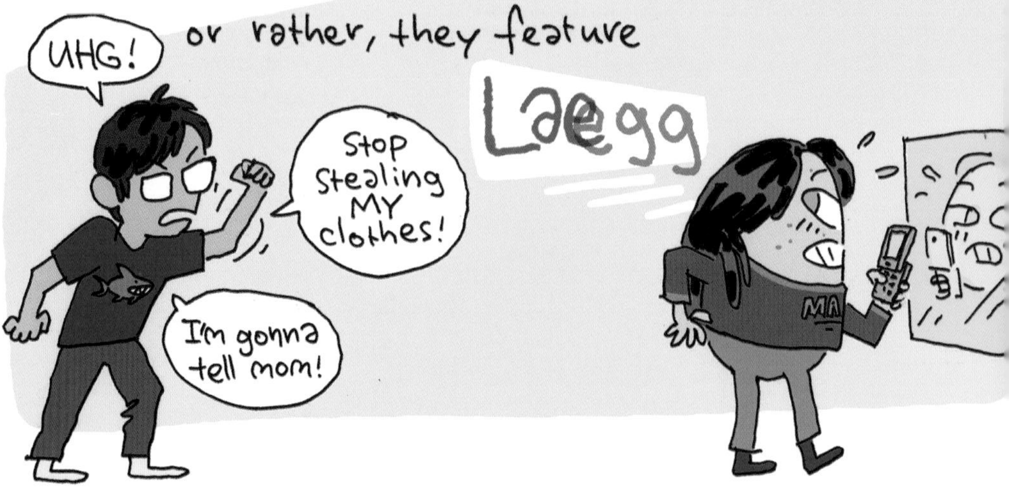
or rather, they feature
Laegg
UHG!
Stop stealing MY clothes!
I'm gonna tell mom!

elementary school science chat

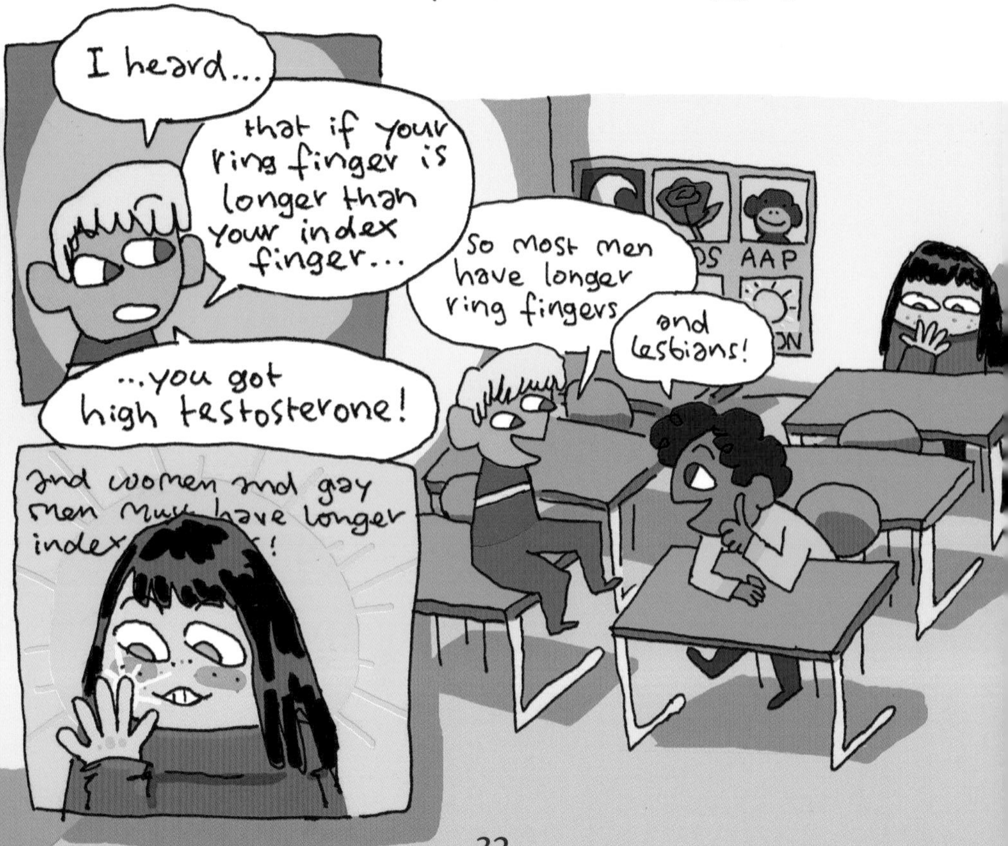
I heard...
that if your ring finger is longer than your index finger...
...you got high testosterone!
So most men have longer ring fingers
and lesbians!
and women and gay men
have longer
index
AAP

exposition

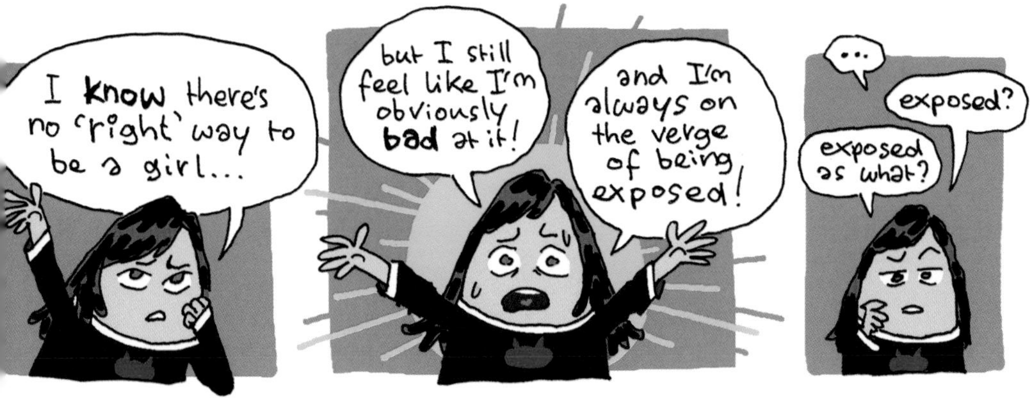

I **know** there's no 'right' way to be a girl...
but I still feel like I'm obviously **bad** at it!
and I'm always on the verge of being exposed!
...
exposed?
exposed as what?

girl costume

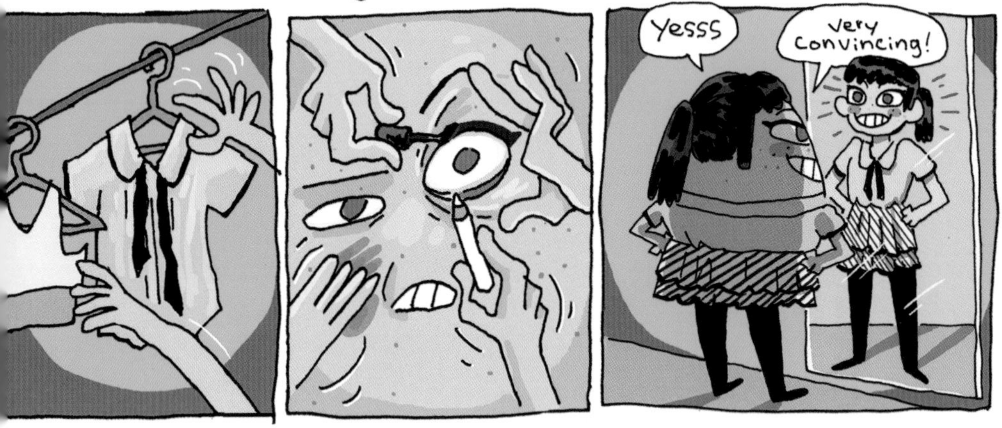

Yesss
very convincing!

teenage envy

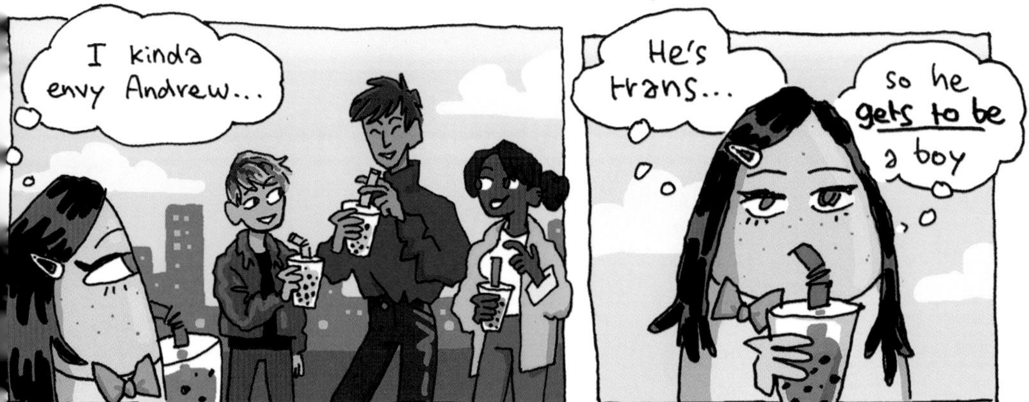

I kinda envy Andrew...
He's trans...
so he gets to be a boy

art school portrait posing

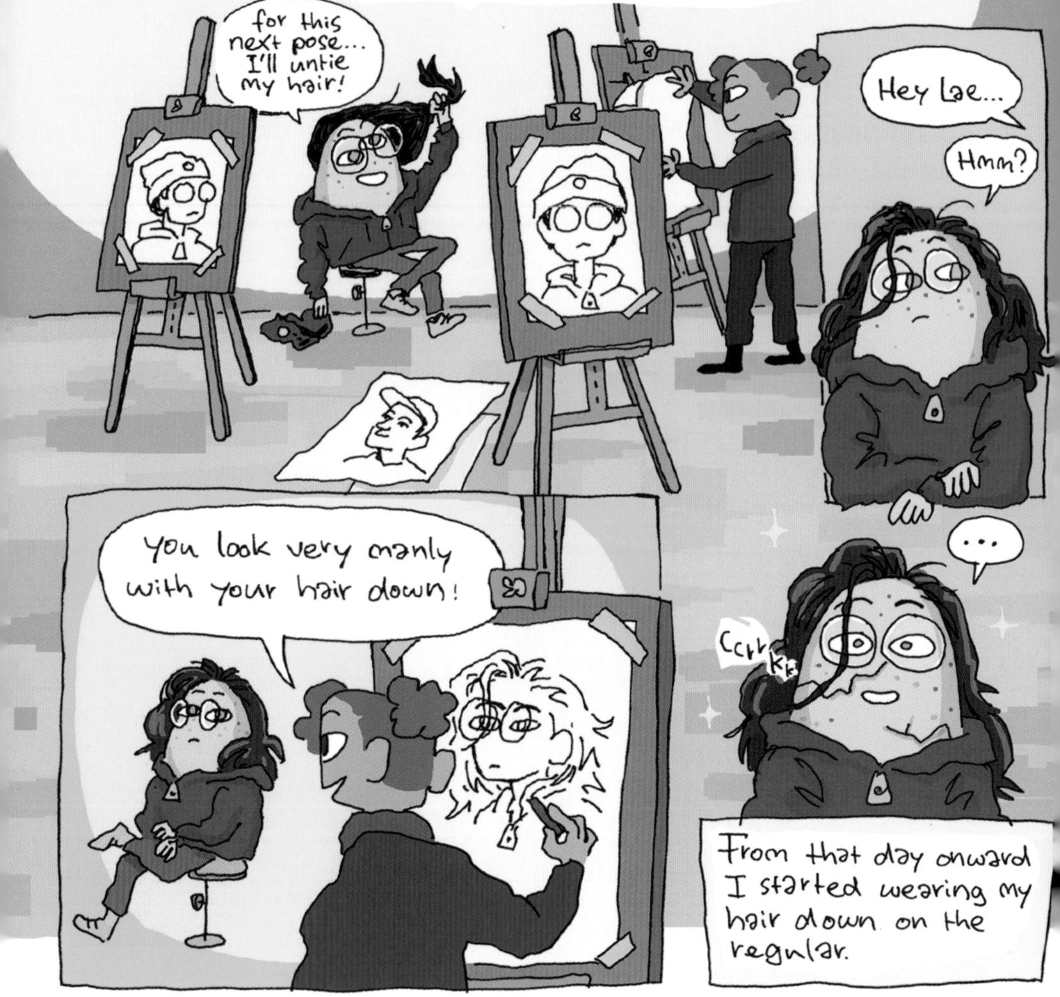
for this next pose... I'll untie my hair!
Hey Lae...
Hmm?
You look very manly with your hair down!
...
From that day onward I started wearing my hair down on the regular.

what the world wants

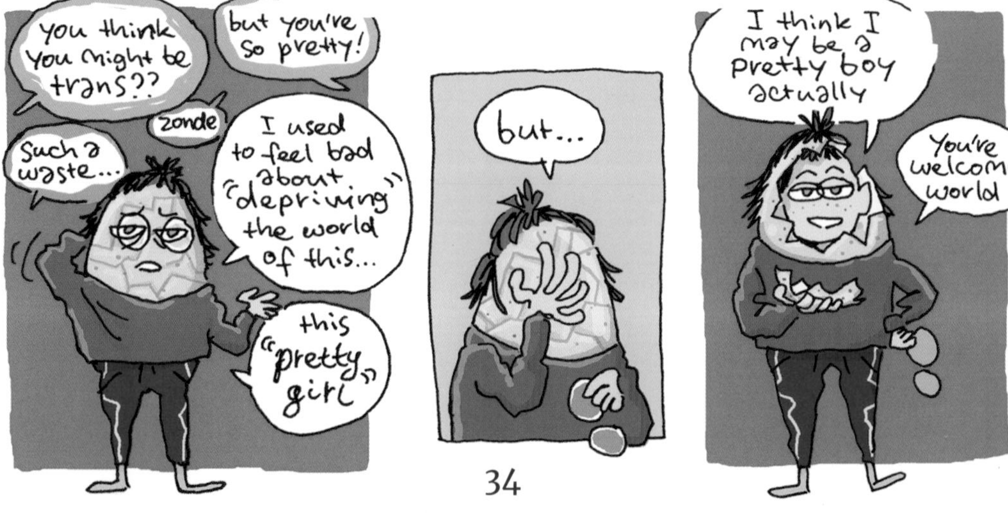
you think you might be trans??
but you're so pretty!
zonde
Such a waste...
I used to feel bad about "depriving" the world of this...
this "pretty girl"
but...
I think I may be a pretty boy actually
You're welcome world

LIAM COBALLES
(HE/HIM)

Liam is a queer Filipino trans man from Skokie, Illinois. He studied traditional animation at Columbia College Chicago, and currently he lives in Burbank, California, with his partner, roommates, and cat, Gigi. He works as a Production Coordinator at VSI Los Angeles, a post-production studio that works on English dubbing for live action and animated series and films. When he isn't drawing, he's watching YouTube and reading manga.

Find him on Instagram or Twitter:
@natural_nin

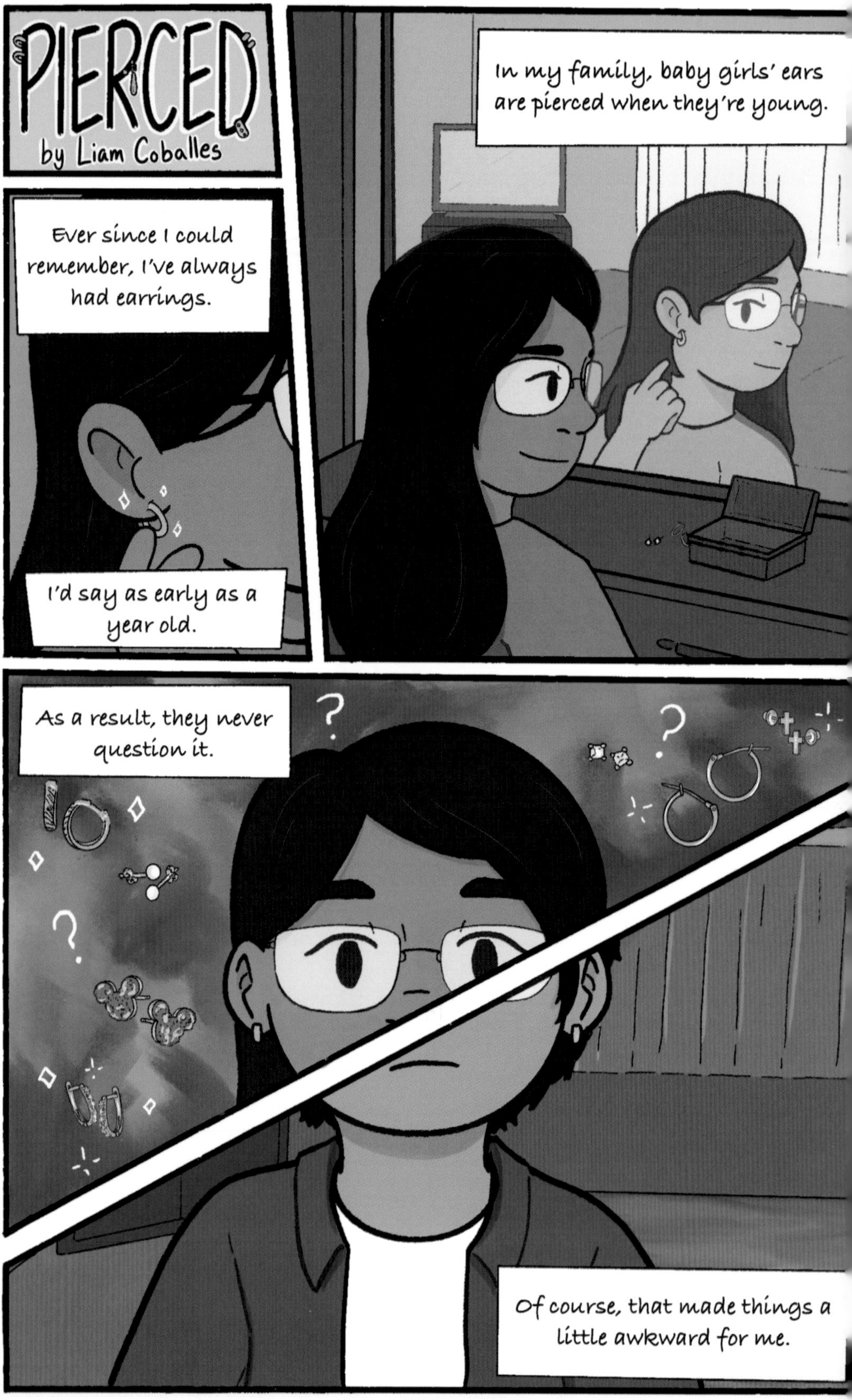
PIERCED
by Liam Coballes
In my family, baby girls' ears are pierced when they're young.
Ever since I could remember, I've always had earrings.
I'd say as early as a year old.
As a result, they never question it.
Of course, that made things a little awkward for me.

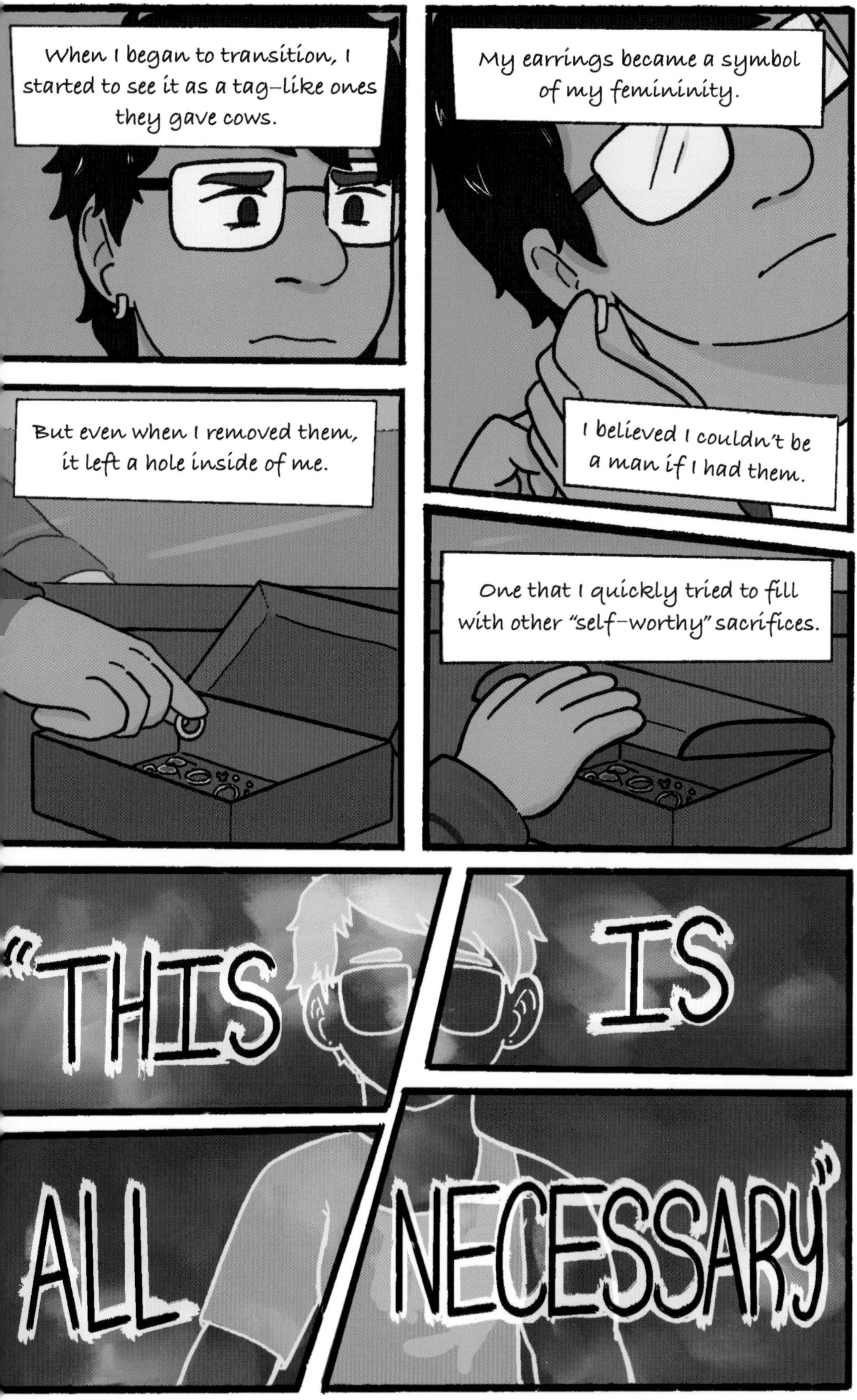
When I began to transition, I started to see it as a tag—like ones they gave cows.
My earrings became a symbol of my femininity.
I believed I couldn't be a man if I had them.
But even when I removed them, it left a hole inside of me.
One that I quickly tried to fill with other "self-worthy" sacrifices.
"THIS
IS
ALL
NECESSARY"

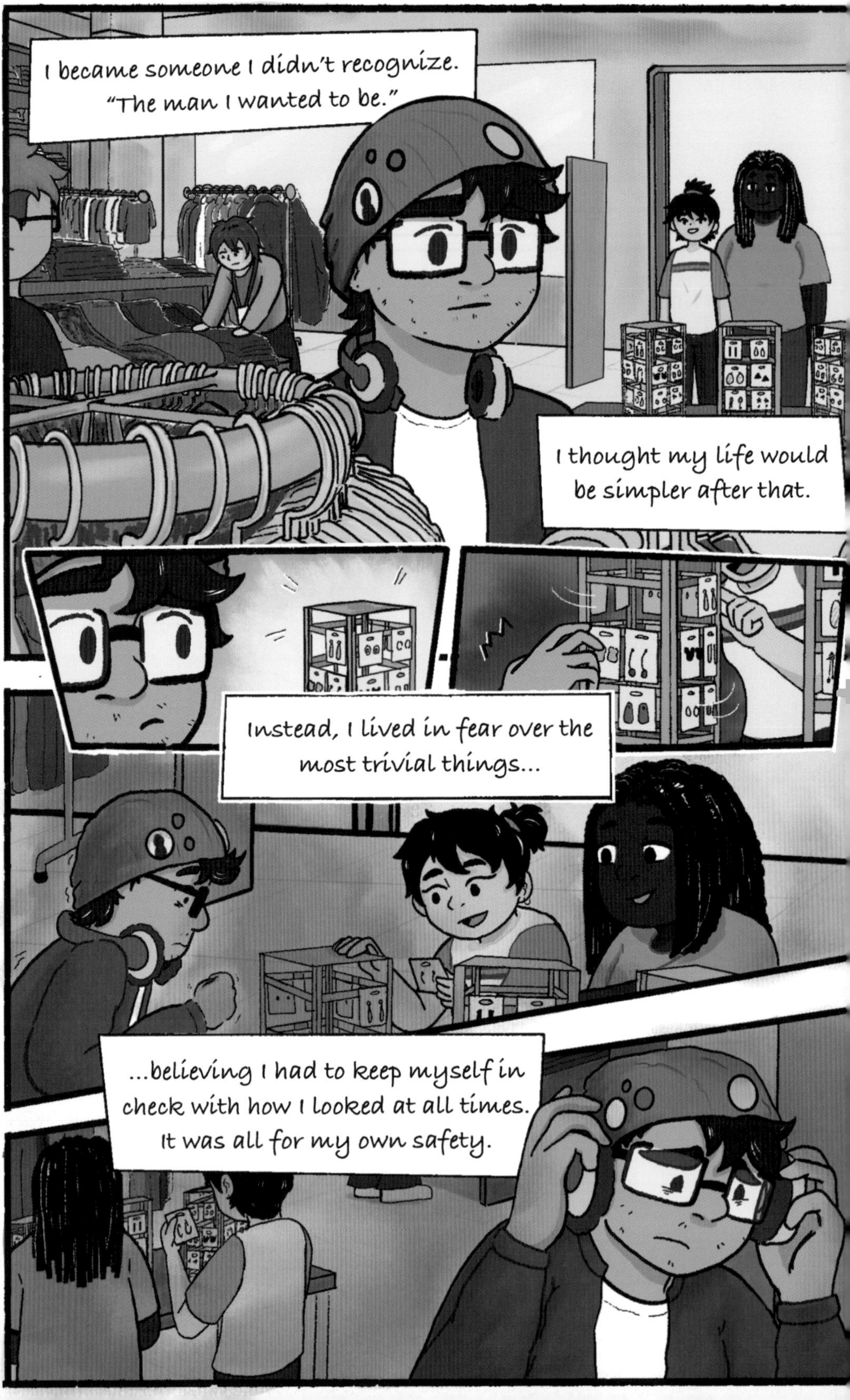
I became someone I didn't recognize. "The man I wanted to be."
I thought my life would be simpler after that.
Instead, I lived in fear over the most trivial things...
...believing I had to keep myself in check with how I looked at all times. It was all for my own safety.

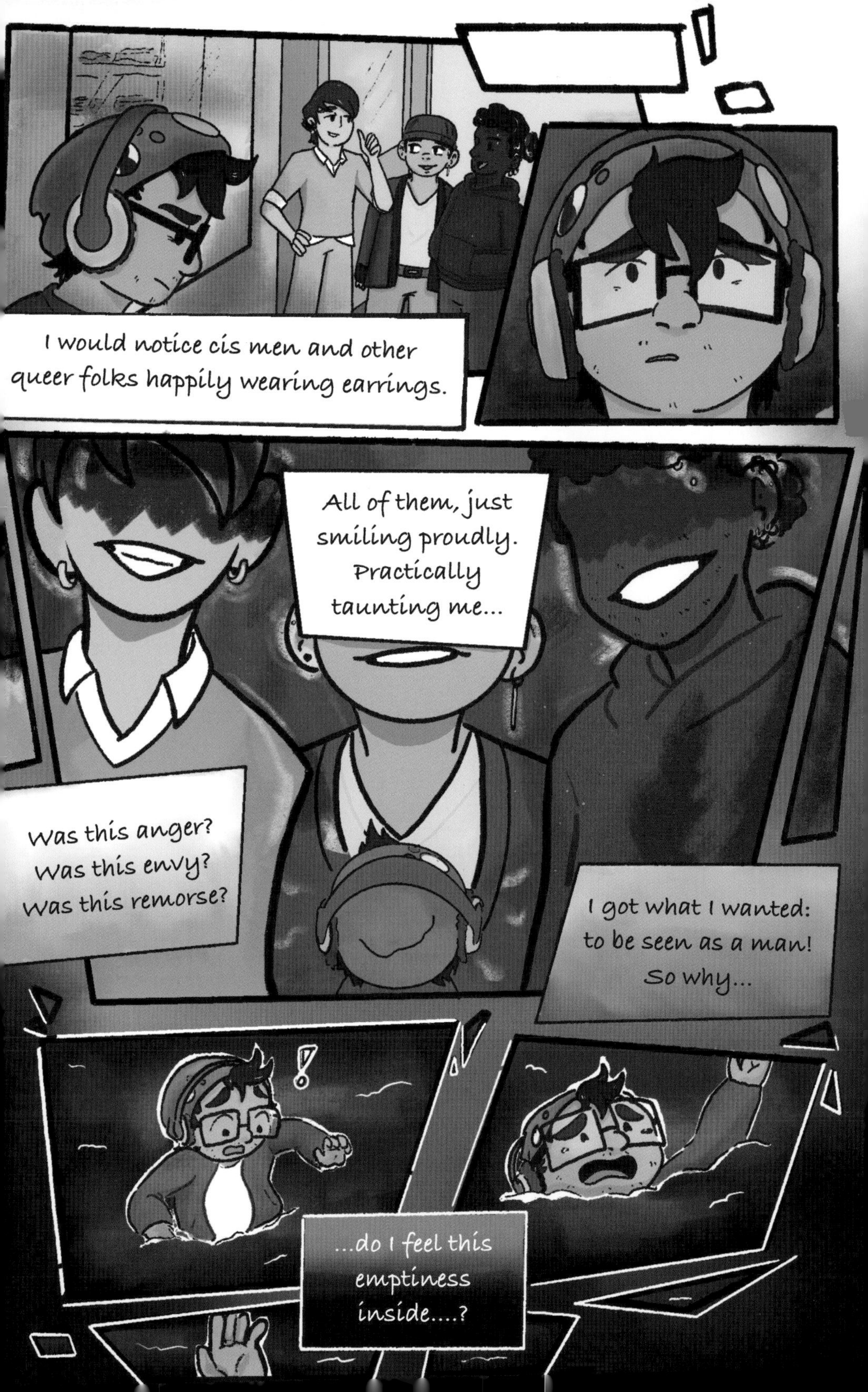
I would notice cis men and other queer folks happily wearing earrings.
All of them, just smiling proudly. Practically taunting me...
Was this anger? Was this envy? Was this remorse?
I got what I wanted: to be seen as a man! So why...
!
...do I feel this emptiness inside....?

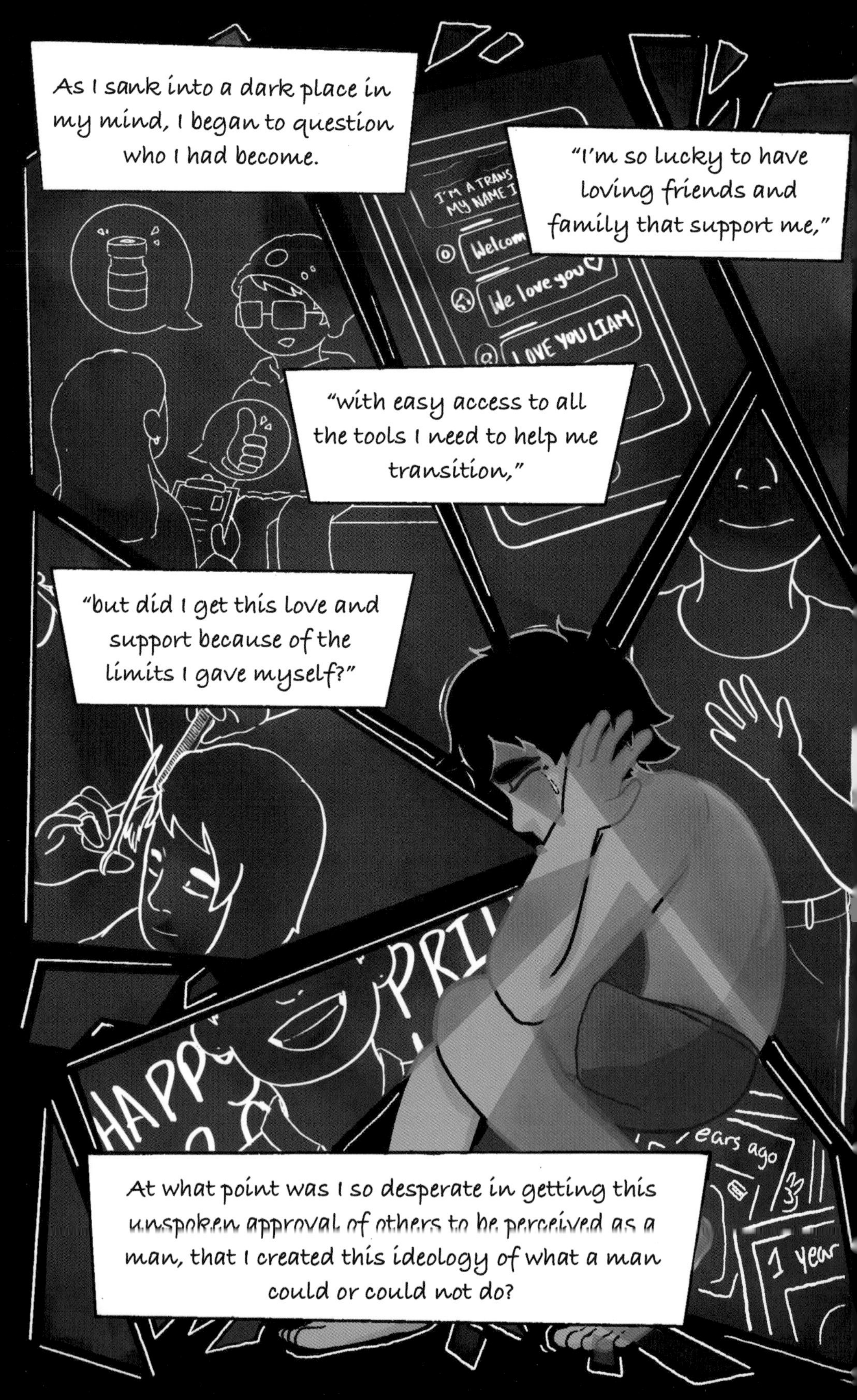
As I sank into a dark place in my mind, I began to question who I had become.
"I'm so lucky to have loving friends and family that support me,"
We love you
LOVE YOU LIAM
"with easy access to all the tools I need to help me transition,"
"but did I get this love and support because of the limits I gave myself?"
1 year
At what point was I so desperate in getting this unspoken approval of others to be perceived as a man, that I created this ideology of what a man could or could not do?

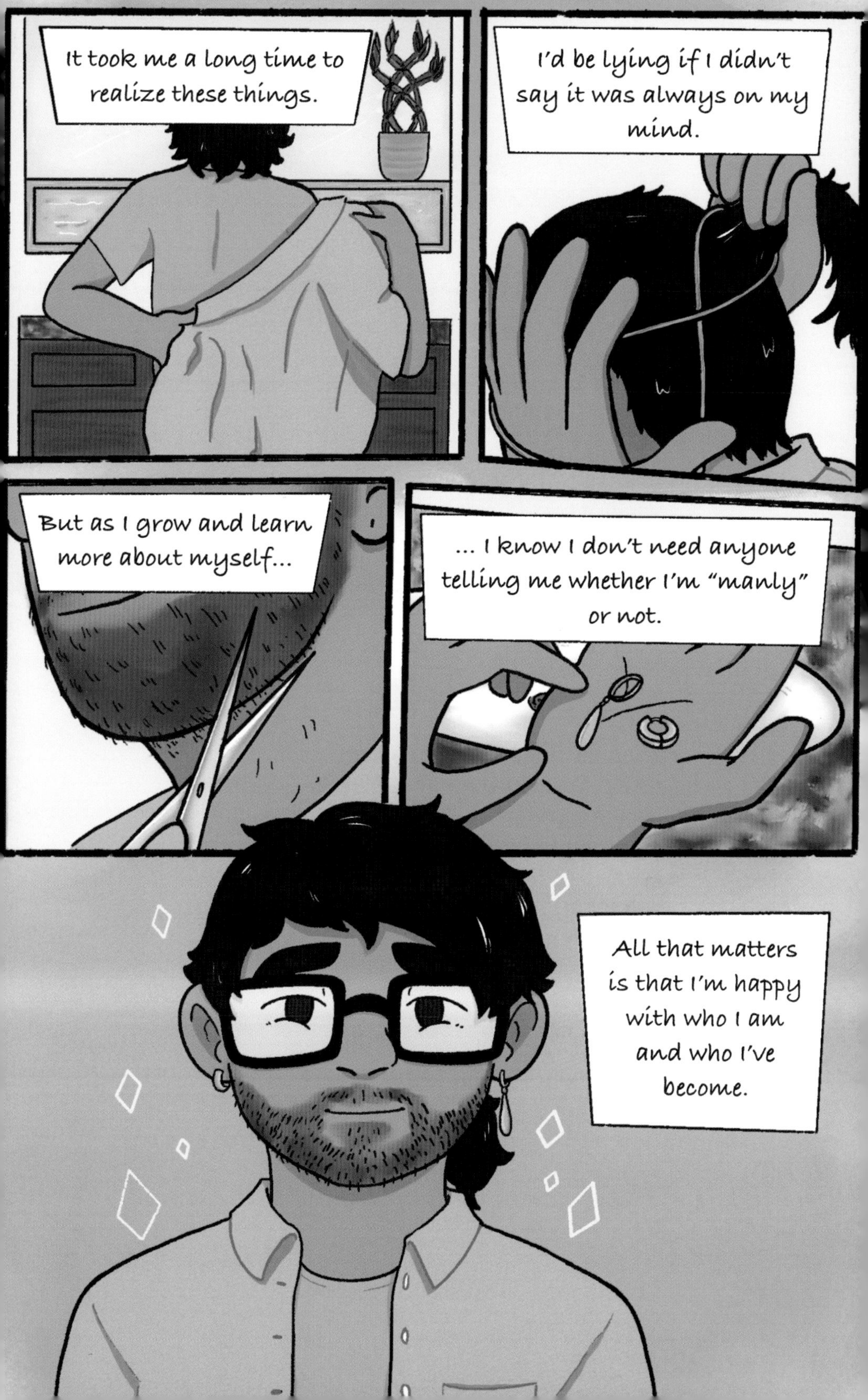
It took me a long time to realize these things.
I'd be lying if I didn't say it was always on my mind.
But as I grow and learn more about myself...
... I know I don't need anyone telling me whether I'm "manly" or not.
All that matters is that I'm happy with who I am and who I've become.

ZHEN
(THEY/THEM)

Zhen is a queer, trans, autistic Chinese artist raised in Atlanta, Georgia. With a background in graphic design, they now work full time as an independent artist and creator. When they're not busy creating something, they're usually deep in thought about life and other existential matters . . . or silly nonsense and curiosities that have no answer.

You can find them on Instagram:
@worldofzhen

UNDEFINED

BY ZHEN TSO

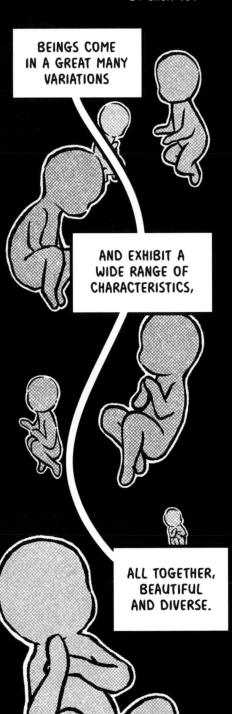

BEINGS COME IN A GREAT MANY VARIATIONS

AND EXHIBIT A WIDE RANGE OF CHARACTERISTICS,

ALL TOGETHER, BEAUTIFUL AND DIVERSE.

UNFORTUNATELY, FROM THE MOMENT WE ENTER INTO THE WORLD— INTO SOCIETY—WE GET SORTED INTO ONE OF TWO CATEGORIES.

IT'S AN OVERSIMPLIFIED SYSTEM APPLIED TO ALL, REGARDLESS OF WHETHER IT'S A GOOD FIT.

SO WHEN IT WAS MY TIME, LIKE ALL THE OTHERS, I WAS SORTED AND SENT OFF INTO THE WORLD.

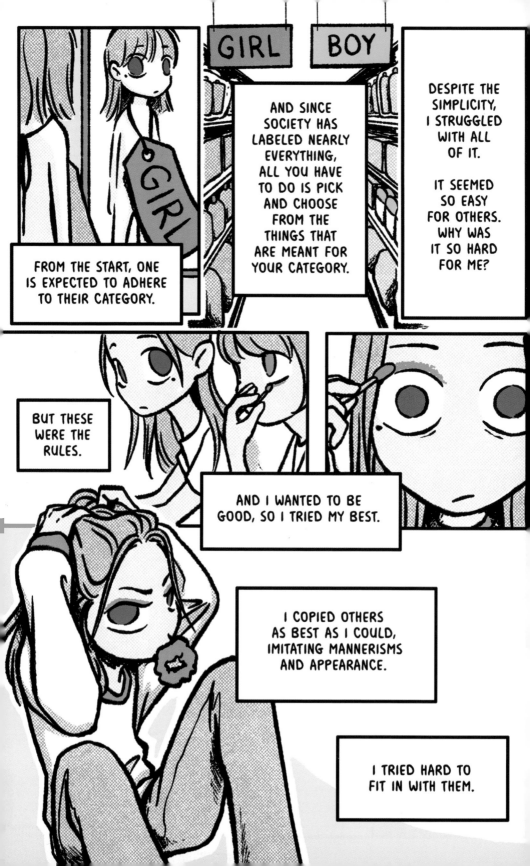

GIRL   BOY

FROM THE START, ONE IS EXPECTED TO ADHERE TO THEIR CATEGORY.

AND SINCE SOCIETY HAS LABELED NEARLY EVERYTHING, ALL YOU HAVE TO DO IS PICK AND CHOOSE FROM THE THINGS THAT ARE MEANT FOR YOUR CATEGORY.

DESPITE THE SIMPLICITY, I STRUGGLED WITH ALL OF IT.

IT SEEMED SO EASY FOR OTHERS. WHY WAS IT SO HARD FOR ME?

BUT THESE WERE THE RULES.

AND I WANTED TO BE GOOD, SO I TRIED MY BEST.

I COPIED OTHERS AS BEST AS I COULD, IMITATING MANNERISMS AND APPEARANCE.

I TRIED HARD TO FIT IN WITH THEM.

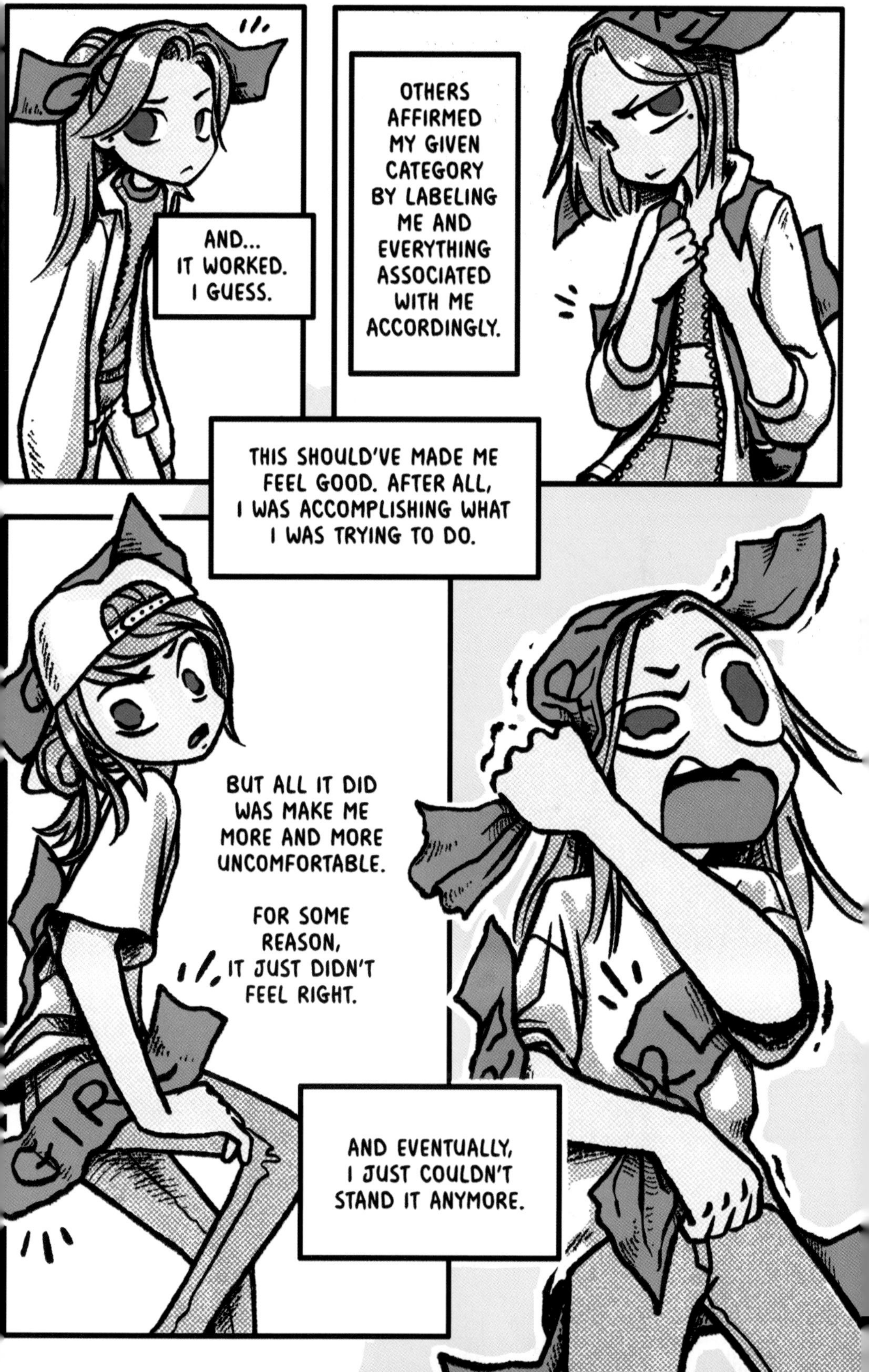
AND... IT WORKED. I GUESS.
OTHERS AFFIRMED MY GIVEN CATEGORY BY LABELING ME AND EVERYTHING ASSOCIATED WITH ME ACCORDINGLY.
THIS SHOULD'VE MADE ME FEEL GOOD. AFTER ALL, I WAS ACCOMPLISHING WHAT I WAS TRYING TO DO.
BUT ALL IT DID WAS MAKE ME MORE AND MORE UNCOMFORTABLE.
FOR SOME REASON, IT JUST DIDN'T FEEL RIGHT.
AND EVENTUALLY, I JUST COULDN'T STAND IT ANYMORE.

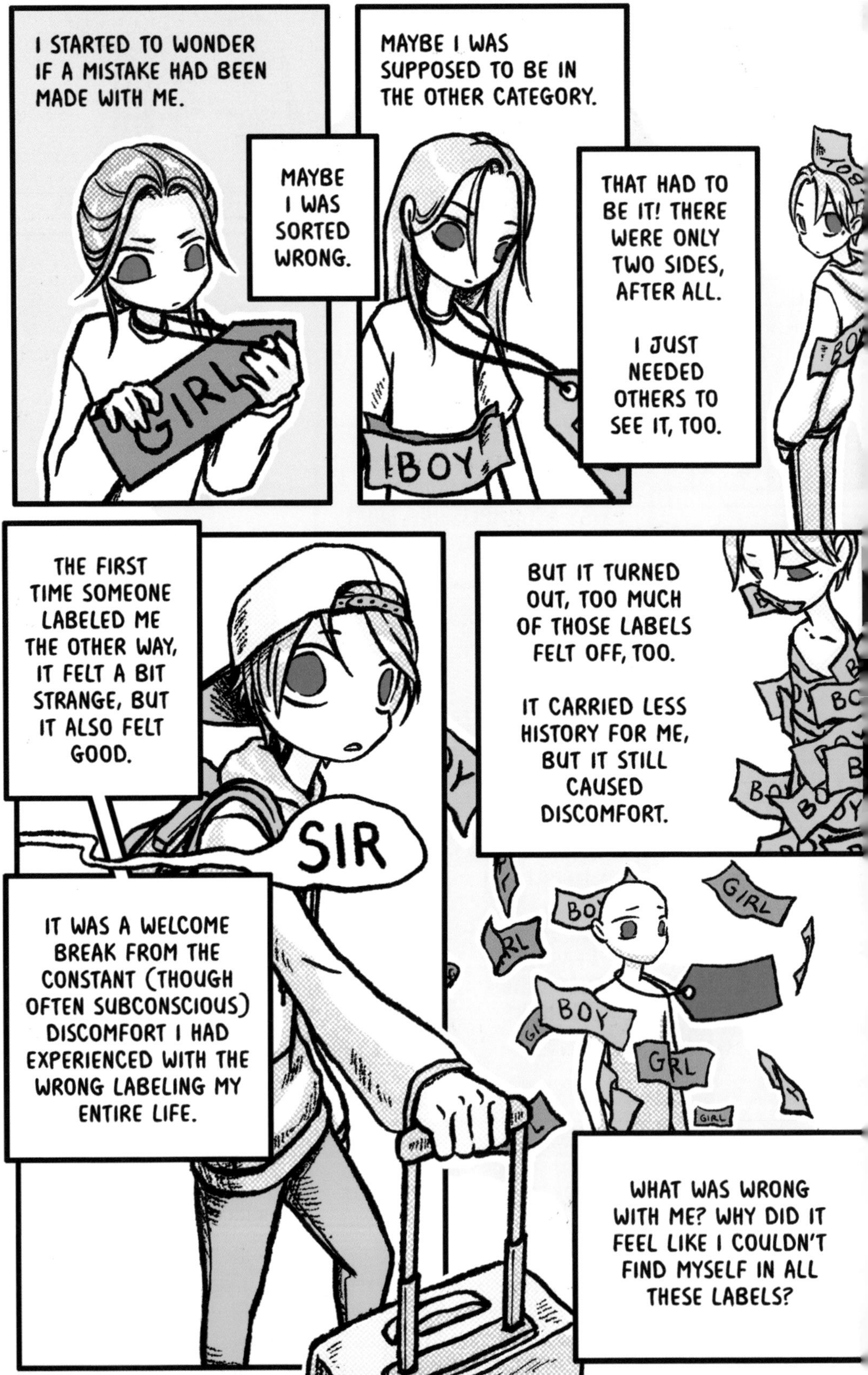

I STARTED TO WONDER IF A MISTAKE HAD BEEN MADE WITH ME.
GIRL
MAYBE I WAS SORTED WRONG.
MAYBE I WAS SUPPOSED TO BE IN THE OTHER CATEGORY.
BOY
THAT HAD TO BE IT! THERE WERE ONLY TWO SIDES, AFTER ALL.
I JUST NEEDED OTHERS TO SEE IT, TOO.
BOY
BOY
THE FIRST TIME SOMEONE LABELED ME THE OTHER WAY, IT FELT A BIT STRANGE, BUT IT ALSO FELT GOOD.
SIR
BUT IT TURNED OUT, TOO MUCH OF THOSE LABELS FELT OFF, TOO.
IT CARRIED LESS HISTORY FOR ME, BUT IT STILL CAUSED DISCOMFORT.
IT WAS A WELCOME BREAK FROM THE CONSTANT (THOUGH OFTEN SUBCONSCIOUS) DISCOMFORT I HAD EXPERIENCED WITH THE WRONG LABELING MY ENTIRE LIFE.
GIRL
BOY
BOY
GRL
GIRL
WHAT WAS WRONG WITH ME? WHY DID IT FEEL LIKE I COULDN'T FIND MYSELF IN ALL THESE LABELS?

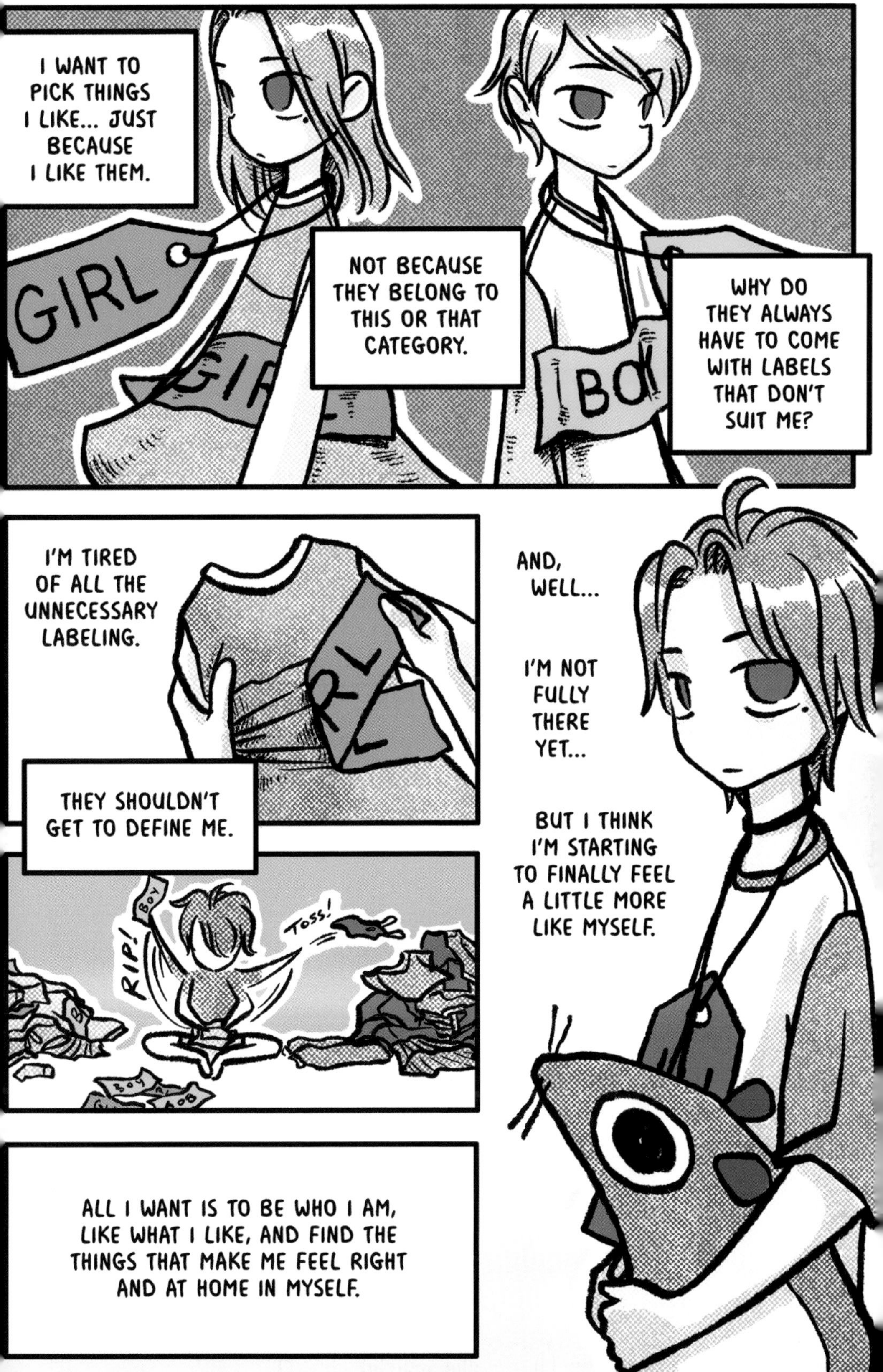
I WANT TO PICK THINGS I LIKE... JUST BECAUSE I LIKE THEM.
GIRL
GIRL
NOT BECAUSE THEY BELONG TO THIS OR THAT CATEGORY.
BOY
WHY DO THEY ALWAYS HAVE TO COME WITH LABELS THAT DON'T SUIT ME?
I'M TIRED OF ALL THE UNNECESSARY LABELING.
THEY SHOULDN'T GET TO DEFINE ME.
RIP!
BOY
TOSS!
AND, WELL...
I'M NOT FULLY THERE YET...
BUT I THINK I'M STARTING TO FINALLY FEEL A LITTLE MORE LIKE MYSELF.
ALL I WANT IS TO BE WHO I AM, LIKE WHAT I LIKE, AND FIND THE THINGS THAT MAKE ME FEEL RIGHT AND AT HOME IN MYSELF.

ASHI
(HE/THEY)

Ashi is a Taiwanese-Filipino artist based in Canada. He publishes a webcomic called *Life is Confusing* on Tapas. Other than drawing, he enjoys playing video games in his spare time.

You can find them on Instagram:
@ashi_cookie

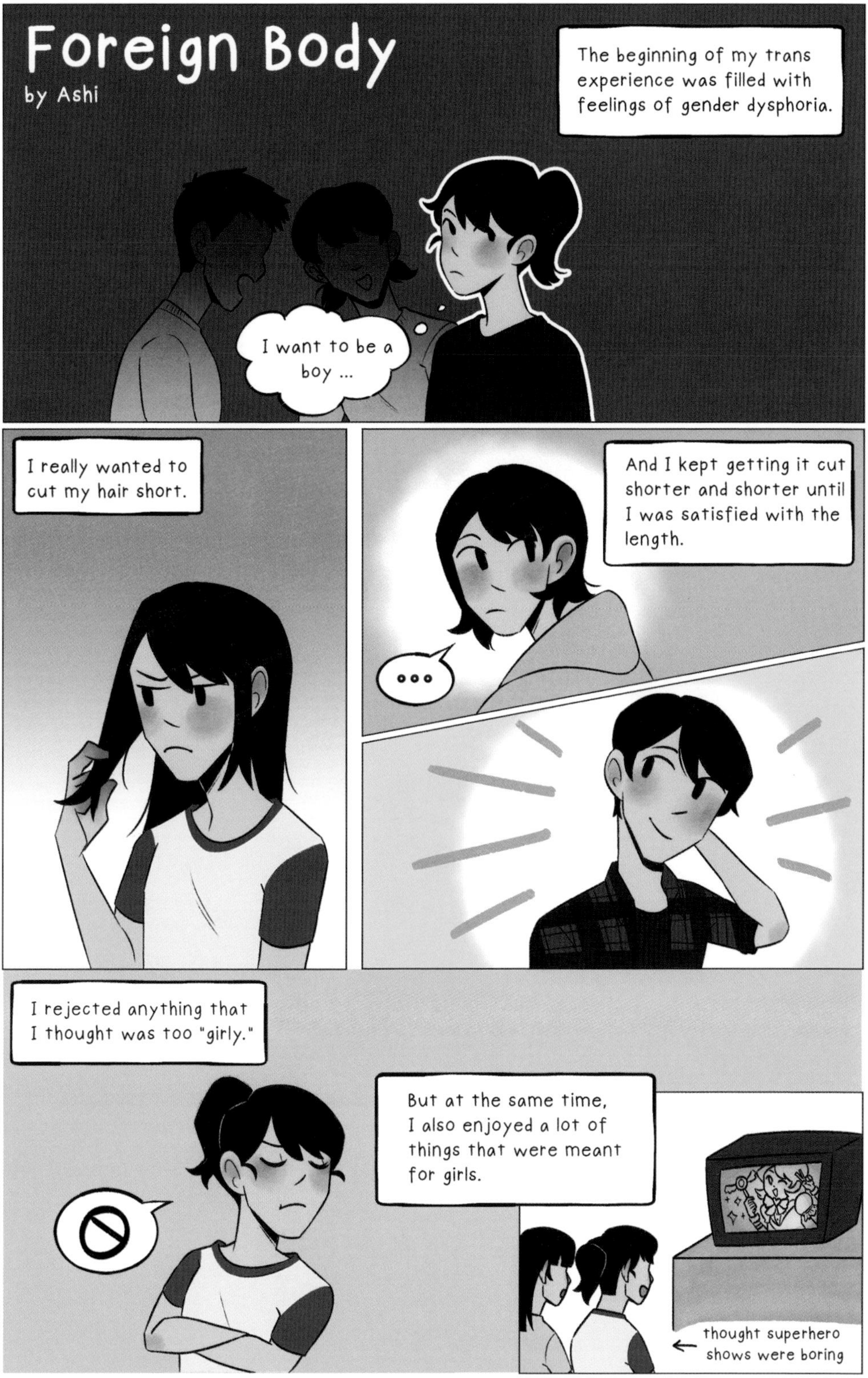
Foreign Body
by Ashi
The beginning of my trans experience was filled with feelings of gender dysphoria.
I want to be a boy ...
I really wanted to cut my hair short.
And I kept getting it cut shorter and shorter until I was satisfied with the length.
...
I rejected anything that I thought was too "girly."
But at the same time, I also enjoyed a lot of things that were meant for girls.
thought superhero shows were boring

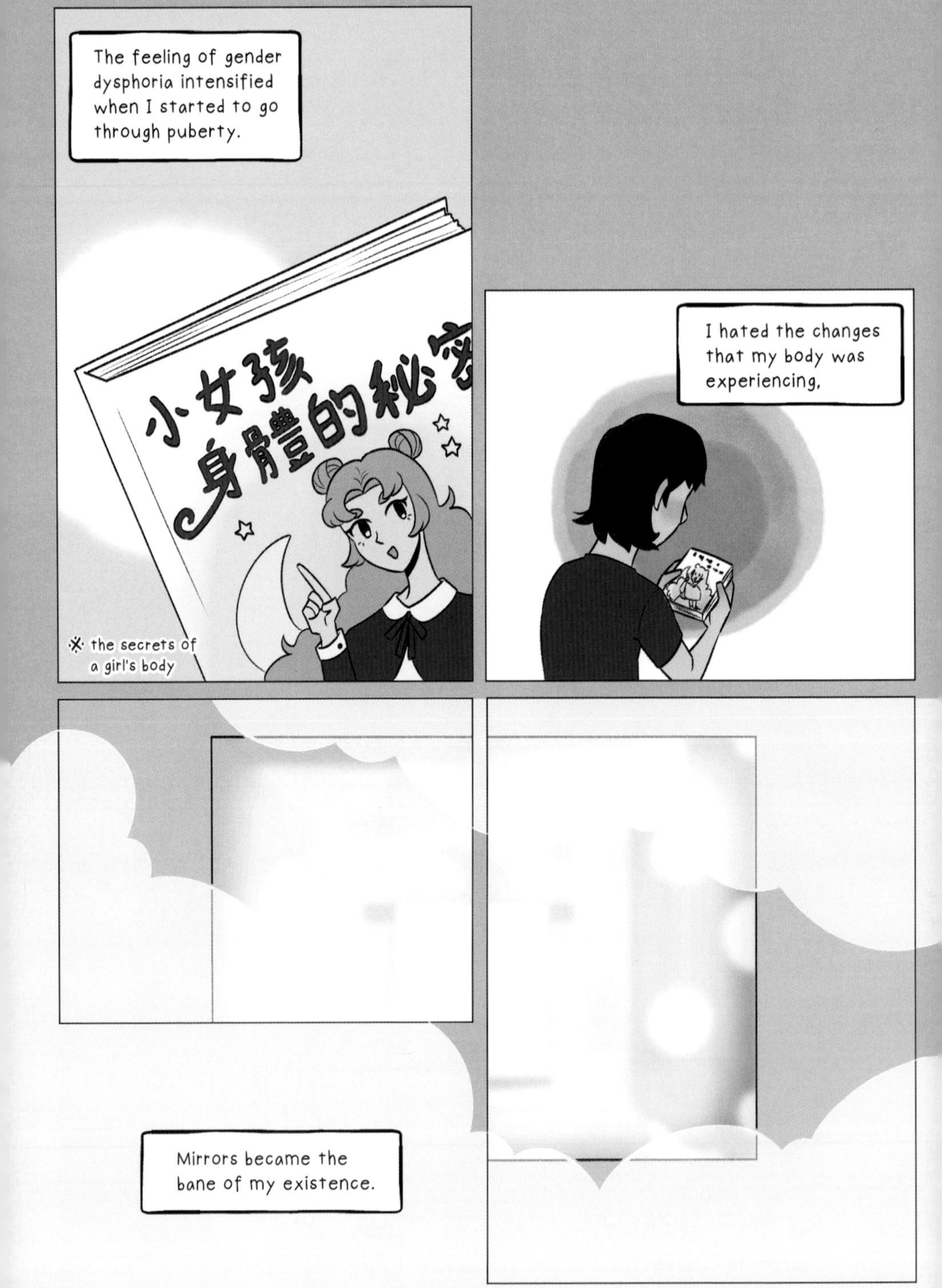
The feeling of gender dysphoria intensified when I started to go through puberty.
小女孩
身體的秘
※ the secrets of a girl's body
I hated the changes that my body was experiencing,
Mirrors became the bane of my existence.

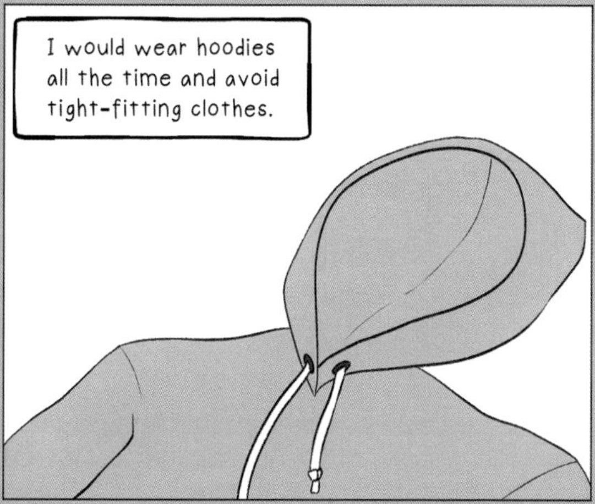
I would wear hoodies all the time and avoid tight-fitting clothes.

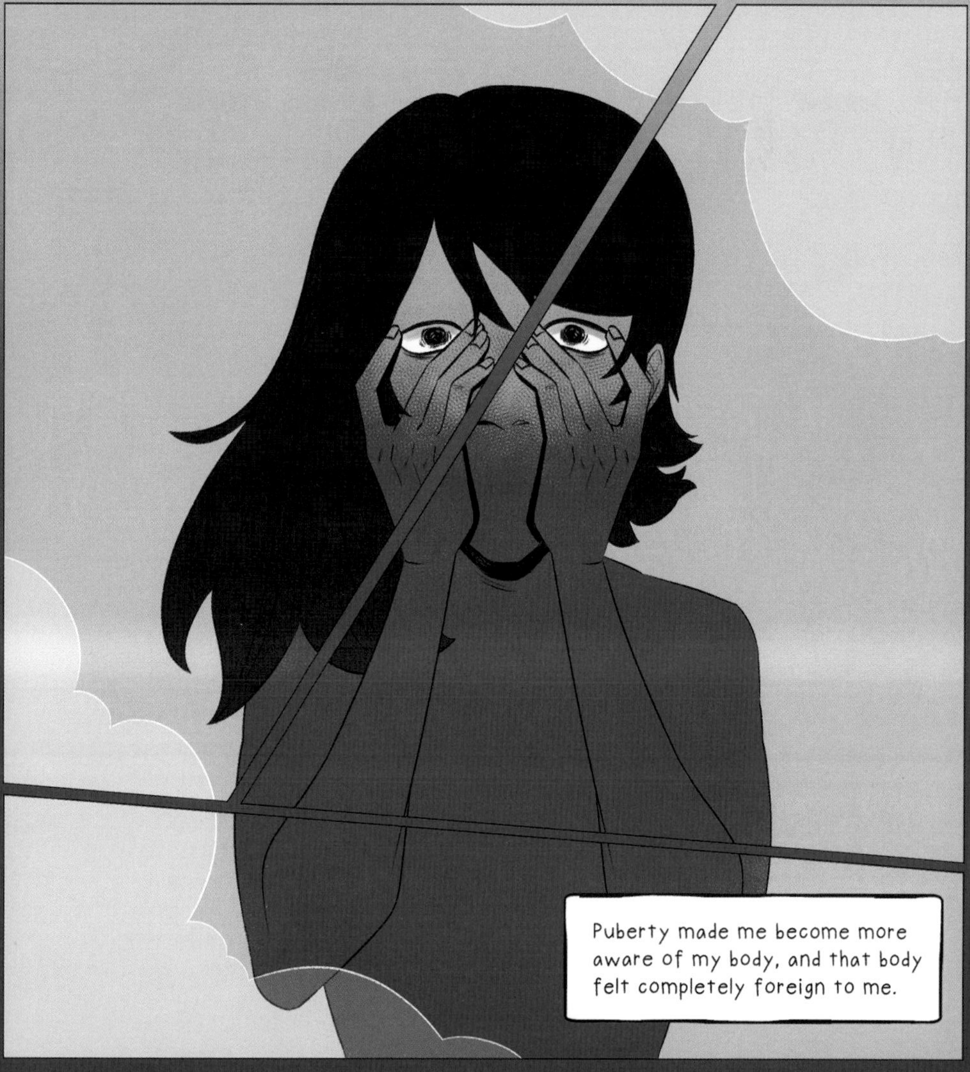
Puberty made me become more aware of my body, and that body felt completely foreign to me.

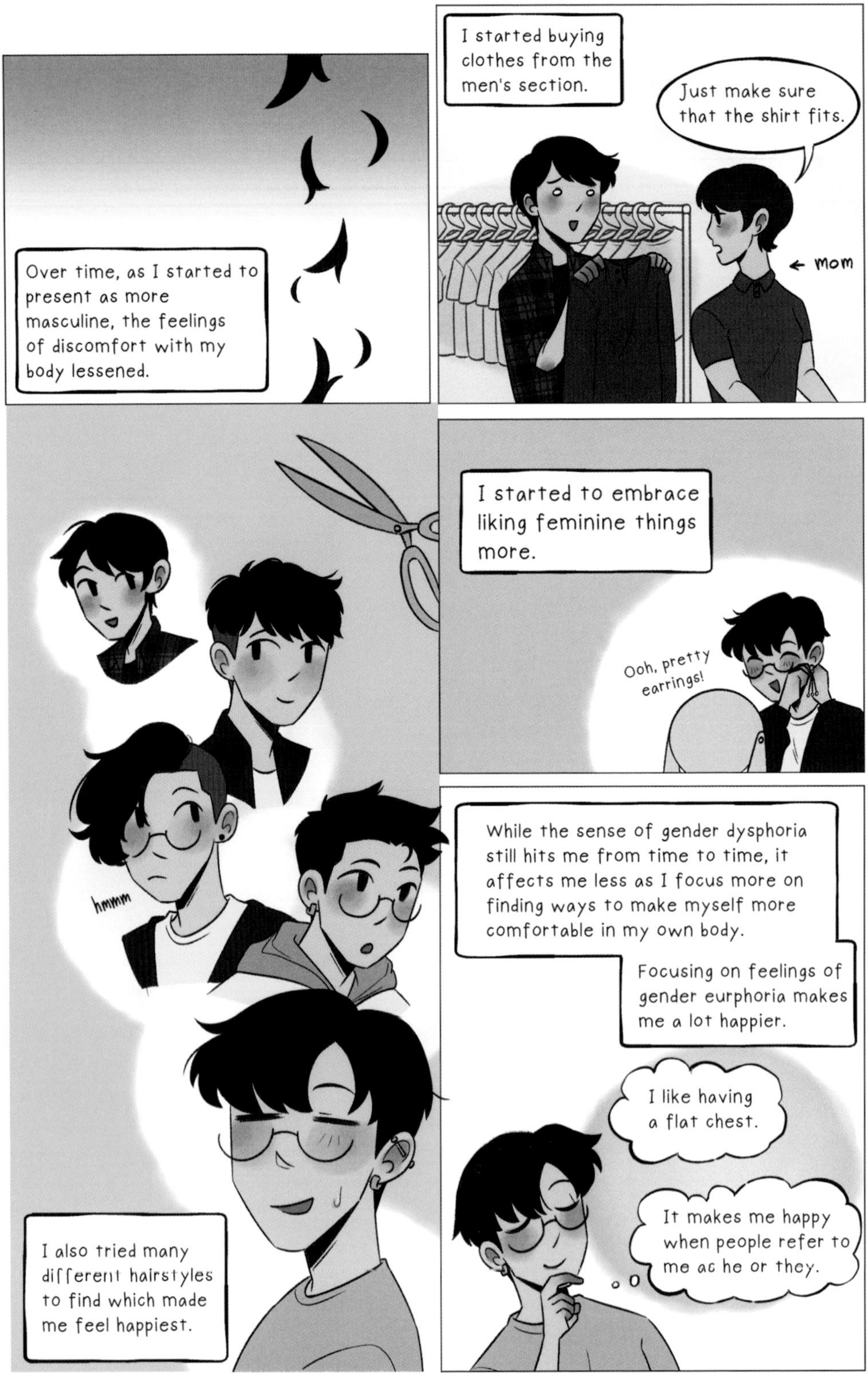
Over time, as I started to present as more masculine, the feelings of discomfort with my body lessened.
I started buying clothes from the men's section.
Just make sure that the shirt fits.
← mom
I started to embrace liking feminine things more.
Ooh, pretty earrings!
hmmm
I also tried many different hairstyles to find which made me feel happiest.
While the sense of gender dysphoria still hits me from time to time, it affects me less as I focus more on finding ways to make myself more comfortable in my own body.
Focusing on feelings of gender eurphoria makes me a lot happier.
I like having a flat chest.
It makes me happy when people refer to me as he or they.

VIXTOPHER
(THEY/THEM)

Vixtopher is a Chicago-based illustrator. They take inspiration from their Mexican-American heritage, science fiction, and the queer community. Their work focuses on exploring character development in futuristic and surreal settings.

You can find them on Instagram:
@vixtopher

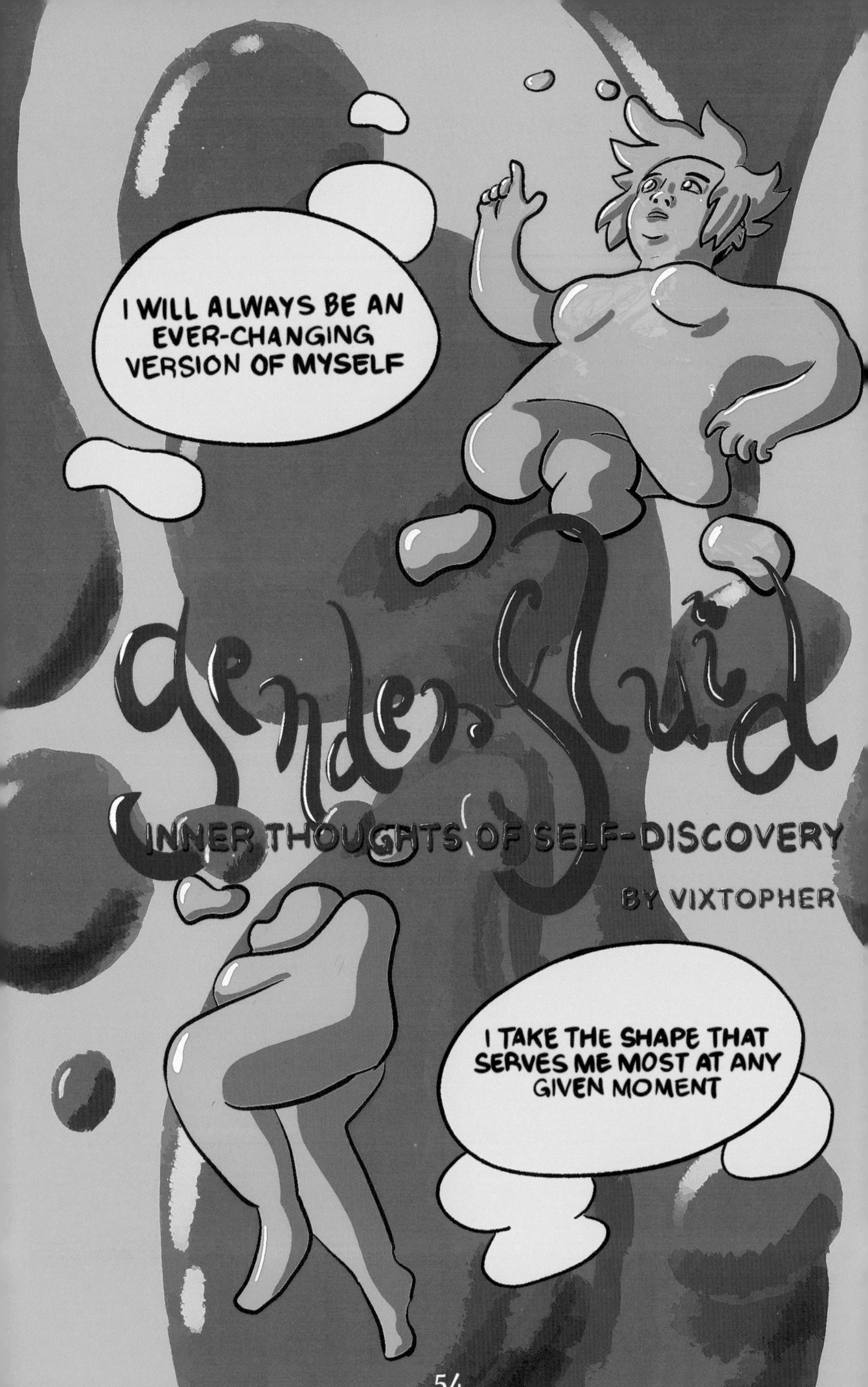
I WILL ALWAYS BE AN EVER-CHANGING VERSION OF MYSELF
genderfluid
INNER THOUGHTS OF SELF-DISCOVERY
BY VIXTOPHER
I TAKE THE SHAPE THAT SERVES ME MOST AT ANY GIVEN MOMENT

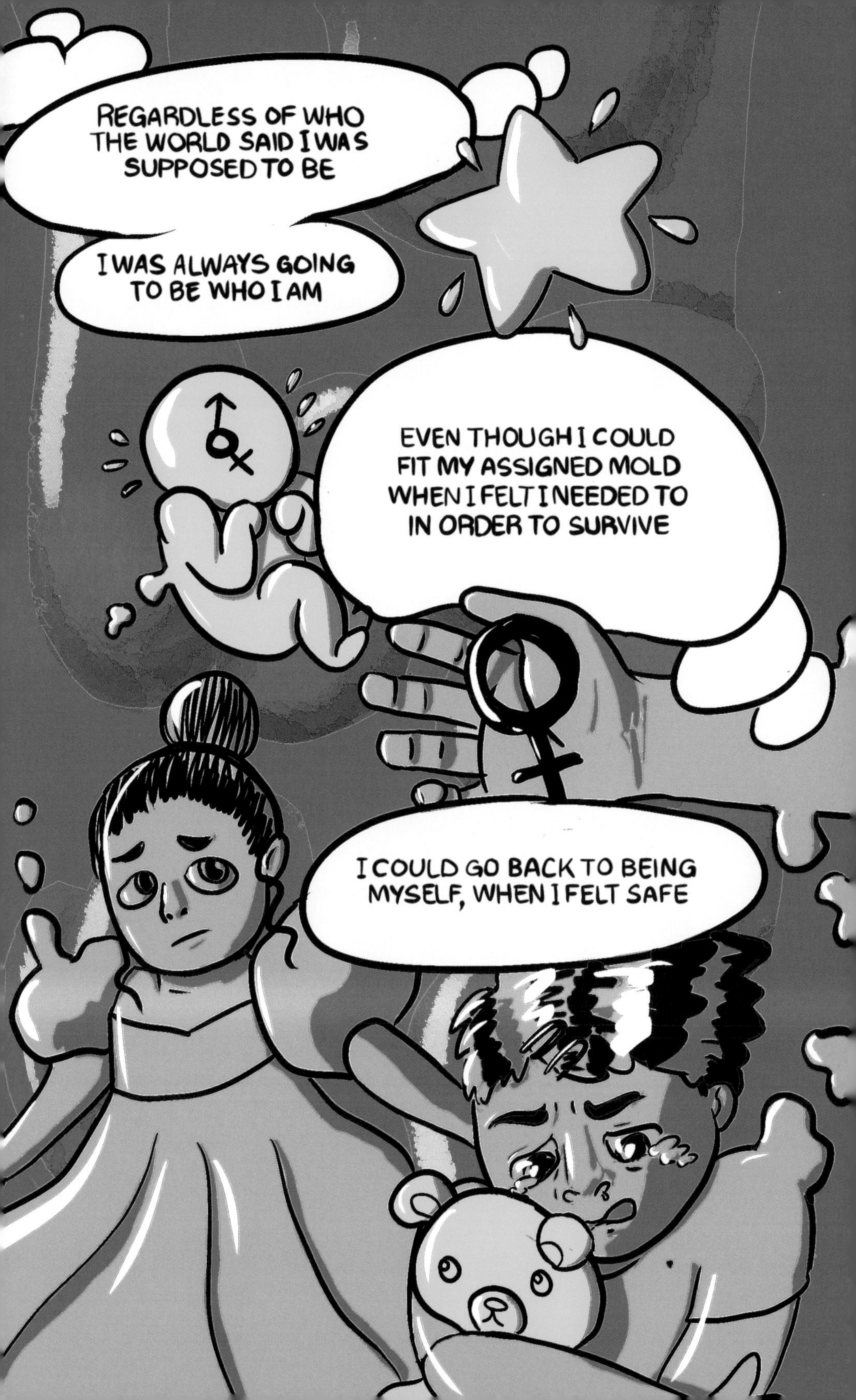
REGARDLESS OF WHO THE WORLD SAID I WAS SUPPOSED TO BE
I WAS ALWAYS GOING TO BE WHO I AM
EVEN THOUGH I COULD FIT MY ASSIGNED MOLD WHEN I FELT I NEEDED TO IN ORDER TO SURVIVE
I COULD GO BACK TO BEING MYSELF, WHEN I FELT SAFE

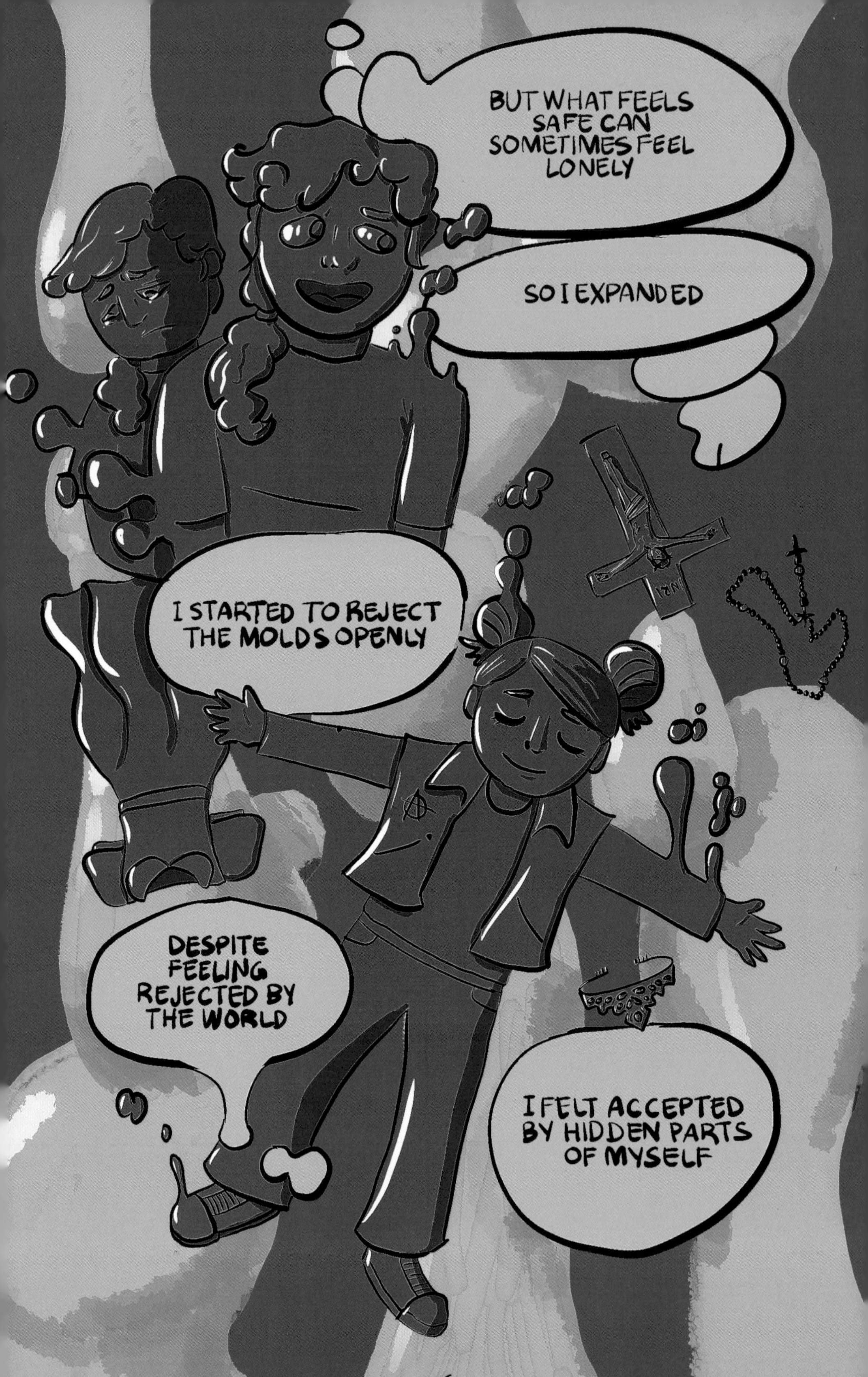
BUT WHAT FEELS SAFE CAN SOMETIMES FEEL LONELY
SO I EXPANDED
I STARTED TO REJECT THE MOLDS OPENLY
DESPITE FEELING REJECTED BY THE WORLD
I FELT ACCEPTED BY HIDDEN PARTS OF MYSELF

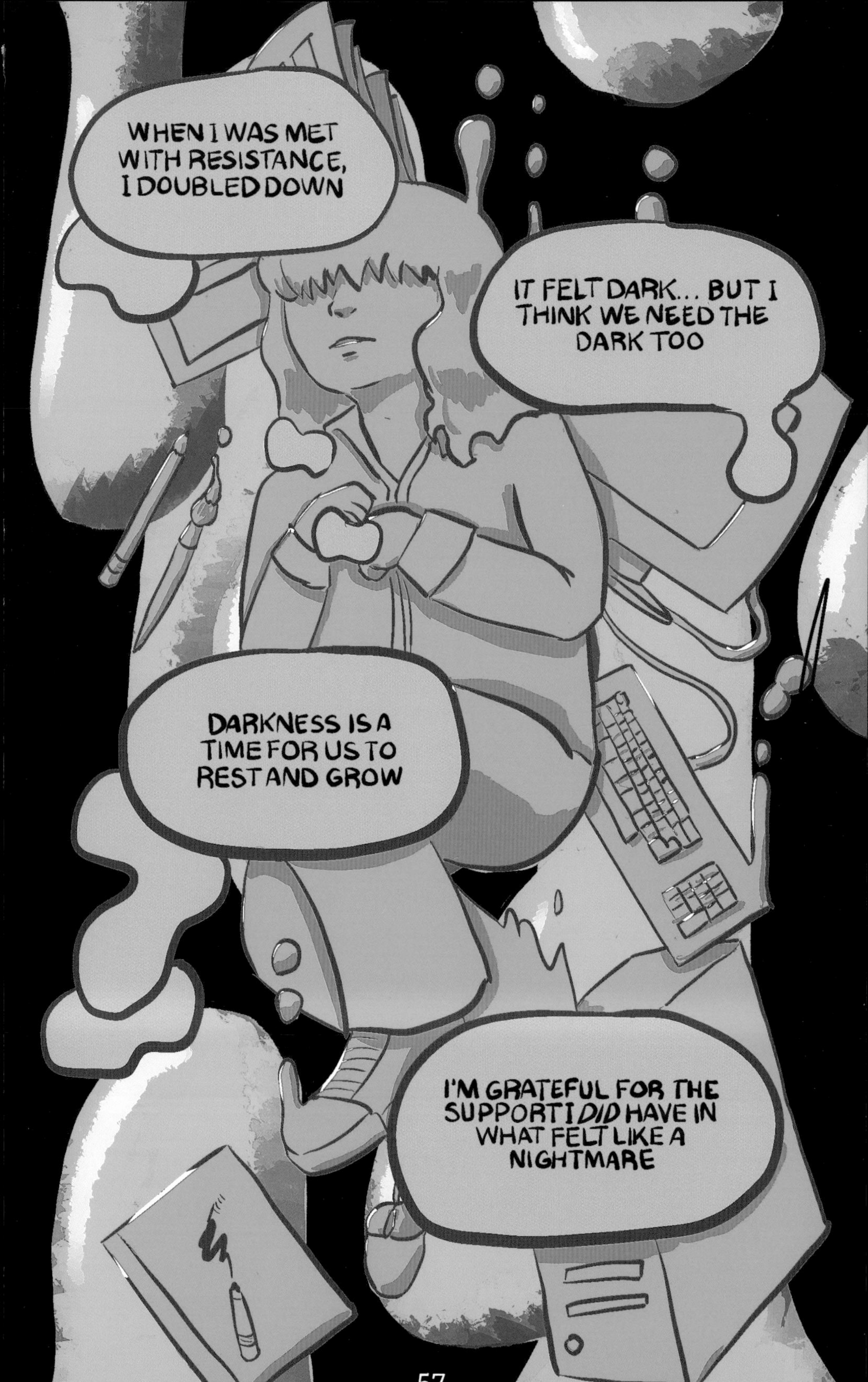
WHEN I WAS MET WITH RESISTANCE, I DOUBLED DOWN
IT FELT DARK... BUT I THINK WE NEED THE DARK TOO
DARKNESS IS A TIME FOR US TO REST AND GROW
I'M GRATEFUL FOR THE SUPPORT I *DID* HAVE IN WHAT FELT LIKE A NIGHTMARE

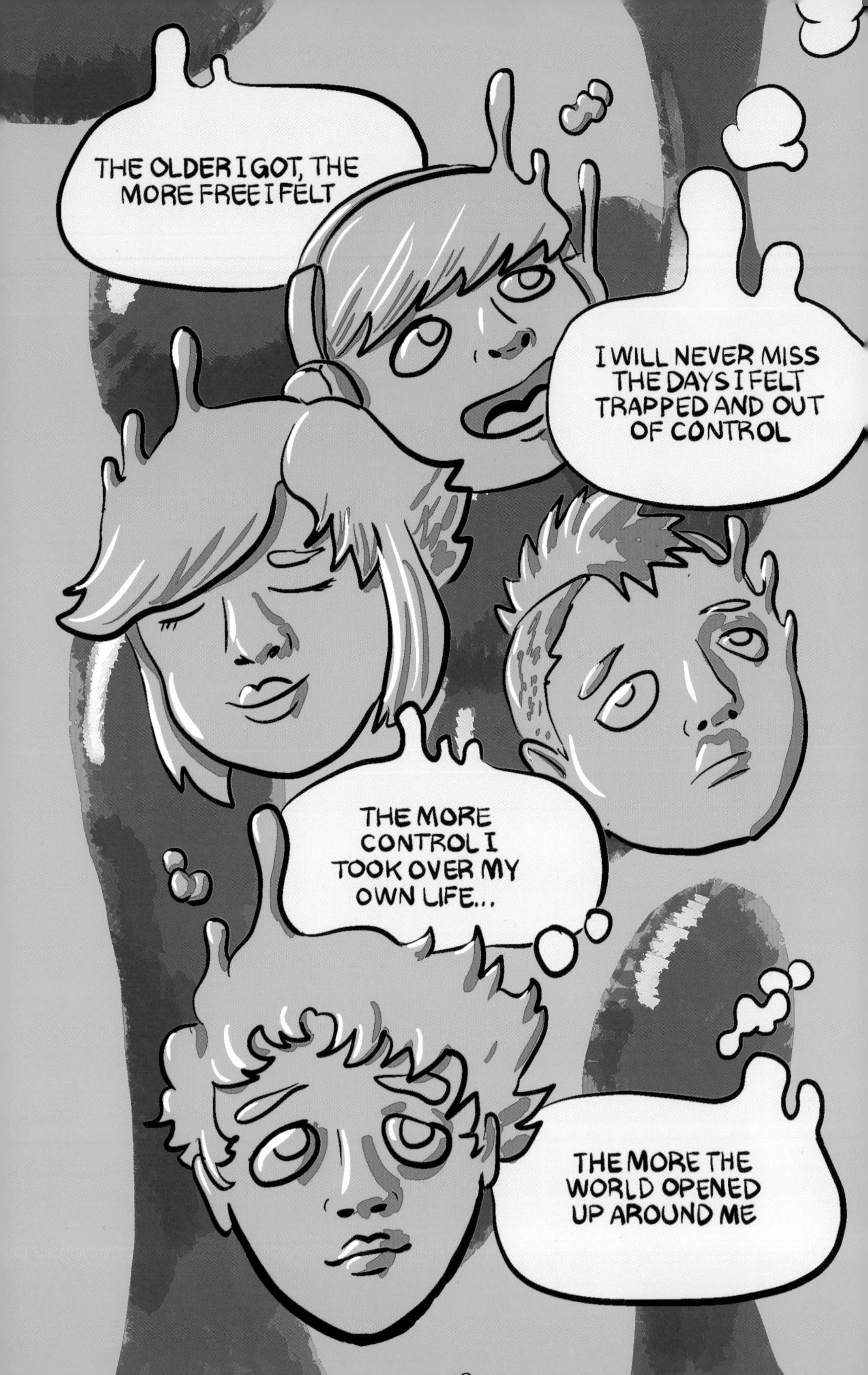
THE OLDER I GOT, THE MORE FREE I FELT
I WILL NEVER MISS THE DAYS I FELT TRAPPED AND OUT OF CONTROL
THE MORE CONTROL I TOOK OVER MY OWN LIFE...
THE MORE THE WORLD OPENED UP AROUND ME

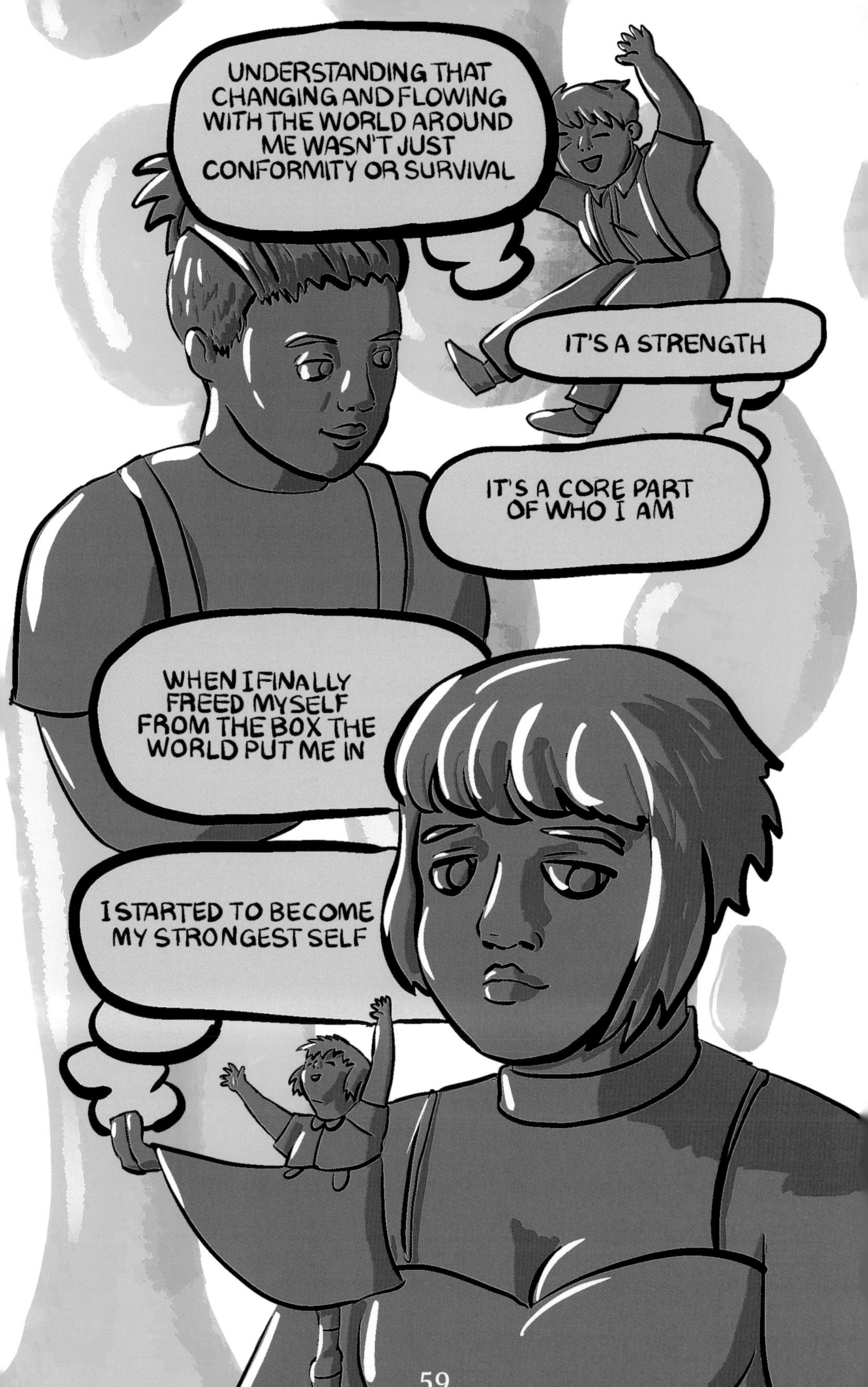
UNDERSTANDING THAT CHANGING AND FLOWING WITH THE WORLD AROUND ME WASN'T JUST CONFORMITY OR SURVIVAL
IT'S A STRENGTH
IT'S A CORE PART OF WHO I AM
WHEN I FINALLY FREED MYSELF FROM THE BOX THE WORLD PUT ME IN
I STARTED TO BECOME MY STRONGEST SELF

VERONICA JANE
(SHE/HER)

Veronica is an emerging trans woman living in the miserable heat of Australia with her wife and small cat (who is a very good boy). She creates *Veronica Triumphant*, a comic about her life as a trans woman and the parts of her life that have nothing to do with being a trans woman.

You can find her online at:
veronicajane.net

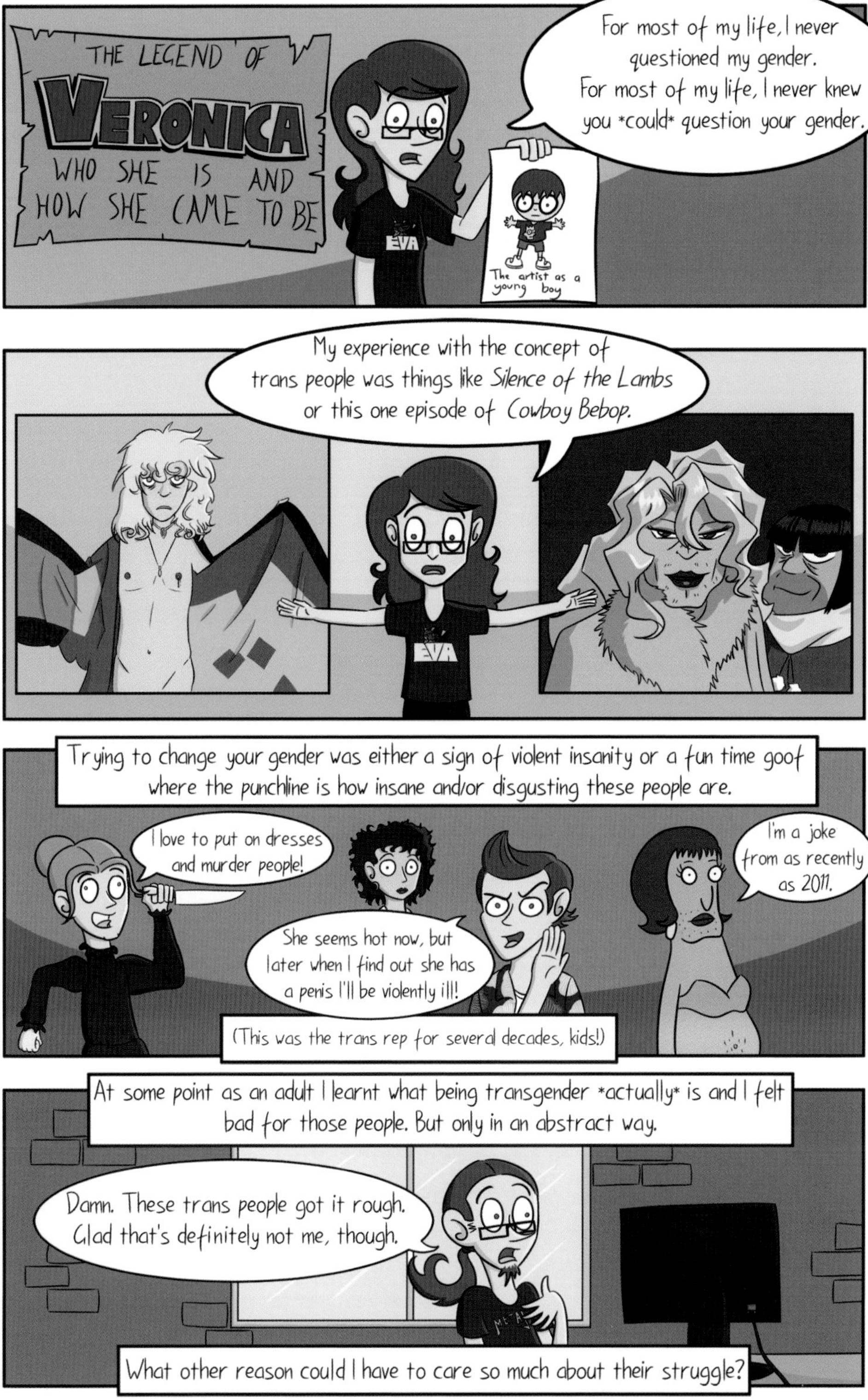
THE LEGEND OF
VERONICA
WHO SHE IS AND HOW SHE CAME TO BE
For most of my life, I never questioned my gender.
For most of my life, I never knew you *could* question your gender.
The artist as a young boy
My experience with the concept of trans people was things like Silence of the Lambs or this one episode of Cowboy Bebop.
Trying to change your gender was either a sign of violent insanity or a fun time goof where the punchline is how insane and/or disgusting these people are.
I love to put on dresses and murder people!
I'm a joke from as recently as 2011.
She seems hot now, but later when I find out she has a penis I'll be violently ill!
(This was the trans rep for several decades, kids!)
At some point as an adult I learnt what being transgender *actually* is and I felt bad for those people. But only in an abstract way.
Damn. These trans people got it rough. Glad that's definitely not me, though.
What other reason could I have to care so much about their struggle?

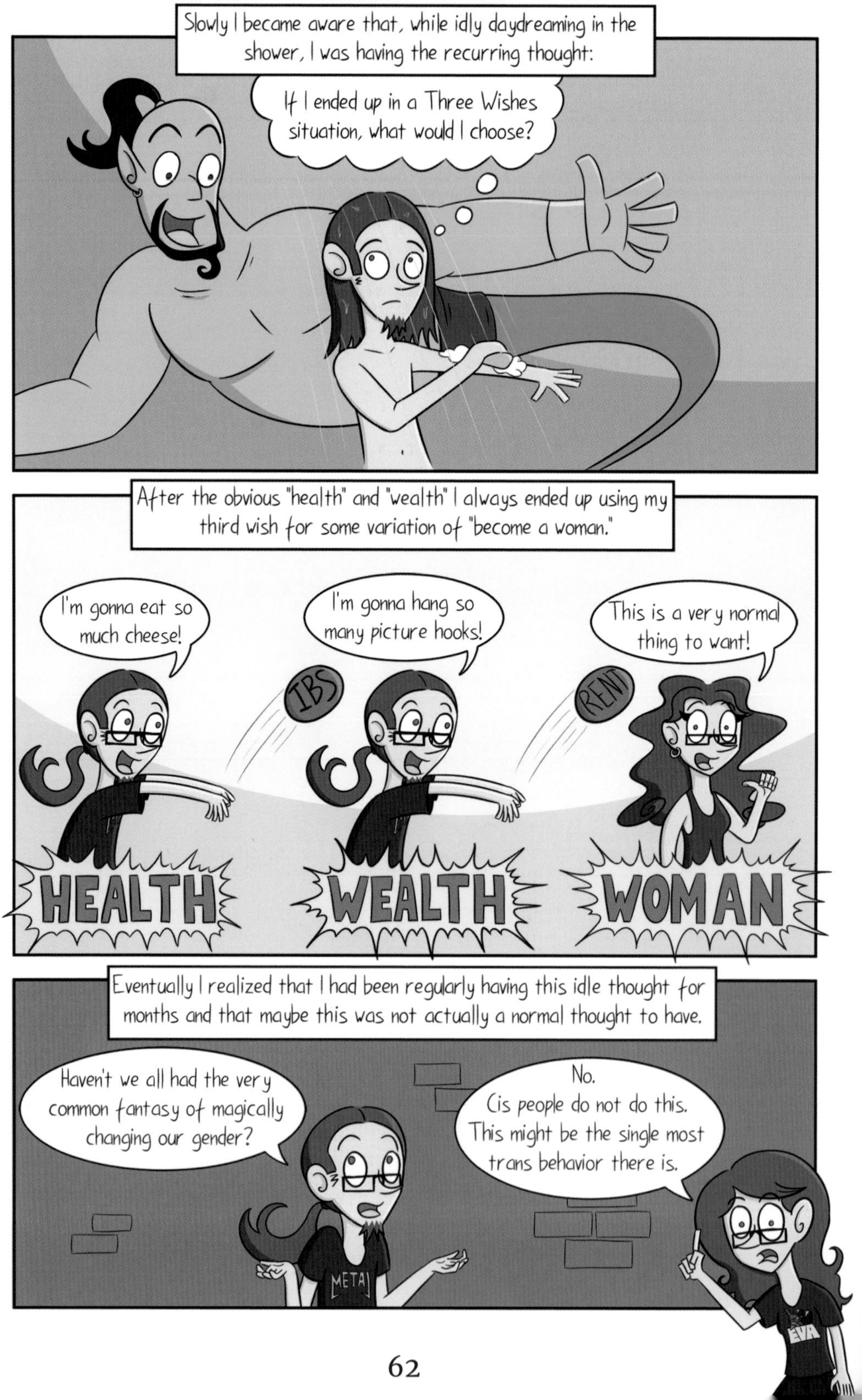
Slowly I became aware that, while idly daydreaming in the shower, I was having the recurring thought:
If I ended up in a Three Wishes situation, what would I choose?
After the obvious "health" and "wealth" I always ended up using my third wish for some variation of "become a woman."
I'm gonna eat so much cheese!
I'm gonna hang so many picture hooks!
This is a very normal thing to want!
IBS
RENT
HEALTH
WEALTH
WOMAN
Eventually I realized that I had been regularly having this idle thought for months and that maybe this was not actually a normal thought to have.
Haven't we all had the very common fantasy of magically changing our gender?
No.
Cis people do not do this.
This might be the single most trans behavior there is.
METAL
EVA

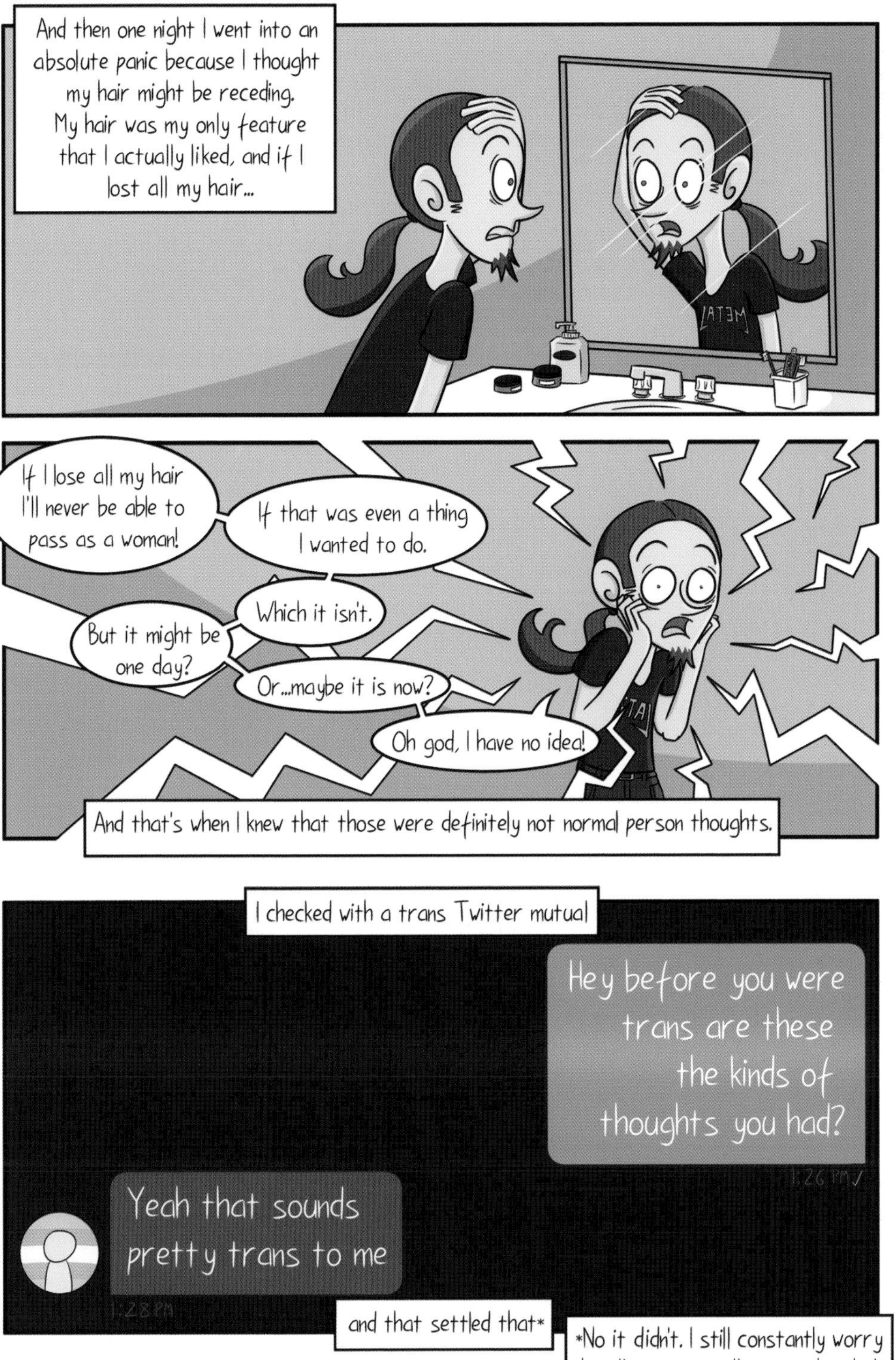
And then one night I went into an absolute panic because I thought my hair might be receding. My hair was my only feature that I actually liked, and if I lost all my hair...
If I lose all my hair I'll never be able to pass as a woman!
If that was even a thing I wanted to do.
Which it isn't.
But it might be one day?
Or...maybe it is now?
Oh god, I have no idea!
And that's when I knew that those were definitely not normal person thoughts.
I checked with a trans Twitter mutual
Hey before you were trans are these the kinds of thoughts you had?
1:26 PM
Yeah that sounds pretty trans to me
1:28 PM
and that settled that*
*No it didn't. I still constantly worry that I'm not actually trans, but let's keep things simple here.

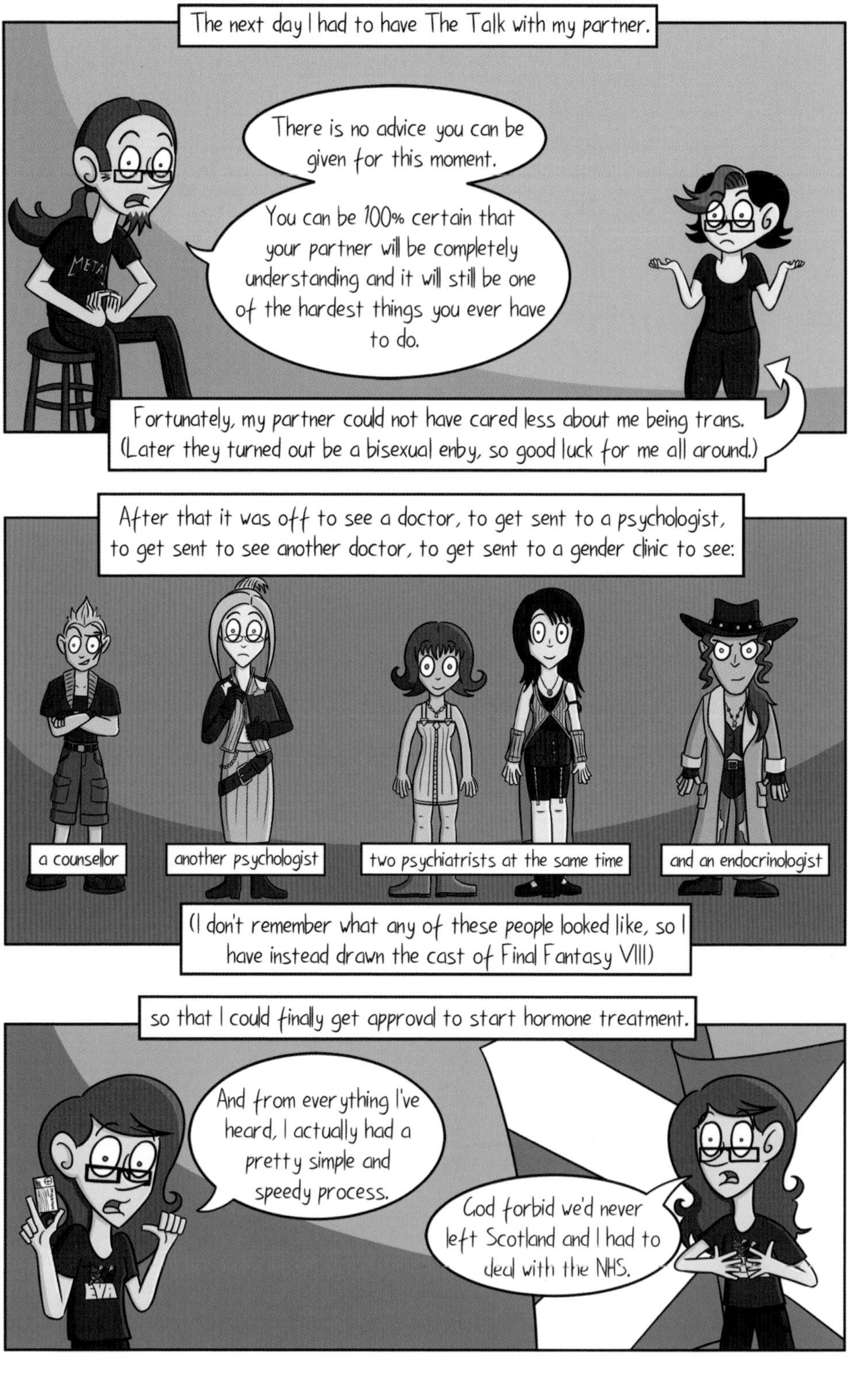

The next day I had to have The Talk with my partner.
There is no advice you can be given for this moment.
You can be 100% certain that your partner will be completely understanding and it will still be one of the hardest things you ever have to do.
Fortunately, my partner could not have cared less about me being trans. (Later they turned out be a bisexual enby, so good luck for me all around.)
After that it was off to see a doctor, to get sent to a psychologist, to get sent to see another doctor, to get sent to a gender clinic to see:
META
a counsellor
another psychologist
two psychiatrists at the same time
and an endocrinologist
(I don't remember what any of these people looked like, so I have instead drawn the cast of Final Fantasy VIII)
so that I could finally get approval to start hormone treatment.
And from everything I've heard, I actually had a pretty simple and speedy process.
God forbid we'd never left Scotland and I had to deal with the NHS.
EVA

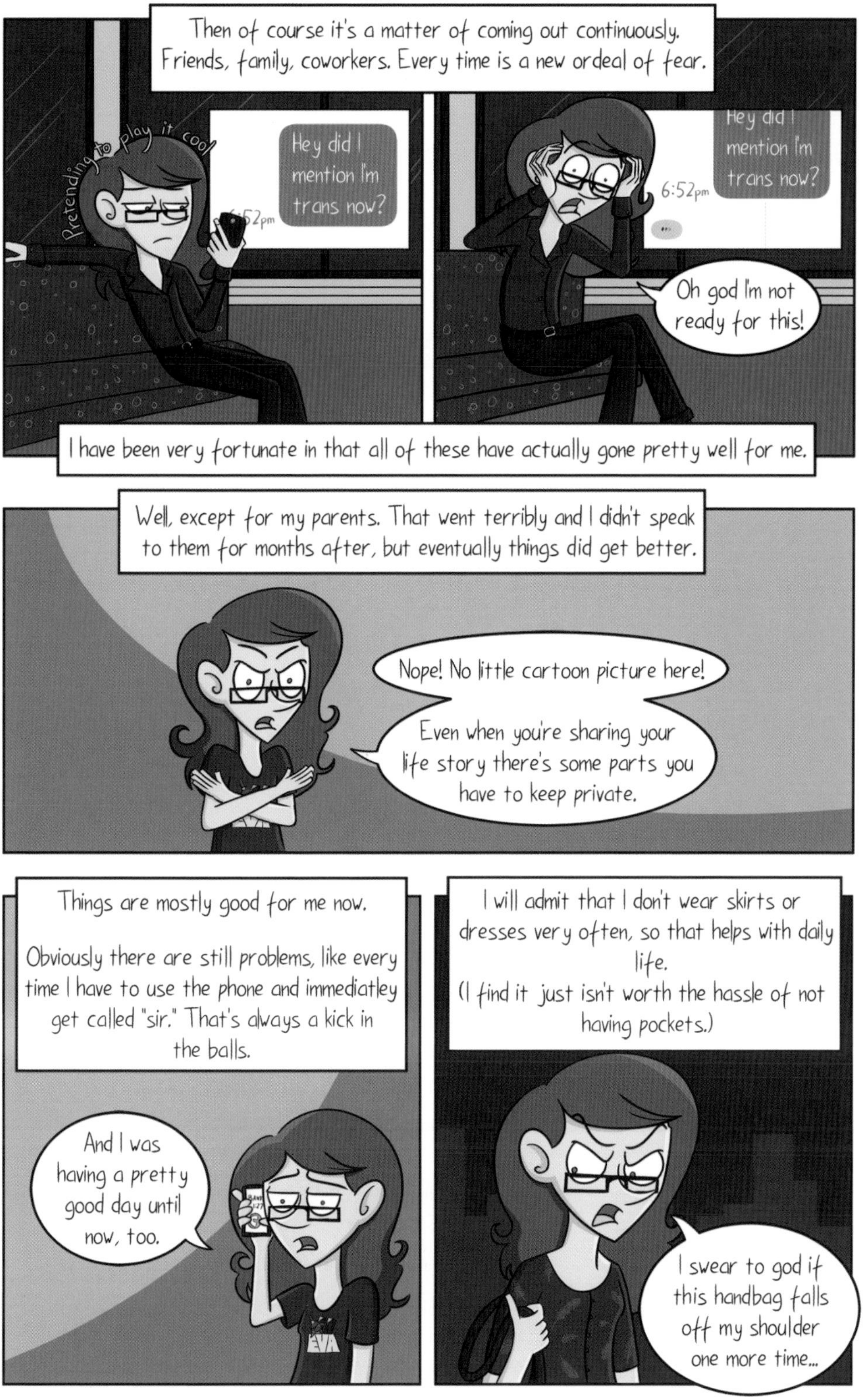
Then of course it's a matter of coming out continuously.
Friends, family, coworkers. Every time is a new ordeal of fear.
Pretending to play it cool
Hey did I mention I'm trans now?
6:52pm
6:52pm
Hey did I mention I'm trans now?
Oh god I'm not ready for this!
I have been very fortunate in that all of these have actually gone pretty well for me.
Well, except for my parents. That went terribly and I didn't speak to them for months after, but eventually things did get better.
Nope! No little cartoon picture here!
Even when you're sharing your life story there's some parts you have to keep private.
Things are mostly good for me now.
Obviously there are still problems, like every time I have to use the phone and immediatley get called "sir." That's always a kick in the balls.
And I was having a pretty good day until now, too.
I will admit that I don't wear skirts or dresses very often, so that helps with daily life.
(I find it just isn't worth the hassle of not having pockets.)
I swear to god if this handbag falls off my shoulder one more time...

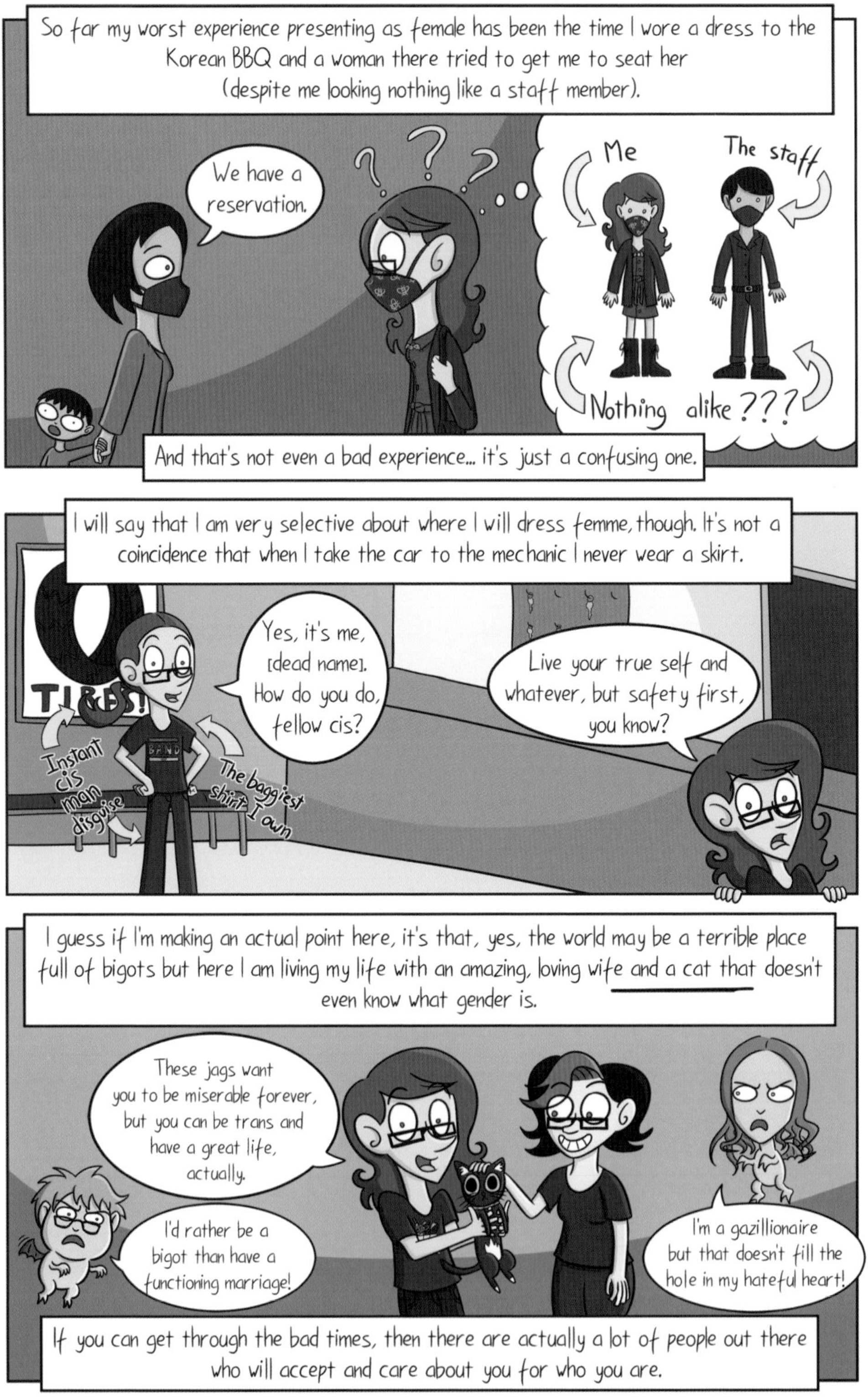
So far my worst experience presenting as female has been the time I wore a dress to the Korean BBQ and a woman there tried to get me to seat her (despite me looking nothing like a staff member).
We have a reservation.
???
Me
The staff
Nothing alike???
And that's not even a bad experience... it's just a confusing one.
I will say that I am very selective about where I will dress femme, though. It's not a coincidence that when I take the car to the mechanic I never wear a skirt.
Yes, it's me, [dead name]. How do you do, fellow cis?
Instant cis man disguise
The baggiest shirt I own
Live your true self and whatever, but safety first, you know?
I guess if I'm making an actual point here, it's that, yes, the world may be a terrible place full of bigots but here I am living my life with an amazing, loving wife and a cat that doesn't even know what gender is.
These jags want you to be miserable forever, but you can be trans and have a great life, actually.
I'd rather be a bigot than have a functioning marriage!
I'm a gazillionaire but that doesn't fill the hole in my hateful heart!
If you can get through the bad times, then there are actually a lot of people out there who will accept and care about you for who you are.

DASHI
(HE/THEY)

A transmasc artist and streamer currently living in Chicago with his horde of bunny plushies, his cat Jiggly Pepper, and his two roommates. He's quirky and chaotic, and when not freelancing you can catch him streaming as the Vtuber Lyspe.

You can find him on Twitter:
@Apakilyspe

LIFE CHOICES

By Dashi

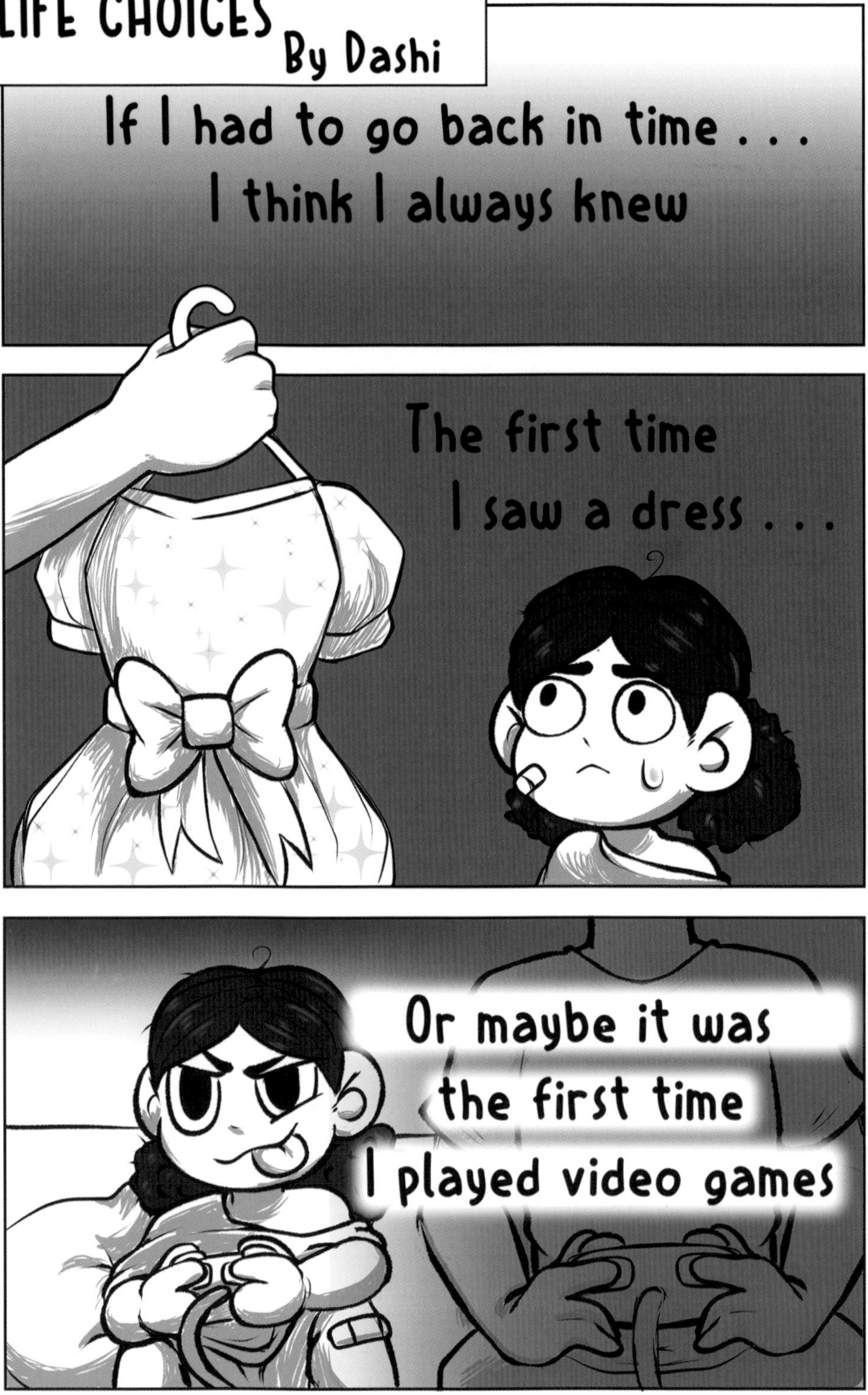
If I had to go back in time . . .
I think I always knew
The first time
I saw a dress . . .
Or maybe it was
the first time
I played video games

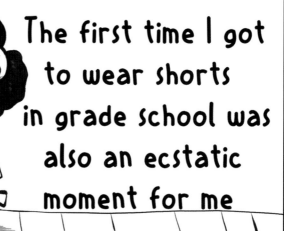

The first time I got to wear shorts in grade school was also an ecstatic moment for me

Don't get me wrong... I caught bugs

Played with dolls

And everything in between

It was overlooked when I was a child....

It was just a "PHASE"

I almost thought the same

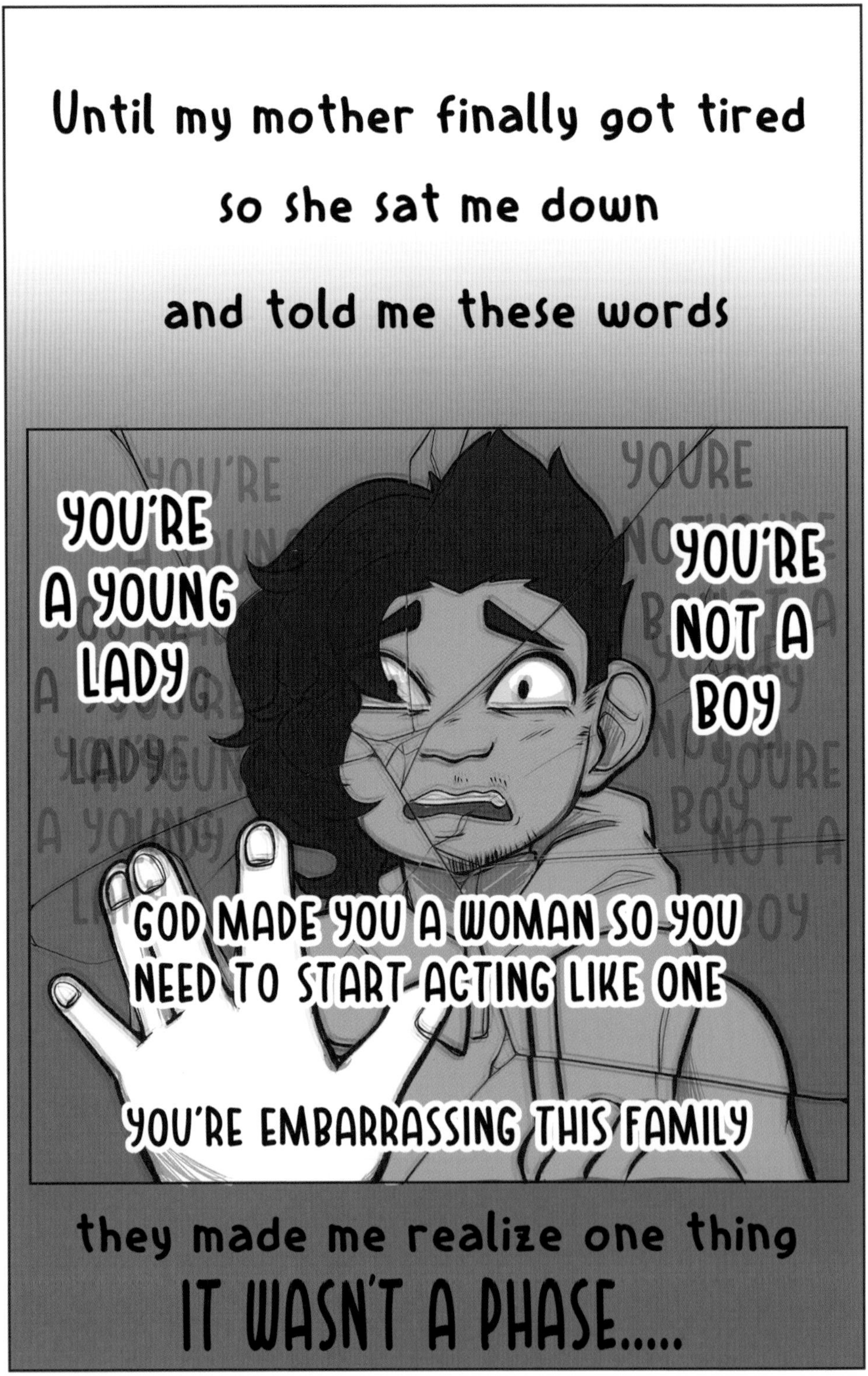
Until my mother finally got tired
so she sat me down
and told me these words
YOU'RE A YOUNG LADY
YOU'RE NOT A BOY
GOD MADE YOU A WOMAN SO YOU NEED TO START ACTING LIKE ONE
YOU'RE EMBARRASSING THIS FAMILY
they made me realize one thing
IT WASN'T A PHASE.....

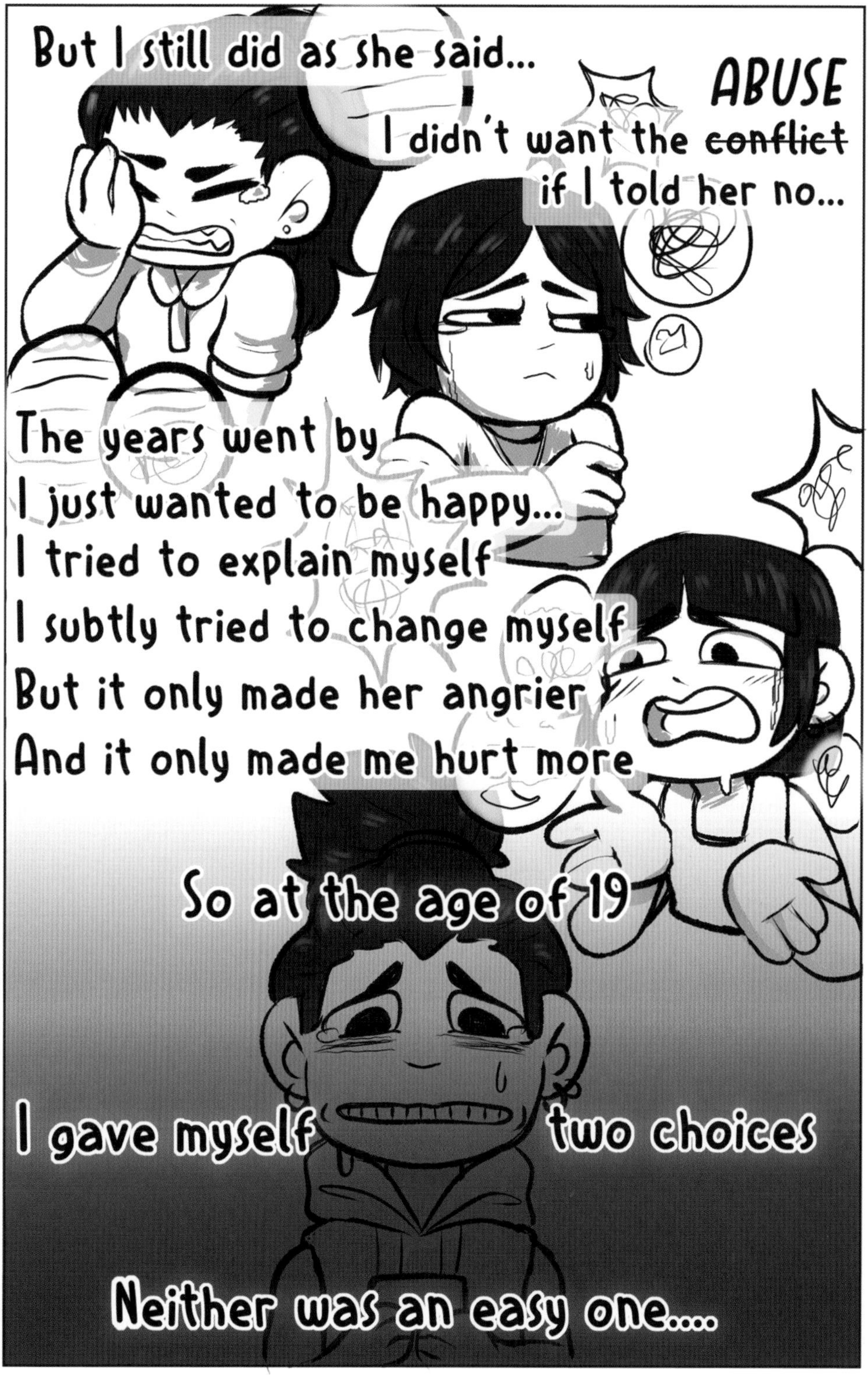

But I still did as she said...
ABUSE
I didn't want the ~~conflict~~
if I told her no...
The years went by
I just wanted to be happy...
I tried to explain myself
I subtly tried to change myself
But it only made her angrier
And it only made me hurt more
So at the age of 19
I gave myself two choices
Neither was an easy one....

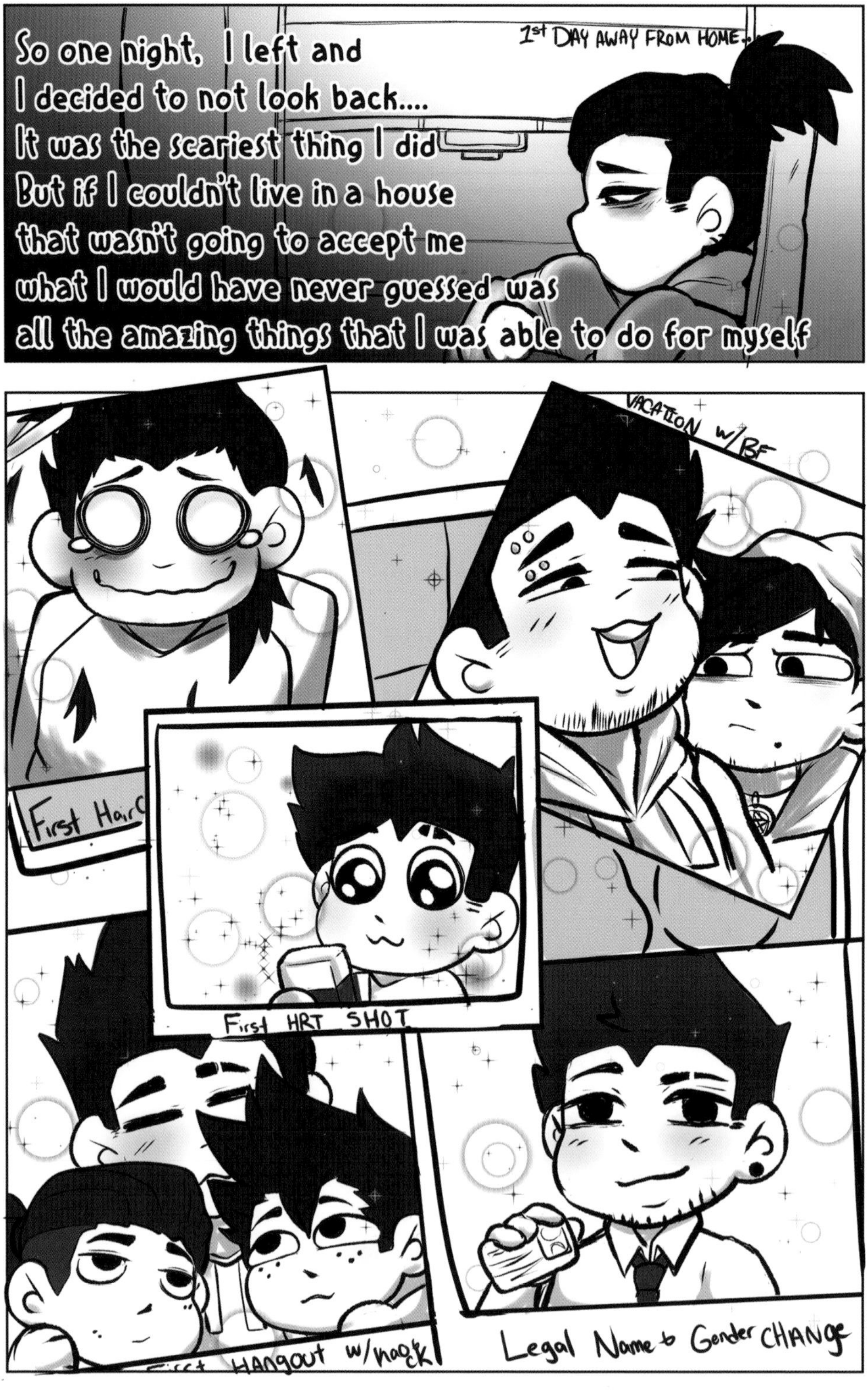
1st DAY AWAY FROM HOME...
So one night, I left and
I decided to not look back....
It was the scariest thing I did
But if I couldn't live in a house
that wasn't going to accept me
what I would have never guessed was
all the amazing things that I was able to do for myself
First Hair
VACATION w/BF
First HRT SHOT
HANGOUT w/nao&ck
Legal Name & Gender CHANGE

For my final words...
I don't condone my actions as
answers for everyone's solution...

But for the years of abuse and
the refusal to be heard
I don't regret the happiness
that I made for myself...

and EVERYONE deserves to be happy

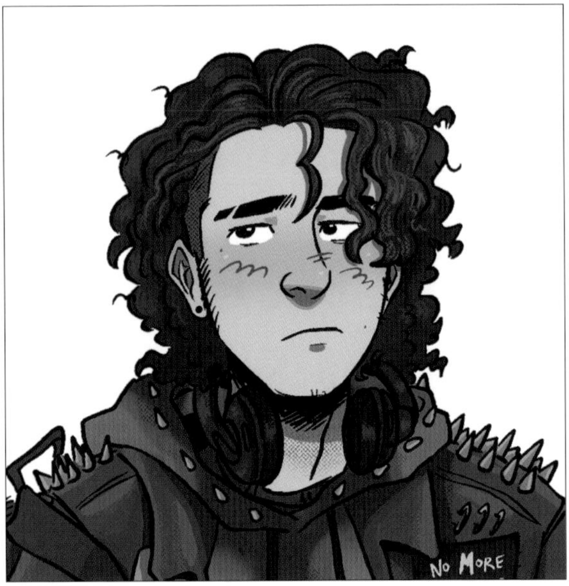
No More

MATTEO MONTERO-MURILLO
(HE/HIM)

Matteo is a trans Mexican artist who also identifies as gay, born and raised in Bethlehem, Pennsylvania. He loves drawing, exploring identity through art, and cats. He has been posting online for years, including several guides for transmascs (and lots of gay art). When he is not drawing, he's usually listening to metal and looking at cute cat photos.

Find him on most social media as:
@mueritos

going home by matteo montero-murillo

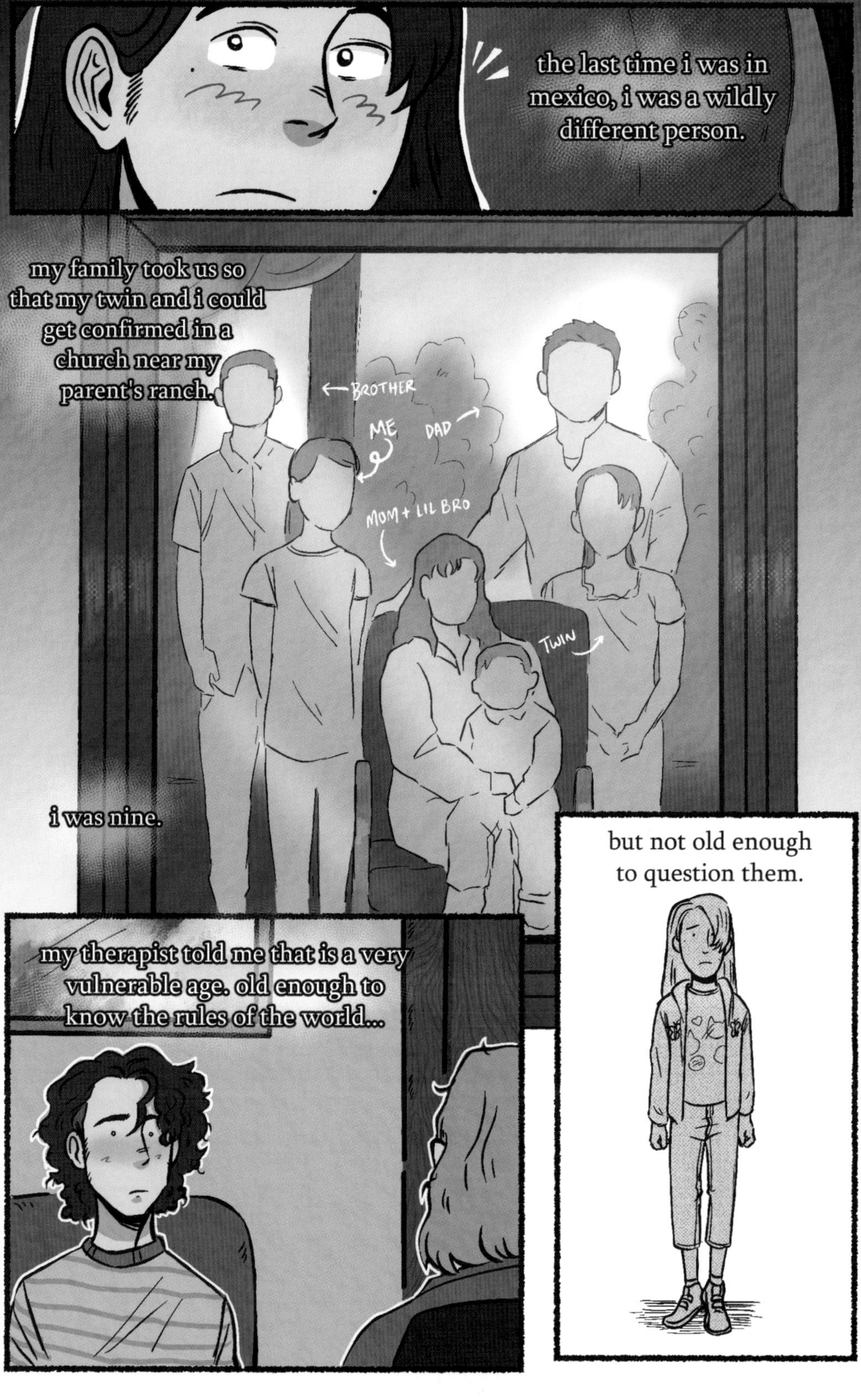
the last time i was in mexico, i was a wildly different person.
my family took us so that my twin and i could get confirmed in a church near my parent's ranch.
←BROTHER
ME
DAD
MOM + LIL BRO
TWIN
i was nine.
my therapist told me that is a very vulnerable age. old enough to know the rules of the world...
but not old enough to question them.

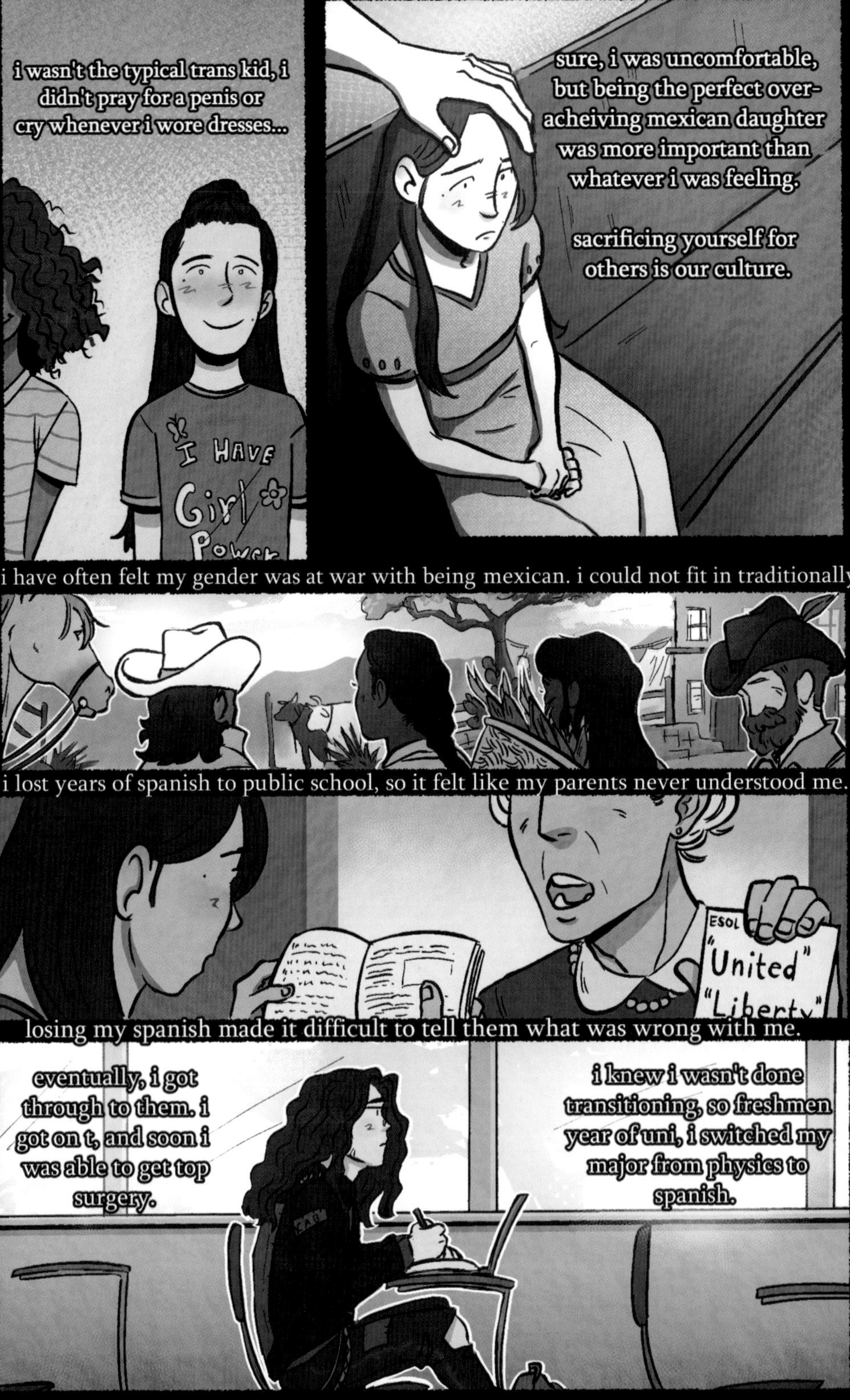
i wasn't the typical trans kid, i didn't pray for a penis or cry whenever i wore dresses...
I HAVE
Girl
sure, i was uncomfortable, but being the perfect over-acheiving mexican daughter was more important than whatever i was feeling.
sacrificing yourself for others is our culture.
i have often felt my gender was at war with being mexican. i could not fit in traditionall
i lost years of spanish to public school, so it felt like my parents never understood me.
ESOL
"United"
losing my spanish made it difficult to tell them what was wrong with me.
eventually, i got through to them. i got on t, and soon i was able to get top surgery.
i knew i wasn't done transitioning, so freshmen year of uni, i switched my major from physics to spanish.

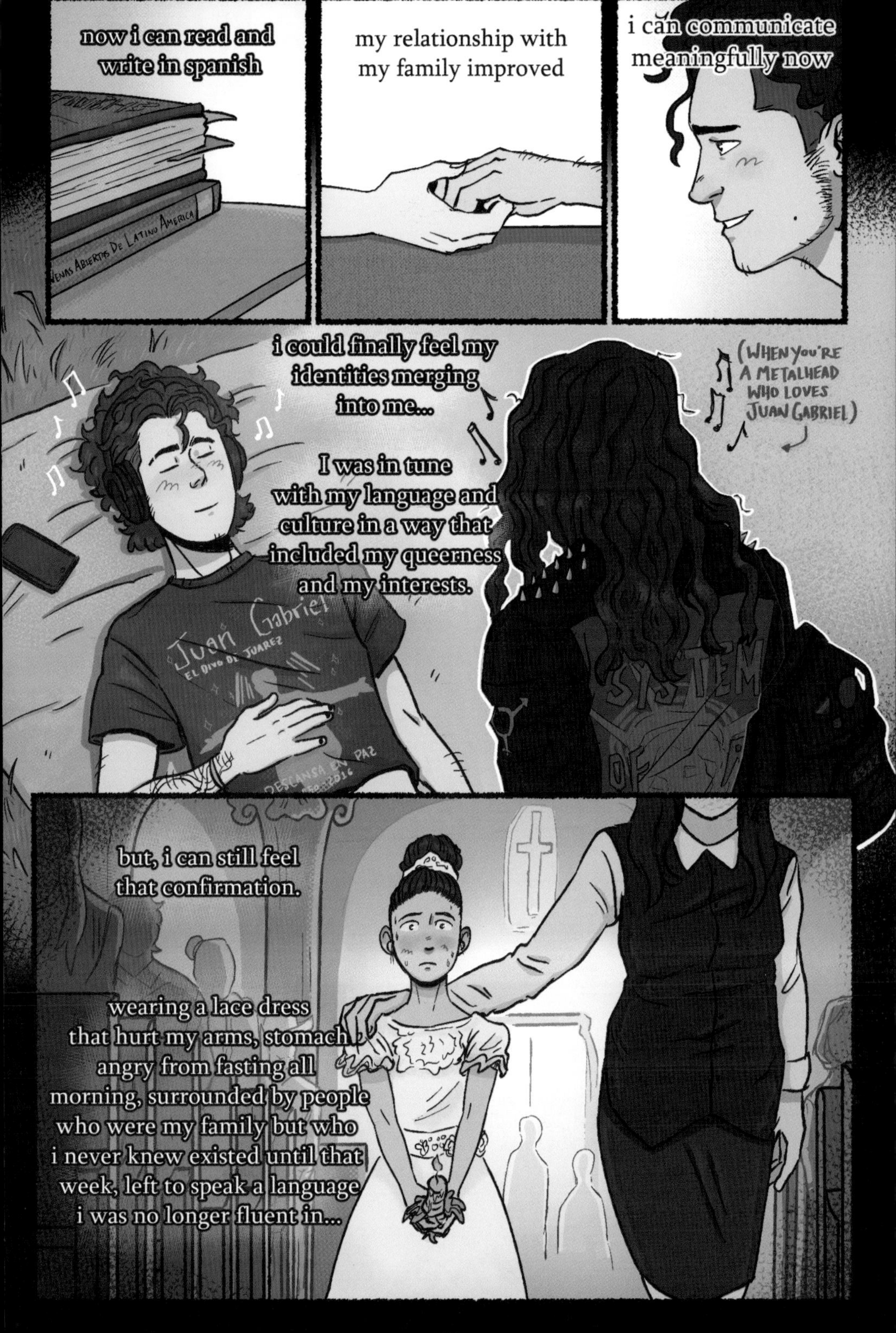
now i can read and write in spanish
Venas Abiertas De Latino America
my relationship with my family improved
i can communicate meaningfully now
i could finally feel my identities merging into me...
I was in tune with my language and culture in a way that included my queerness and my interests.
(WHEN YOU'RE A METALHEAD WHO LOVES JUAN GABRIEL)
Juan Gabriel
EL DIVO DE JUAREZ
DESCANSA EN PAZ
SYSTEM
but, i can still feel that confirmation.
wearing a lace dress that hurt my arms, stomach angry from fasting all morning, surrounded by people who were my family but who i never knew existed until that week, left to speak a language i was no longer fluent in...

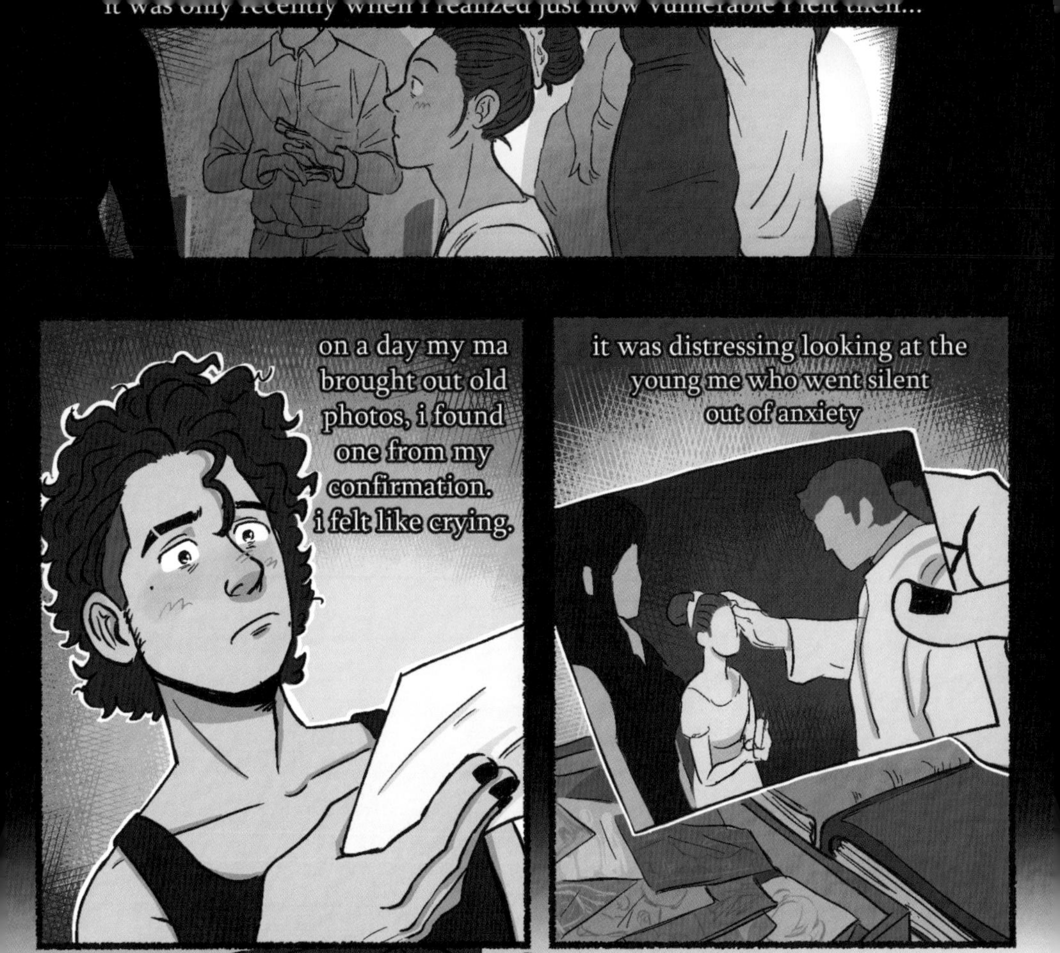
it was only recently when i realized just how vulnerable i felt then...
on a day my ma brought out old photos, i found one from my confirmation. i felt like crying.
it was distressing looking at the young me who went silent out of anxiety

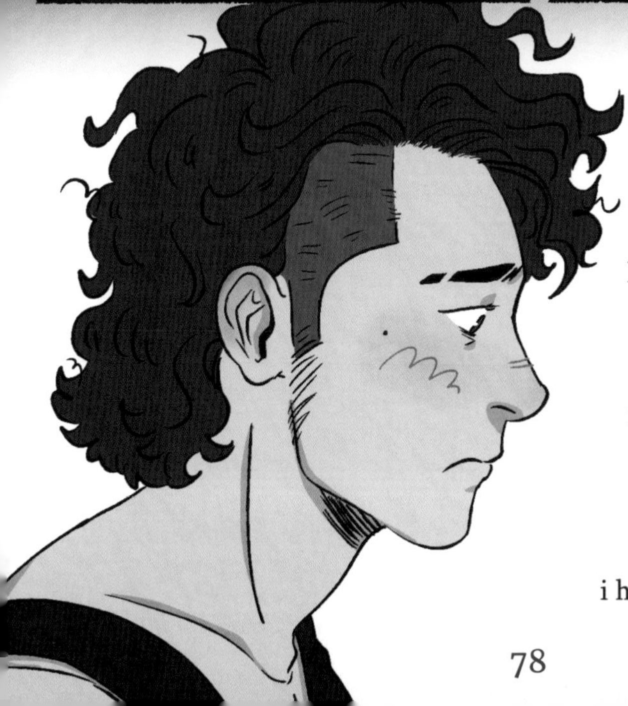

but i couldn't cry.

as life-saving as testosterone has been for me, it made using my old ways to reach catharsis impossible.

i could run from my childhood before, but now that my brain and body had settled, i was forced to actively seek it out.

i had to find new ways to continue healing.

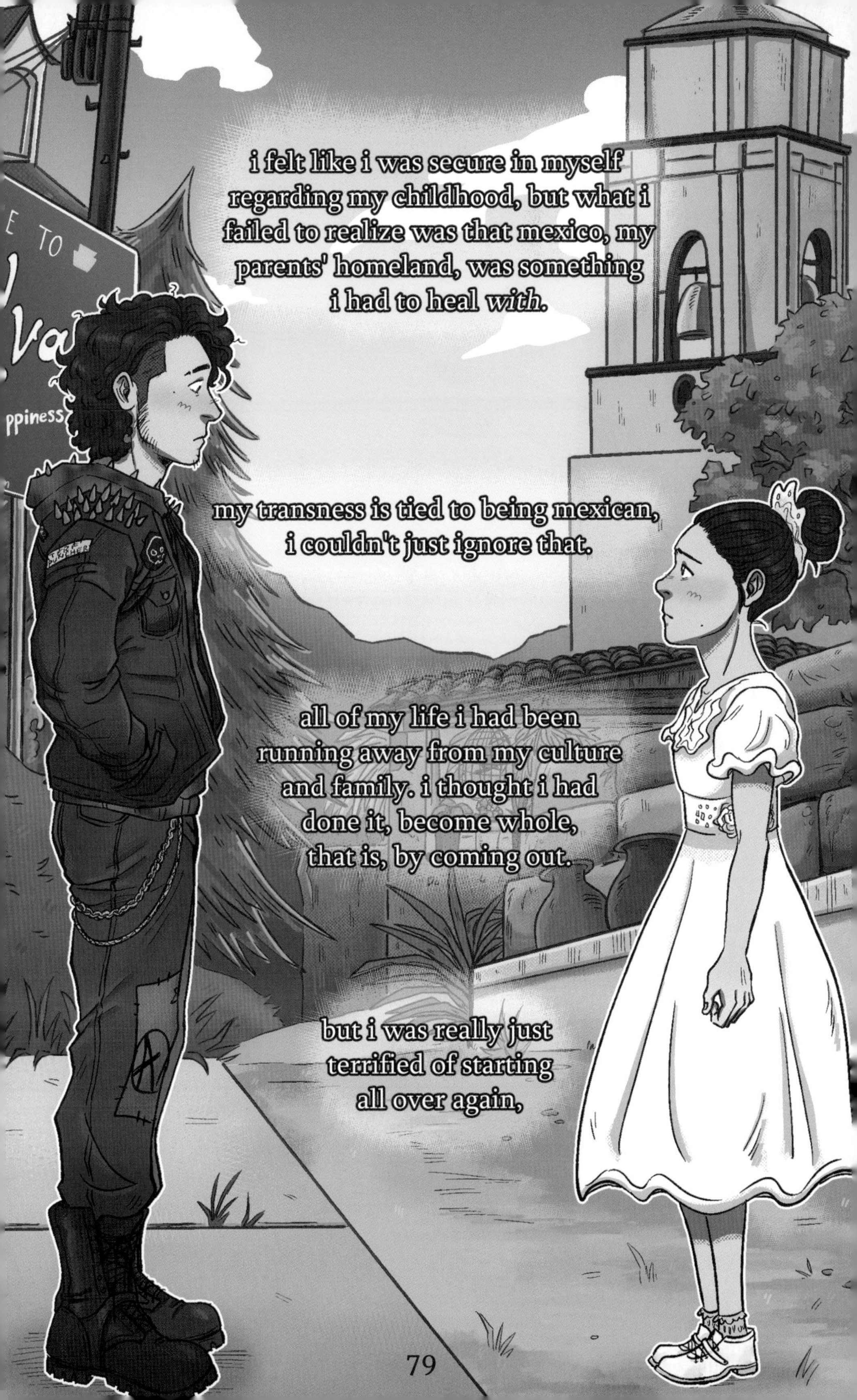
i felt like i was secure in myself regarding my childhood, but what i failed to realize was that mexico, my parents' homeland, was something i had to heal *with*.
my transness is tied to being mexican, i couldn't just ignore that.
all of my life i had been running away from my culture and family. i thought i had done it, become whole, that is, by coming out.
but i was really just terrified of starting all over again,

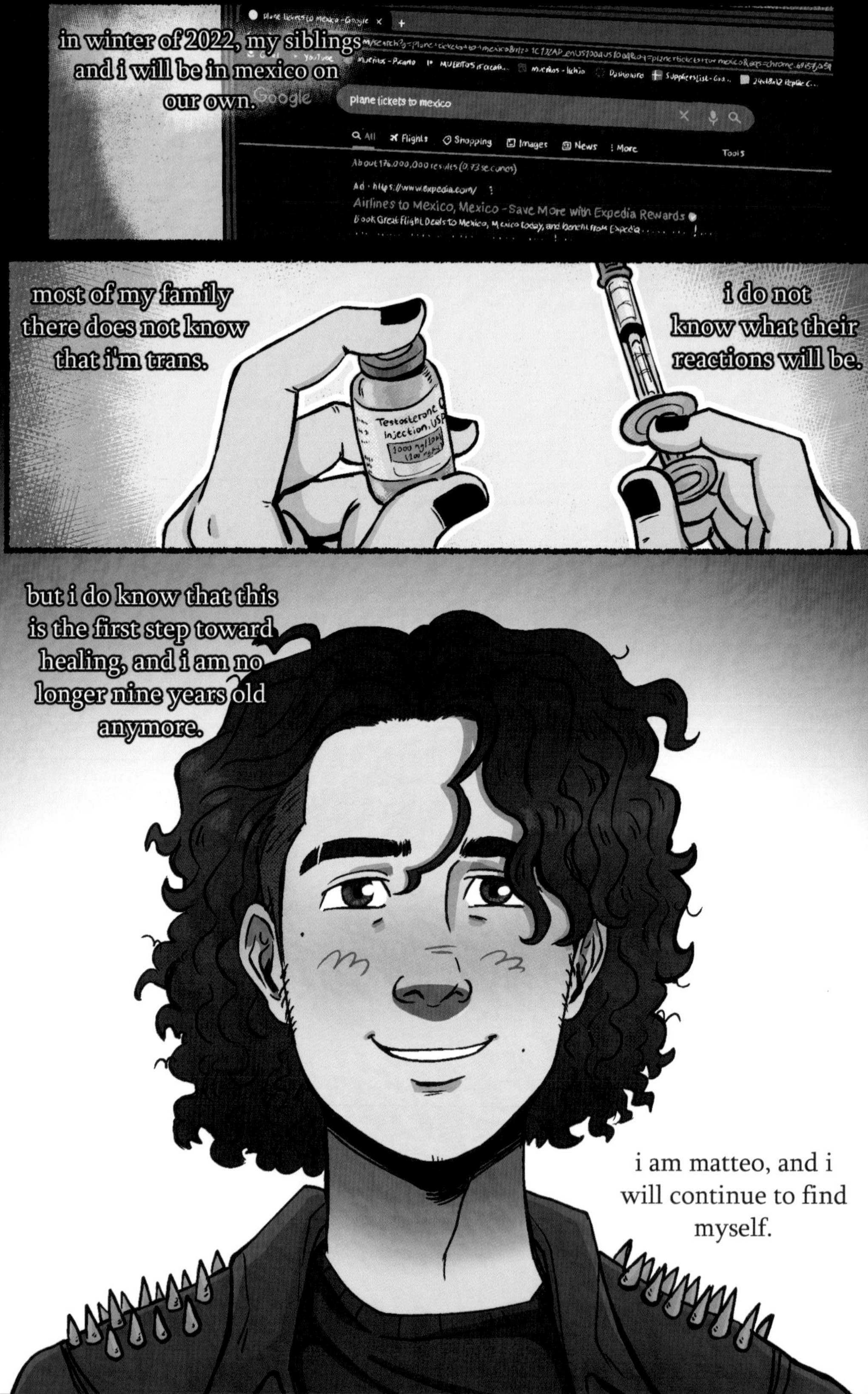
in winter of 2022, my siblings and i will be in mexico on our own.
plane tickets to mexico
All
Flights
Shopping
Images
News
More
Tools
Airlines to Mexico, Mexico - Save More with Expedia Rewards
most of my family there does not know that i'm trans.
Testosterone
Injection, USP
i do not know what their reactions will be.
but i do know that this is the first step toward healing, and i am no longer nine years old anymore.
i am matteo, and i will continue to find myself.

MIN CHRISTENSEN
(THEY/THEM)

Hi, I'm Min Christensen, a Danish comic creator and illustrator born in 1990. In 2015, I got nominated for a Danish comic award for my strip *Fail By Error*, and in 2017, I graduated as a graphic storyteller from the Animation Workshop of Viborg, Denmark. I hope to one day make enough money from my art to be able to afford top surgery and a new tablet.

You can find them on Twitter:
@Flufle

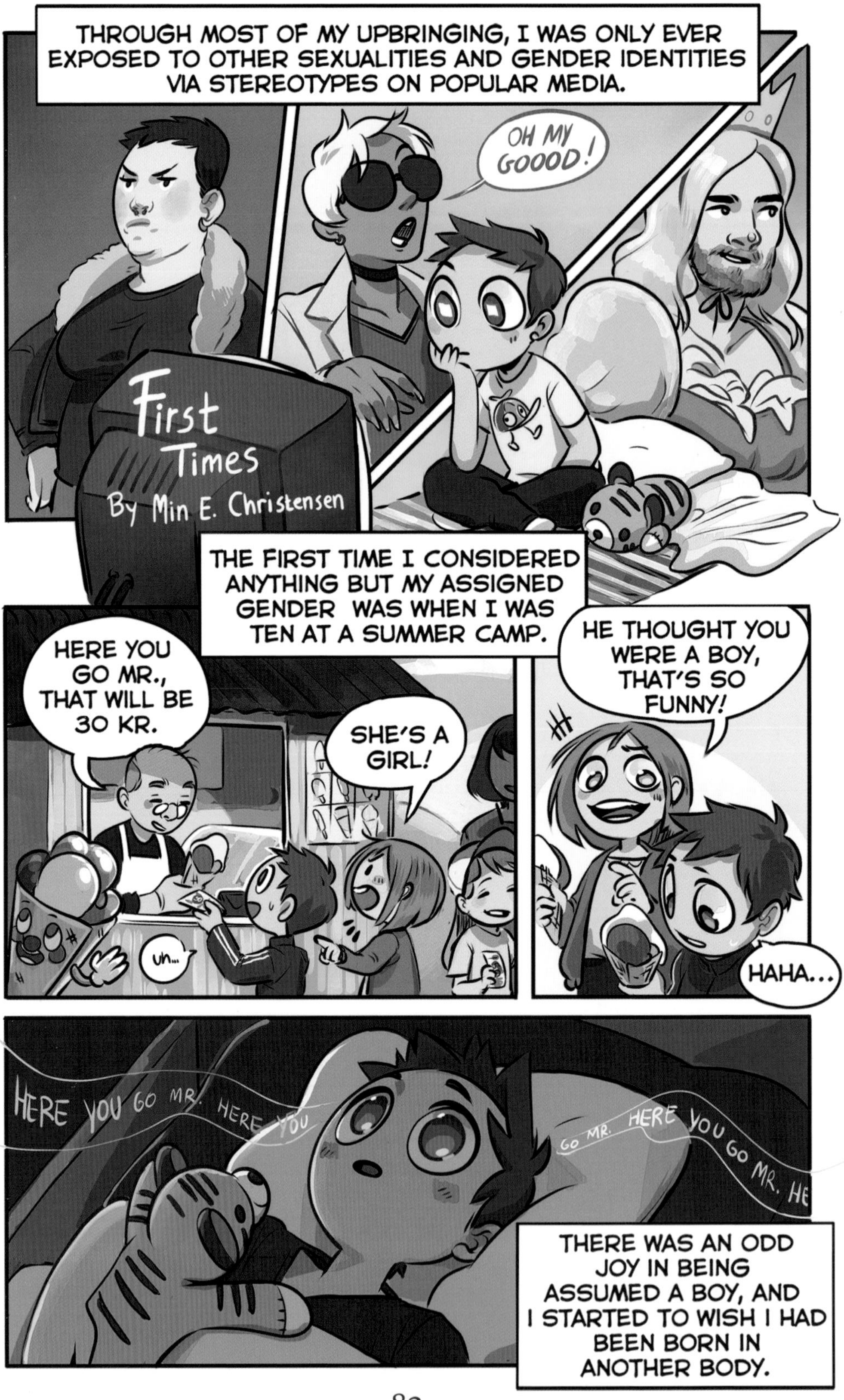
THROUGH MOST OF MY UPBRINGING, I WAS ONLY EVER EXPOSED TO OTHER SEXUALITIES AND GENDER IDENTITIES VIA STEREOTYPES ON POPULAR MEDIA.
OH MY GOOOD!
First Times
By Min E. Christensen
THE FIRST TIME I CONSIDERED ANYTHING BUT MY ASSIGNED GENDER WAS WHEN I WAS TEN AT A SUMMER CAMP.
HERE YOU GO MR., THAT WILL BE 30 KR.
SHE'S A GIRL!
Uh...
HE THOUGHT YOU WERE A BOY, THAT'S SO FUNNY!
HAHA...
HERE YOU GO MR. HERE YOU GO MR. HERE YOU GO MR. HE
THERE WAS AN ODD JOY IN BEING ASSUMED A BOY, AND I STARTED TO WISH I HAD BEEN BORN IN ANOTHER BODY.

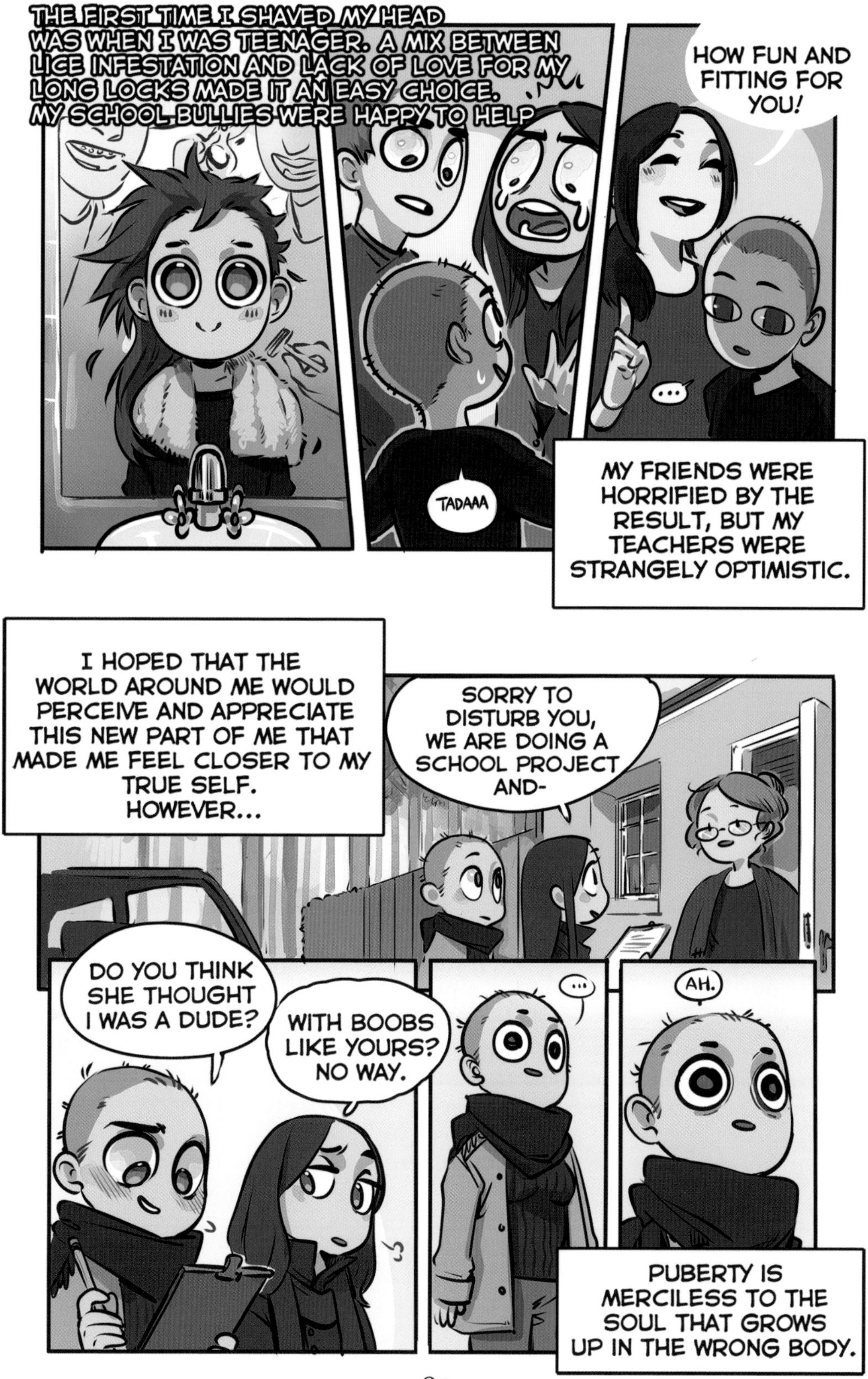
THE FIRST TIME I SHAVED MY HEAD WAS WHEN I WAS TEENAGER. A MIX BETWEEN LICE INFESTATION AND LACK OF LOVE FOR MY LONG LOCKS MADE IT AN EASY CHOICE. MY SCHOOL BULLIES WERE HAPPY TO HELP
TADAAA
HOW FUN AND FITTING FOR YOU!
...
MY FRIENDS WERE HORRIFIED BY THE RESULT, BUT MY TEACHERS WERE STRANGELY OPTIMISTIC.
I HOPED THAT THE WORLD AROUND ME WOULD PERCEIVE AND APPRECIATE THIS NEW PART OF ME THAT MADE ME FEEL CLOSER TO MY TRUE SELF. HOWEVER...
SORRY TO DISTURB YOU, WE ARE DOING A SCHOOL PROJECT AND-
DO YOU THINK SHE THOUGHT I WAS A DUDE?
WITH BOOBS LIKE YOURS? NO WAY.
...
AH.
PUBERTY IS MERCILESS TO THE SOUL THAT GROWS UP IN THE WRONG BODY.

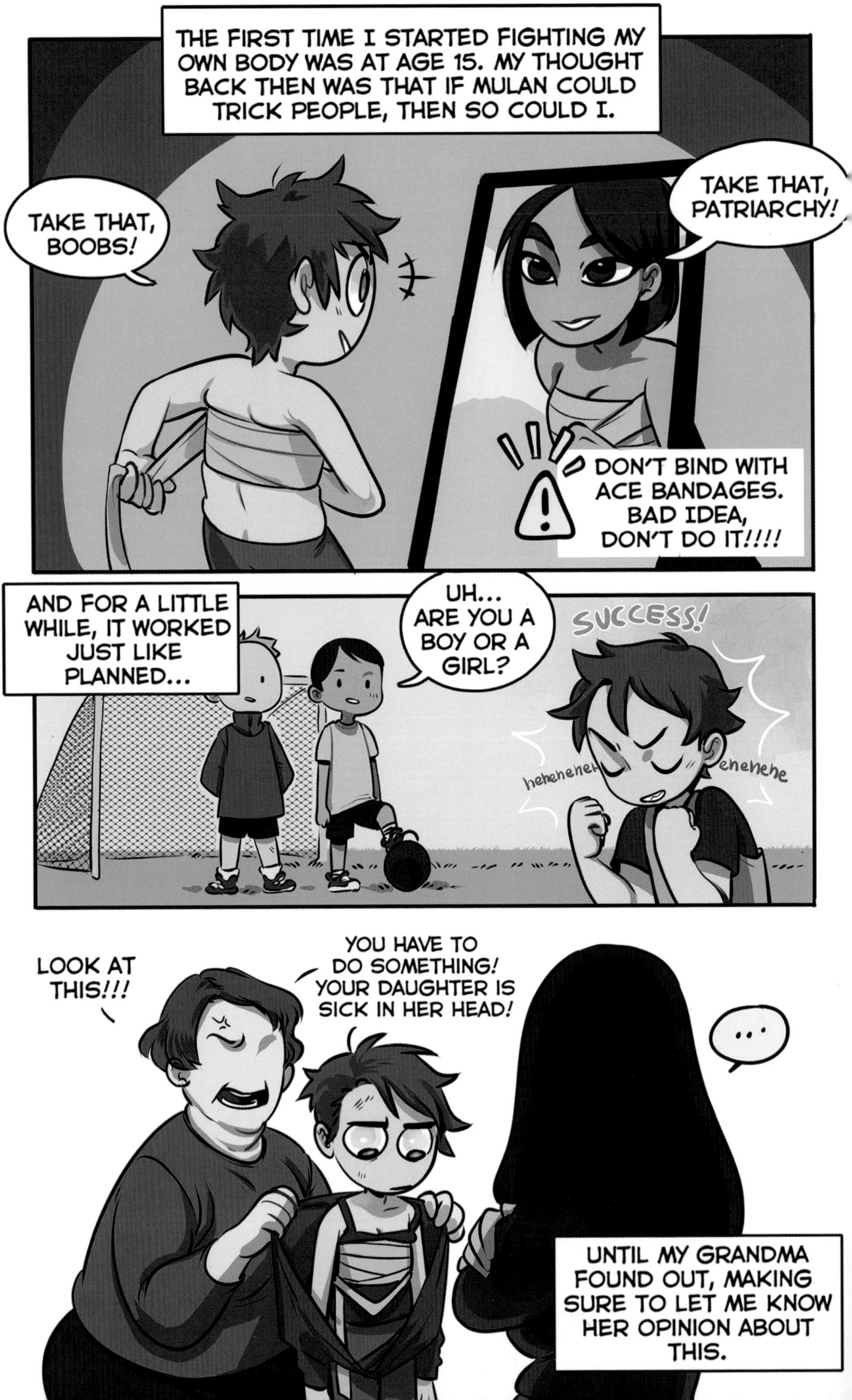
THE FIRST TIME I STARTED FIGHTING MY OWN BODY WAS AT AGE 15. MY THOUGHT BACK THEN WAS THAT IF MULAN COULD TRICK PEOPLE, THEN SO COULD I.
TAKE THAT, BOOBS!
TAKE THAT, PATRIARCHY!
DON'T BIND WITH ACE BANDAGES. BAD IDEA, DON'T DO IT!!!!
AND FOR A LITTLE WHILE, IT WORKED JUST LIKE PLANNED...
UH... ARE YOU A BOY OR A GIRL?
SUCCESS!
hehehehe
ehehehe
LOOK AT THIS!!!
YOU HAVE TO DO SOMETHING! YOUR DAUGHTER IS SICK IN HER HEAD!
...
UNTIL MY GRANDMA FOUND OUT, MAKING SURE TO LET ME KNOW HER OPINION ABOUT THIS.

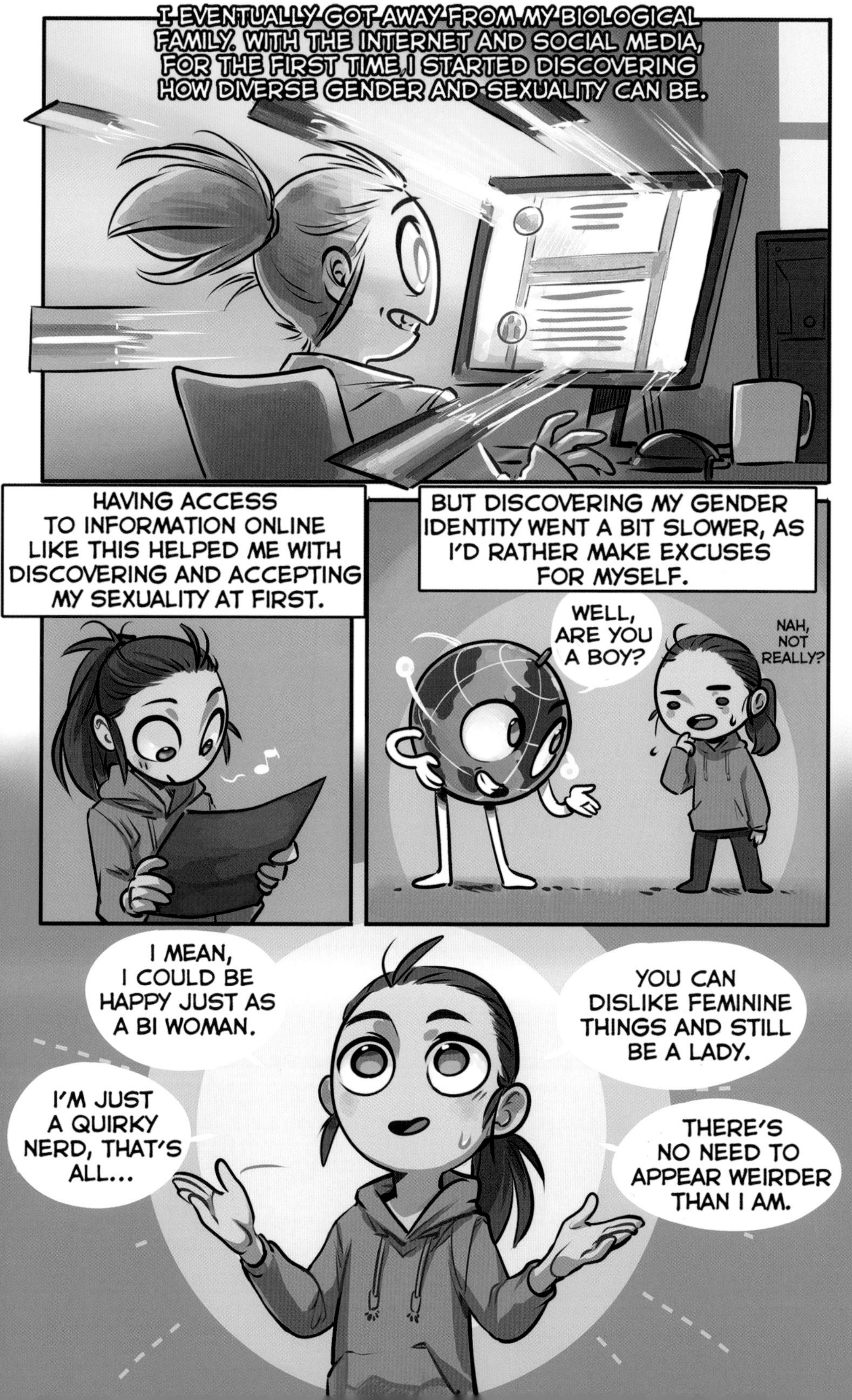
I EVENTUALLY GOT AWAY FROM MY BIOLOGICAL FAMILY. WITH THE INTERNET AND SOCIAL MEDIA, FOR THE FIRST TIME I STARTED DISCOVERING HOW DIVERSE GENDER AND SEXUALITY CAN BE.
HAVING ACCESS TO INFORMATION ONLINE LIKE THIS HELPED ME WITH DISCOVERING AND ACCEPTING MY SEXUALITY AT FIRST.
BUT DISCOVERING MY GENDER IDENTITY WENT A BIT SLOWER, AS I'D RATHER MAKE EXCUSES FOR MYSELF.
WELL, ARE YOU A BOY?
NAH, NOT REALLY?
I MEAN, I COULD BE HAPPY JUST AS A BI WOMAN.
YOU CAN DISLIKE FEMININE THINGS AND STILL BE A LADY.
I'M JUST A QUIRKY NERD, THAT'S ALL...
THERE'S NO NEED TO APPEAR WEIRDER THAN I AM.

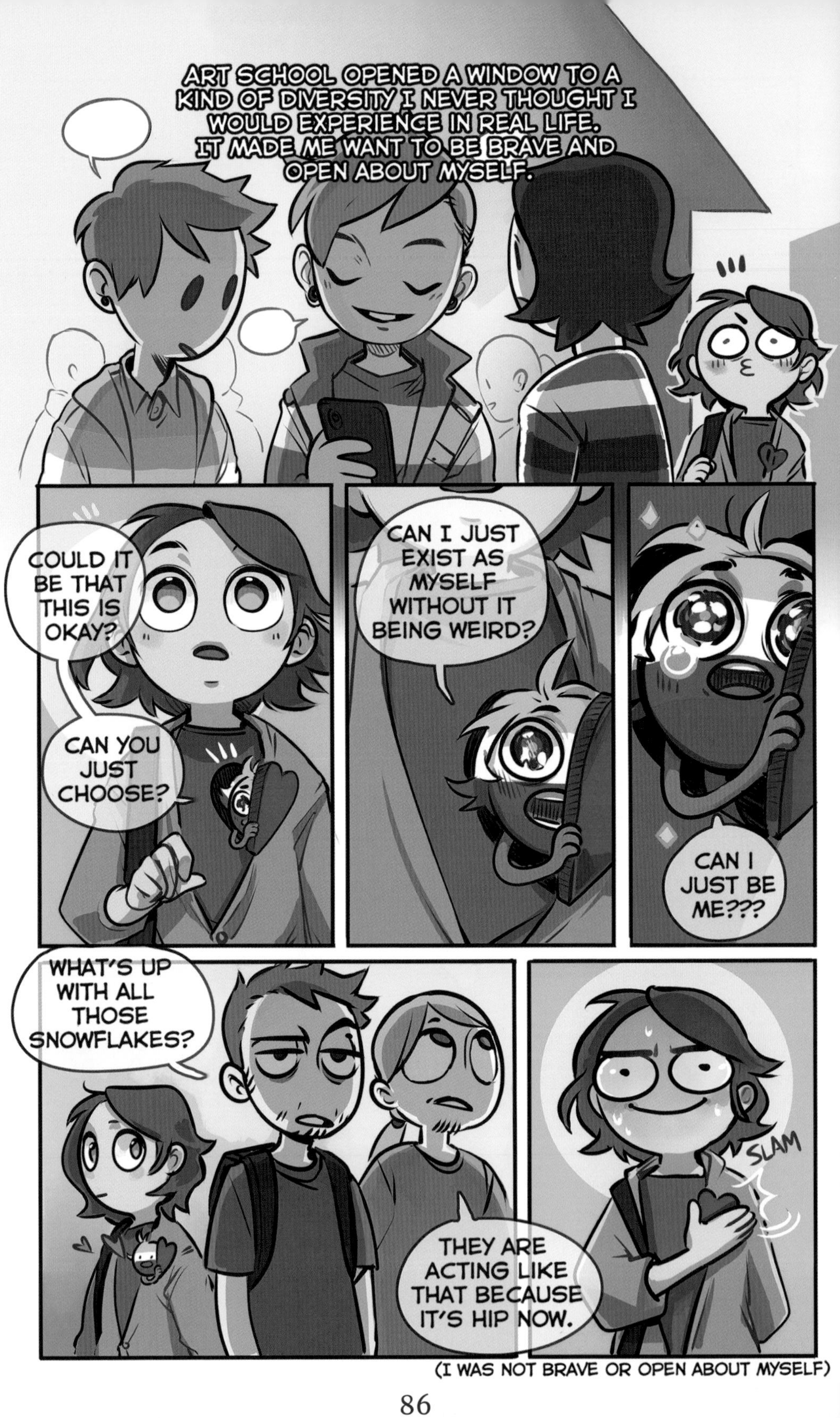
ART SCHOOL OPENED A WINDOW TO A KIND OF DIVERSITY I NEVER THOUGHT I WOULD EXPERIENCE IN REAL LIFE. IT MADE ME WANT TO BE BRAVE AND OPEN ABOUT MYSELF.
COULD IT BE THAT THIS IS OKAY?
CAN YOU JUST CHOOSE?
CAN I JUST EXIST AS MYSELF WITHOUT IT BEING WEIRD?
CAN I JUST BE ME???
WHAT'S UP WITH ALL THOSE SNOWFLAKES?
THEY ARE ACTING LIKE THAT BECAUSE IT'S HIP NOW.
SLAM
(I WAS NOT BRAVE OR OPEN ABOUT MYSELF)

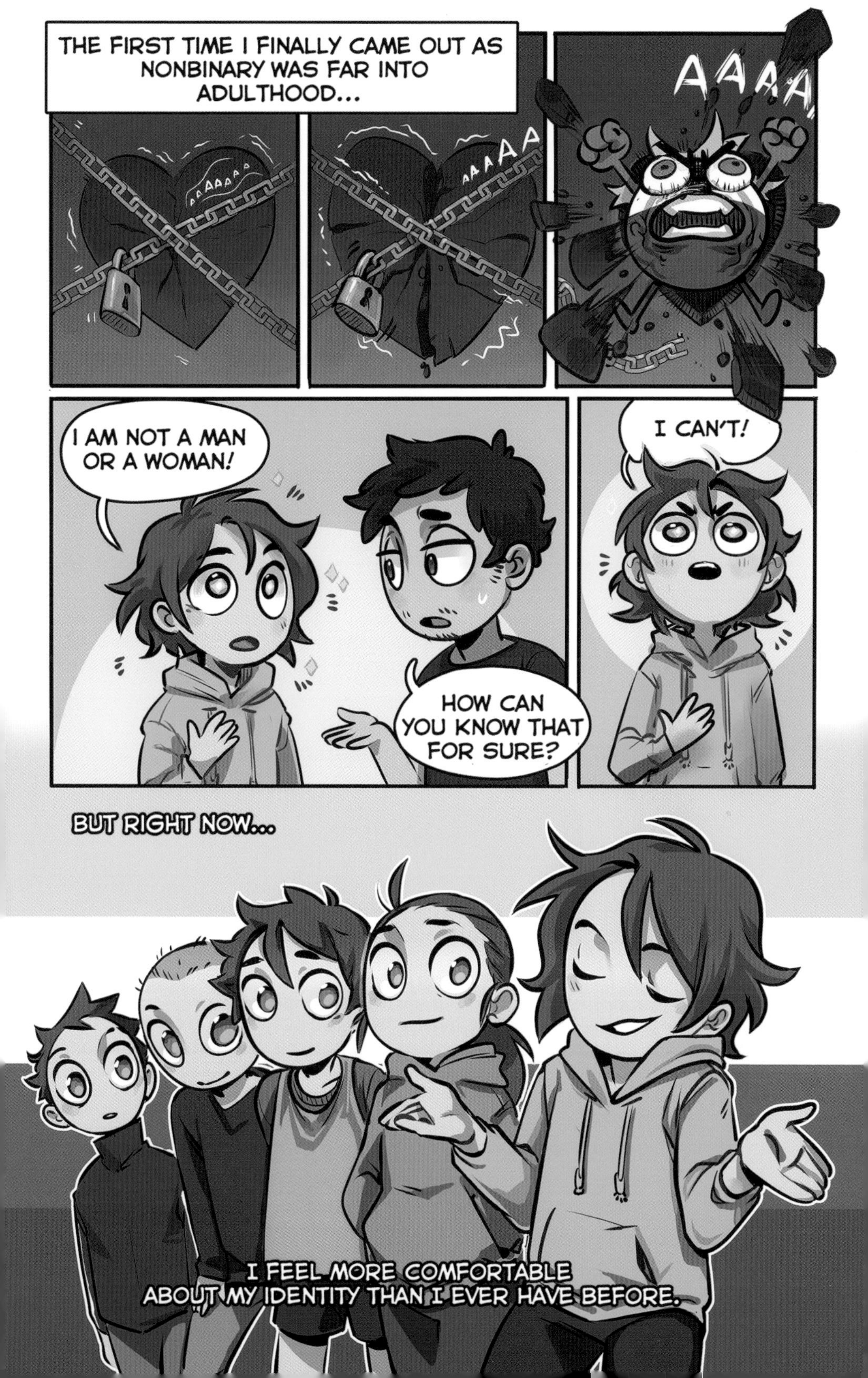
THE FIRST TIME I FINALLY CAME OUT AS NONBINARY WAS FAR INTO ADULTHOOD...
AAAAAA
AAAAAA
AAAA
I AM NOT A MAN OR A WOMAN!
HOW CAN YOU KNOW THAT FOR SURE?
I CAN'T!
BUT RIGHT NOW...
I FEEL MORE COMFORTABLE ABOUT MY IDENTITY THAN I EVER HAVE BEFORE.

JULIE FIVEASH
(THEY/THEM)

Julie Fiveash is Kinyaa'áanii born for Naakai. Their maternal grandfather's clan is Táchii'nii and their paternal grandfather is Bilagaana. Julie Fiveash is a Diné, nonbinary librarian who makes comics about their increasing anxiety issues. Their work has been featured in two *Dirty Diamond* comic collections and was featured in *Portals of Indigenous Futurisms* and *Plants and Animals of Diné Bikéyah* published by Abalone Mountain Press. When they're not reading too much manga, they're missing the desert heat from their small Boston bedroom and working at Harvard University as the Librarian for American Indigenous Studies.

Find them on Instagram and Twitter:
@jooliefiveash

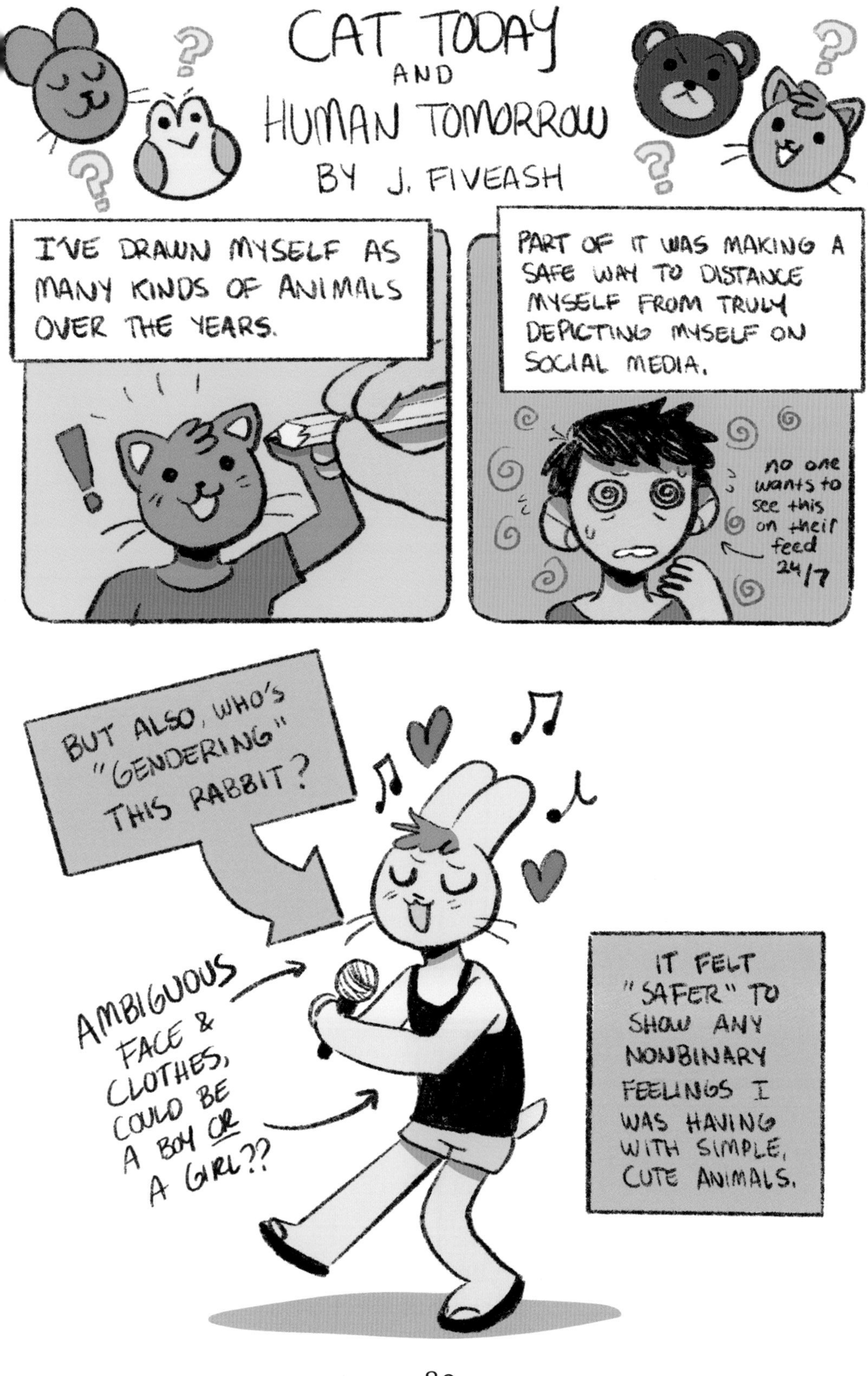
CAT TODAY AND HUMAN TOMORROW
BY J. FIVEASH
I'VE DRAWN MYSELF AS MANY KINDS OF ANIMALS OVER THE YEARS.
PART OF IT WAS MAKING A SAFE WAY TO DISTANCE MYSELF FROM TRULY DEPICTING MYSELF ON SOCIAL MEDIA.
no one wants to see this on their feed 24/7
BUT ALSO, WHO'S "GENDERING" THIS RABBIT?
AMBIGUOUS FACE & CLOTHES, COULD BE A BOY OR A GIRL??
IT FELT "SAFER" TO SHOW ANY NONBINARY FEELINGS I WAS HAVING WITH SIMPLE, CUTE ANIMALS.

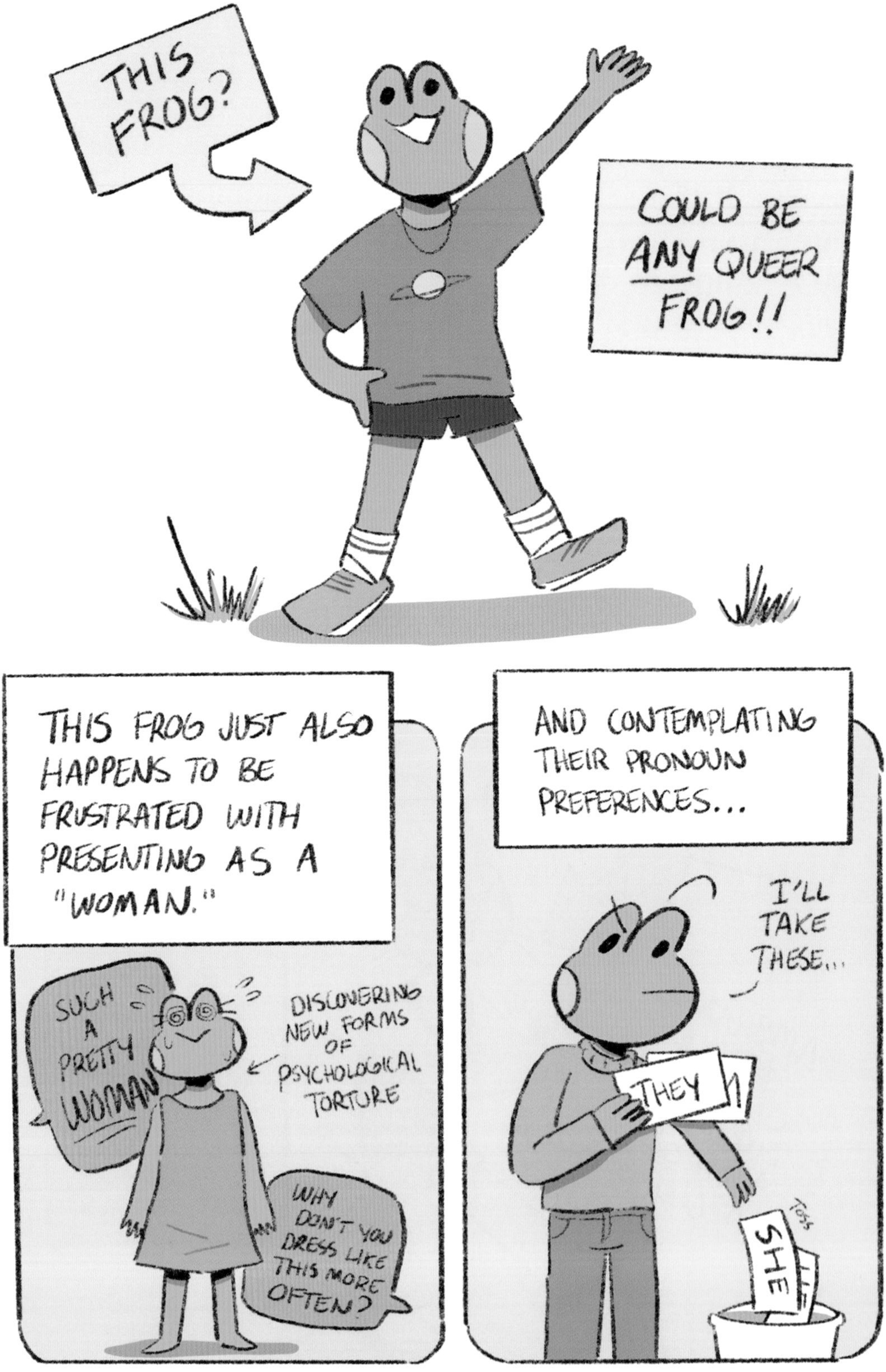
THIS FROG?
COULD BE ANY QUEER FROG!!
THIS FROG JUST ALSO HAPPENS TO BE FRUSTRATED WITH PRESENTING AS A "WOMAN."
SUCH A PRETTY WOMAN
DISCOVERING NEW FORMS OF PSYCHOLOGICAL TORTURE
WHY DON'T YOU DRESS LIKE THIS MORE OFTEN?
AND CONTEMPLATING THEIR PRONOUN PREFERENCES...
I'LL TAKE THESE...
THEY
SHE
TOSS

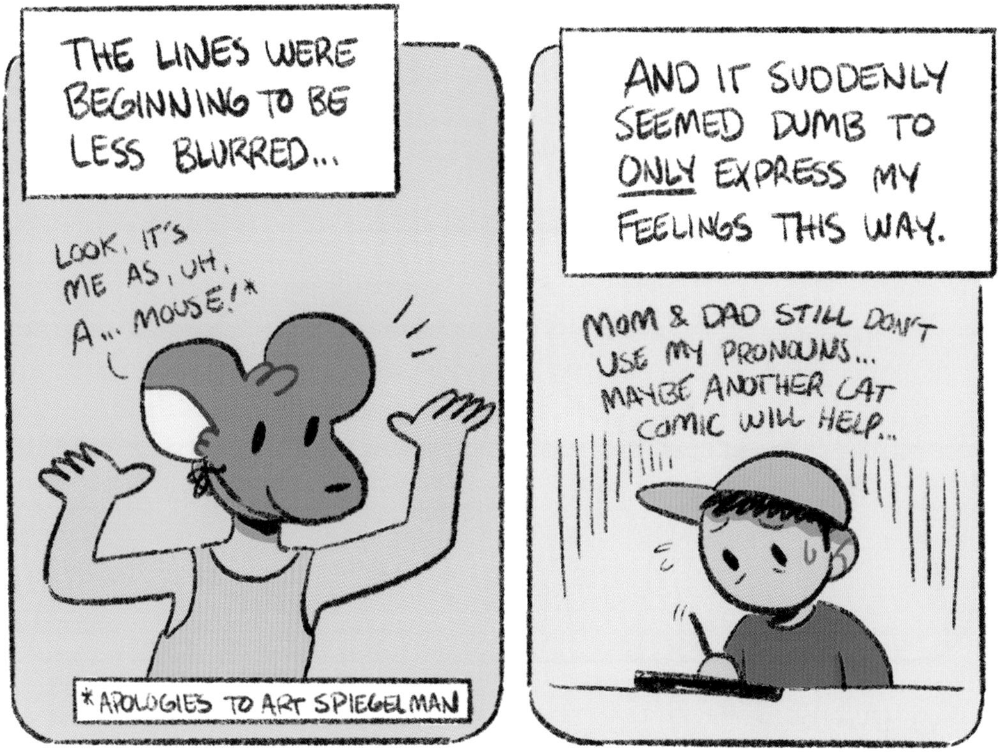
THE LINES WERE BEGINNING TO BE LESS BLURRED...
LOOK, IT'S ME AS, UH, A... MOUSE!*
*APOLOGIES TO ART SPIEGELMAN
AND IT SUDDENLY SEEMED DUMB TO ONLY EXPRESS MY FEELINGS THIS WAY.
MOM & DAD STILL DON'T USE MY PRONOUNS... MAYBE ANOTHER CAT COMIC WILL HELP...

AS MUCH AS I LIKED USING ANIMALS TO PLAY UP FUN AND COMEDIC ASPECTS OF MYSELF, IT WASN'T AUTHENTIC. NOT ENOUGH ANYWAY.

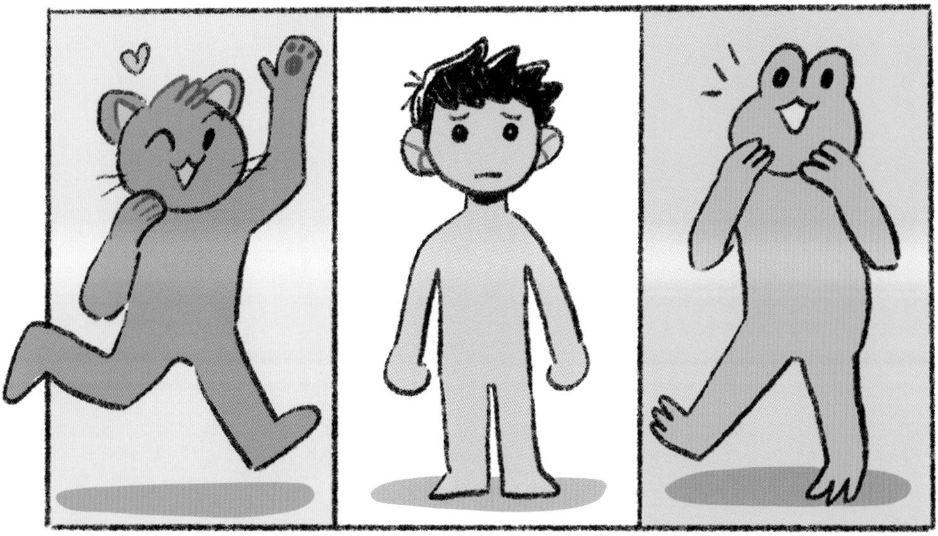

HOW COULD ANYONE RELATE TO <u>ME</u> IF I NEVER SHOWED A <u>REAL</u> ME? <u>WAS</u> THIS REALLY ME??

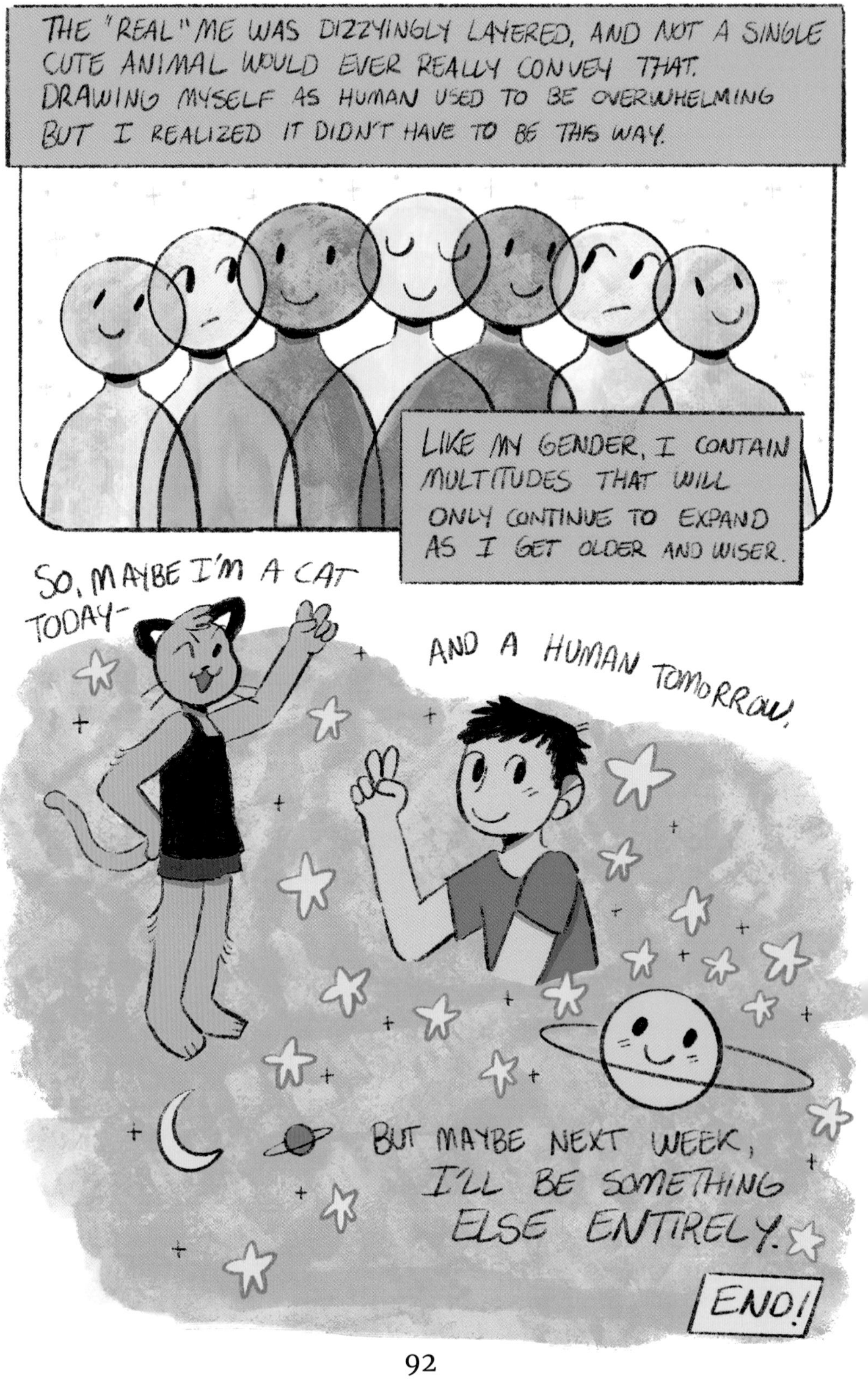
THE "REAL" ME WAS DIZZYINGLY LAYERED, AND NOT A SINGLE CUTE ANIMAL WOULD EVER REALLY CONVEY THAT. DRAWING MYSELF AS HUMAN USED TO BE OVERWHELMING BUT I REALIZED IT DIDN'T HAVE TO BE THIS WAY.
LIKE MY GENDER, I CONTAIN MULTITUDES THAT WILL ONLY CONTINUE TO EXPAND AS I GET OLDER AND WISER.
SO, MAYBE I'M A CAT TODAY-
AND A HUMAN TOMORROW,
BUT MAYBE NEXT WEEK, I'LL BE SOMETHING ELSE ENTIRELY.
END!

COCO OUWERKERK
(SHE/THEY)

Coco finished studying comic design and 2D animation in 2016. At the same time, she published four small press comics and her first original comic series *Acception* with Dutch comic publisher Uitgeverij Syndikaat. Her series is an LGBTQ+ teen drama/comedy story that's free to read on WEBTOON, who've had her under contract since 2019 and will continue to until the story is finished.

You can find them online at:
linktr.ee/Colourbee4

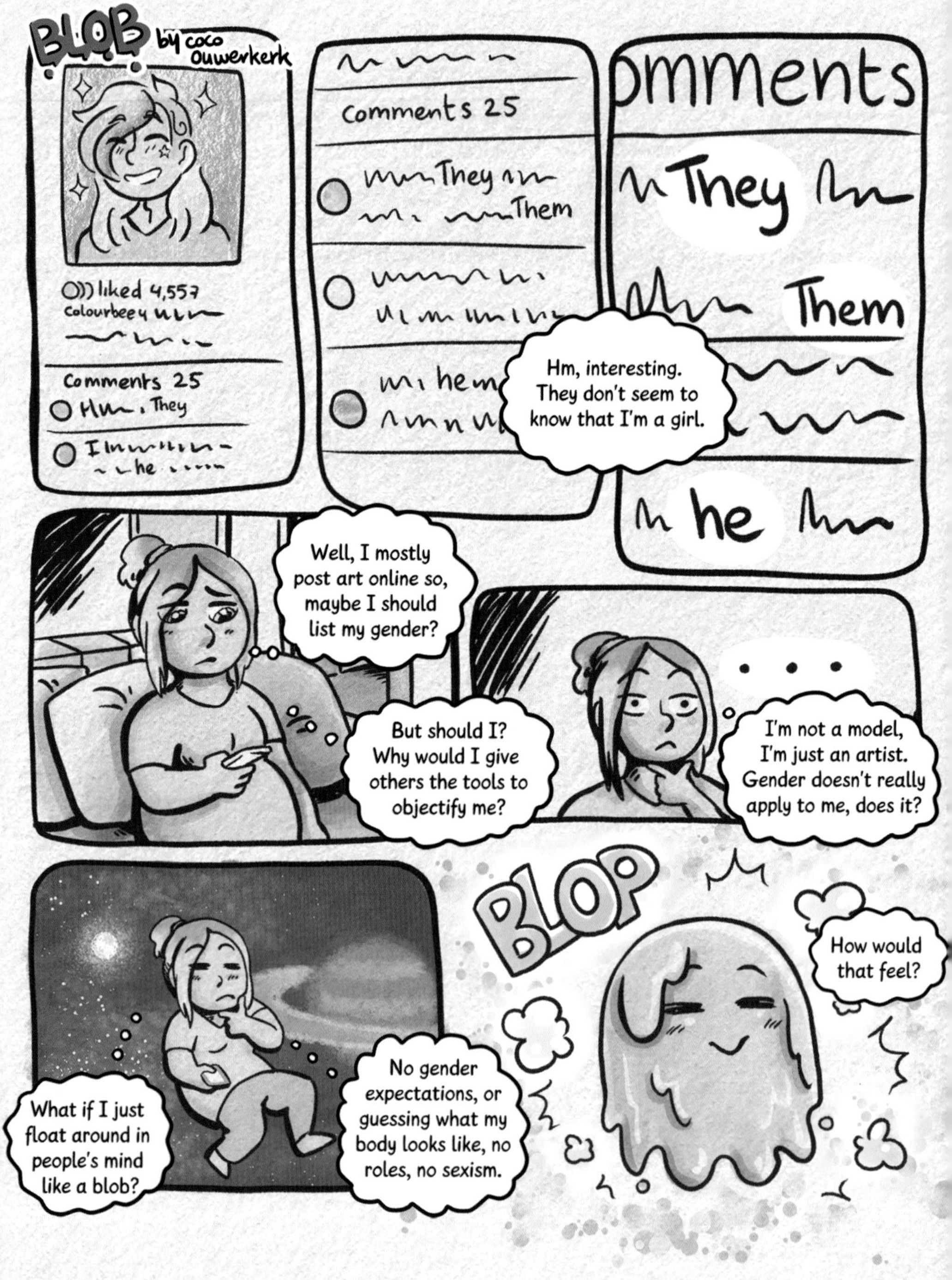
BLOB by coco ouwerkerk
liked 4,557
colourbeey
Comments 25
Hm, They
he
Comments 25
They
Them
he
omments
They
Them
he
Hm, interesting. They don't seem to know that I'm a girl.
Well, I mostly post art online so, maybe I should list my gender?
But should I? Why would I give others the tools to objectify me?
. . .
I'm not a model, I'm just an artist. Gender doesn't really apply to me, does it?
What if I just float around in people's mind like a blob?
No gender expectations, or guessing what my body looks like, no roles, no sexism.
BLOP
How would that feel?

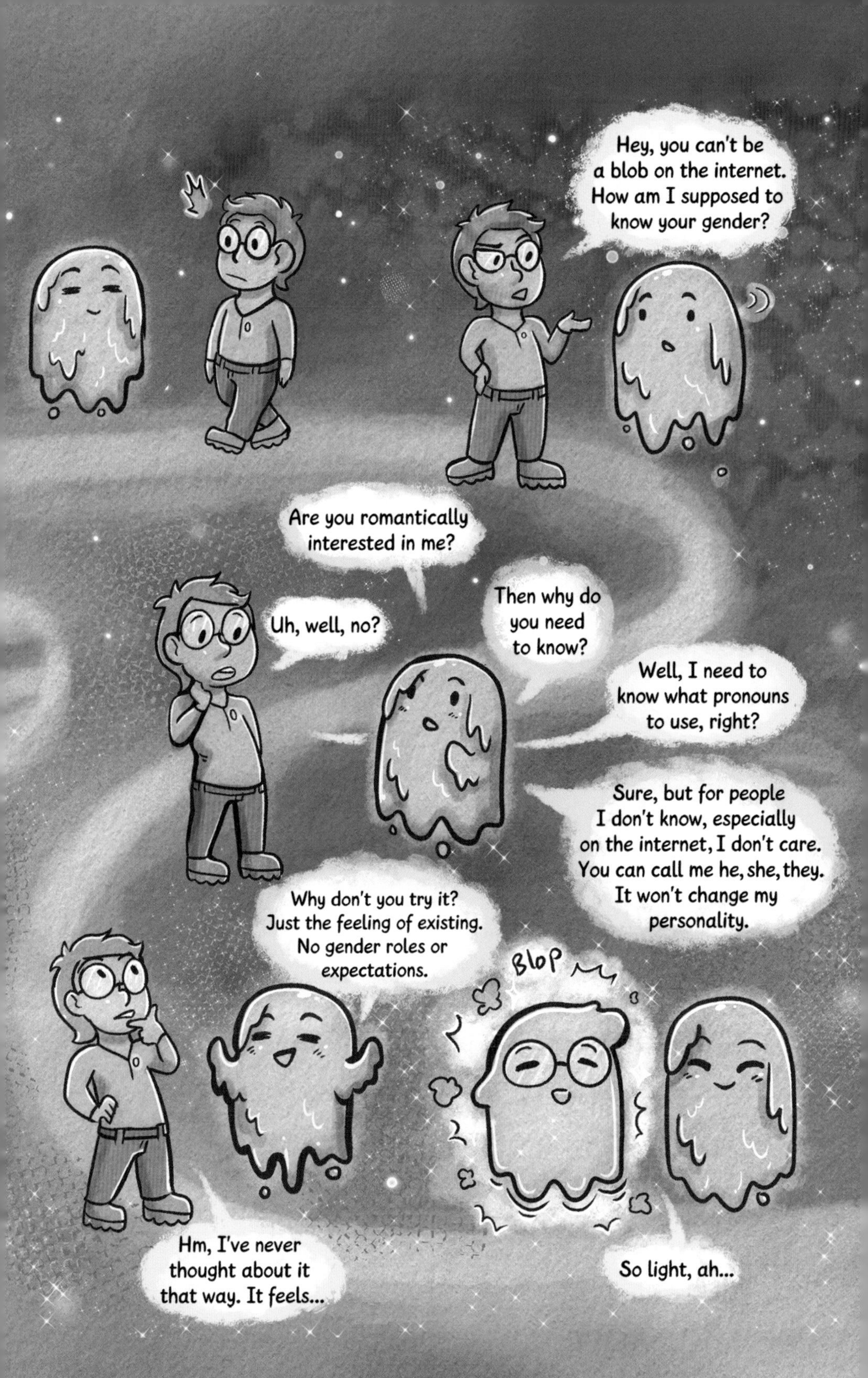
Hey, you can't be a blob on the internet. How am I supposed to know your gender?
Are you romantically interested in me?
Uh, well, no?
Then why do you need to know?
Well, I need to know what pronouns to use, right?
Sure, but for people I don't know, especially on the internet, I don't care. You can call me he, she, they. It won't change my personality.
Why don't you try it? Just the feeling of existing. No gender roles or expectations.
Hm, I've never thought about it that way. It feels...
BLOP
So light, ah...

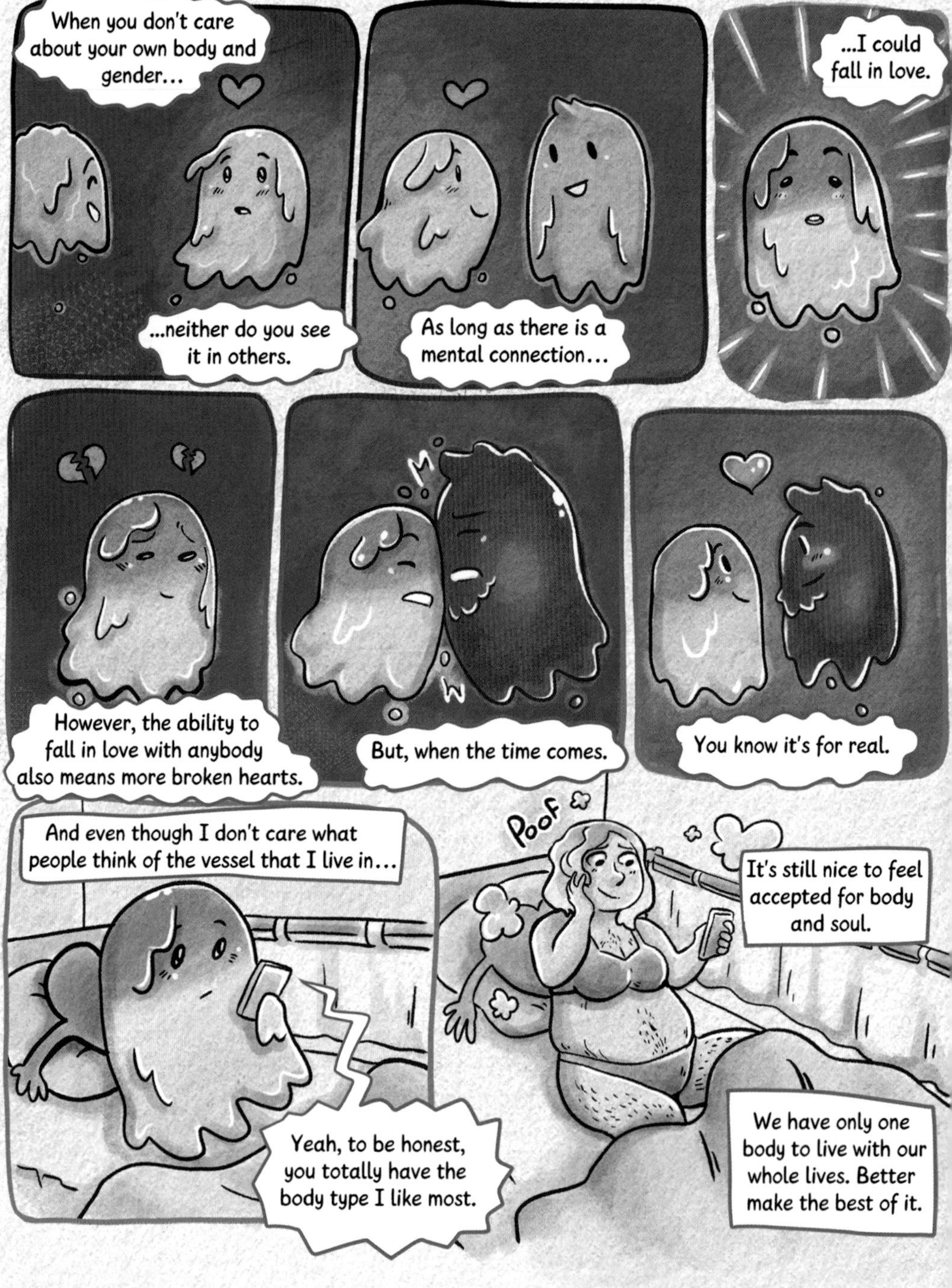
When you don't care about your own body and gender…
…neither do you see it in others.
As long as there is a mental connection…
…I could fall in love.
However, the ability to fall in love with anybody also means more broken hearts.
But, when the time comes.
You know it's for real.
And even though I don't care what people think of the vessel that I live in…
Yeah, to be honest, you totally have the body type I like most.
Poof
It's still nice to feel accepted for body and soul.
We have only one body to live with our whole lives. Better make the best of it.

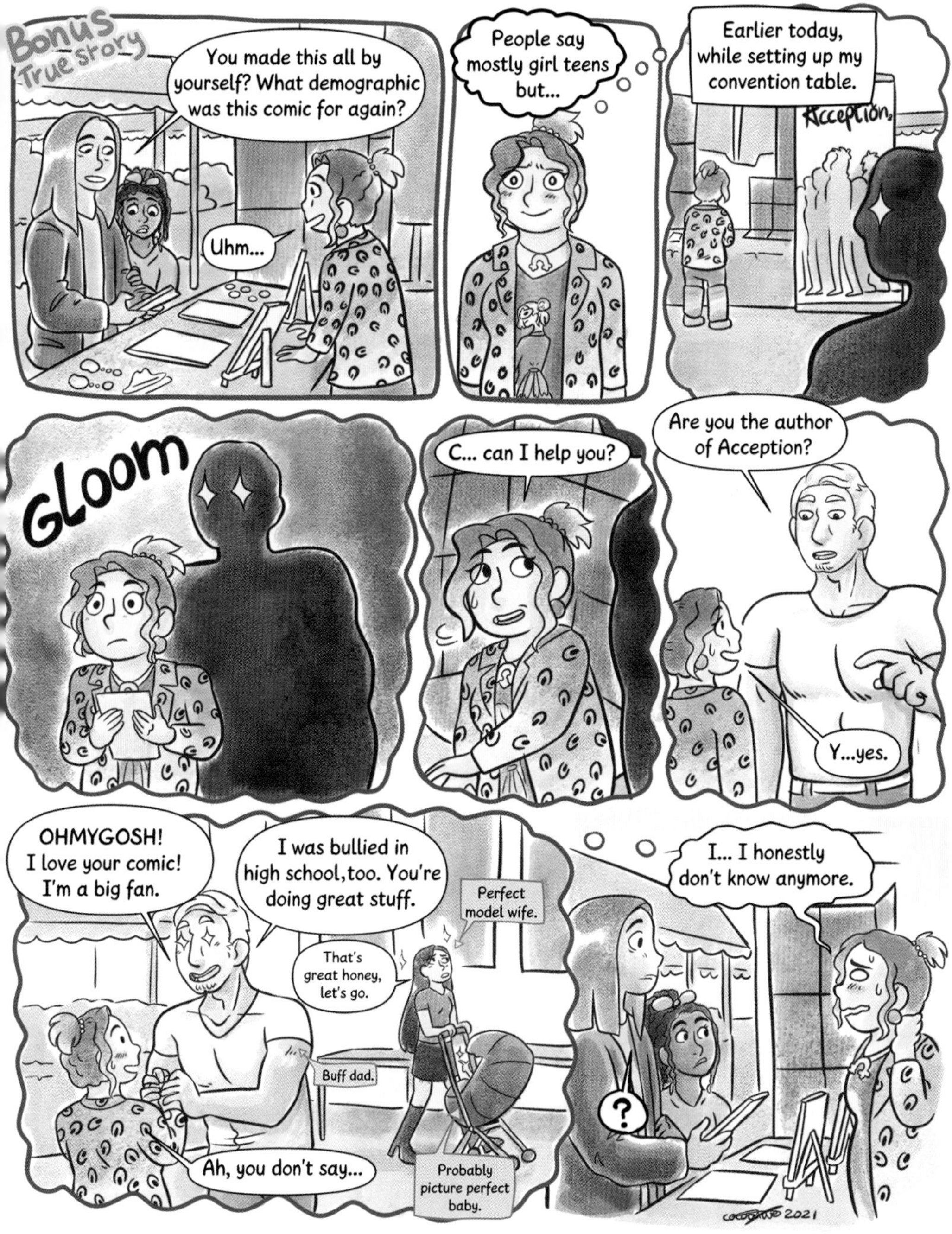
Bonus True story
You made this all by yourself? What demographic was this comic for again?
Uhm...
People say mostly girl teens but...
Earlier today, while setting up my convention table.
Acception
GLOOM
C... can I help you?
Are you the author of Acception?
Y...yes.
OHMYGOSH! I love your comic! I'm a big fan.
I was bullied in high school, too. You're doing great stuff.
Perfect model wife.
That's great honey, let's go.
Buff dad.
Ah, you don't say...
Probably picture perfect baby.
I... I honestly don't know anymore.
?
2021

LAKE FAMA
(THEY/THEM)

Lake is a trans, nonbinary, sapphic storyboard artist working in animation in Los Angeles. They make comics, personal art, and fan art in their free time. Outside of drawing, they're a bird fanatic and have two chaotic pet doves.

You can find them online at:
lakefama.com

Slow and Steady

by Lake Fama

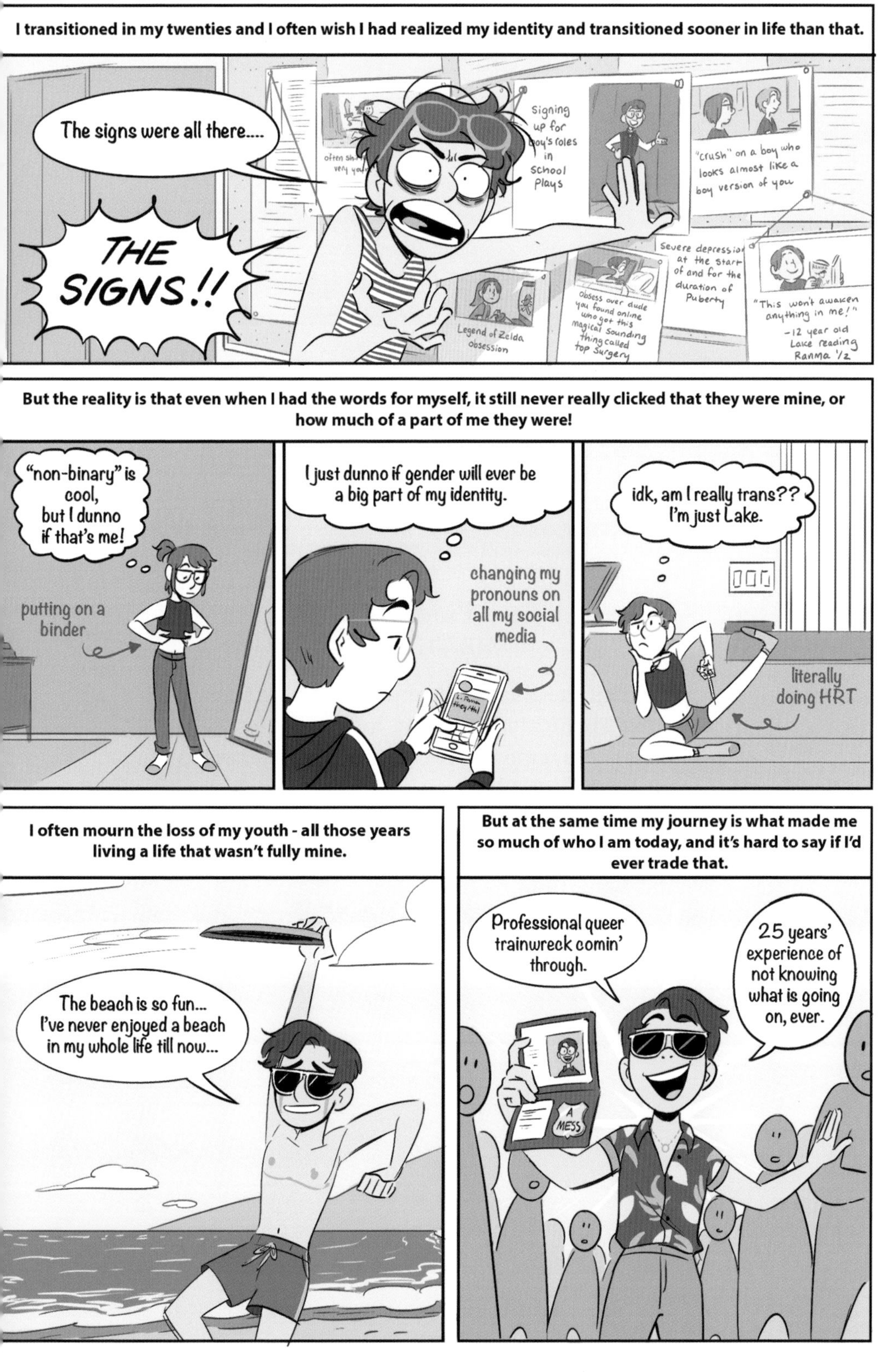

I transitioned in my twenties and I often wish I had realized my identity and transitioned sooner in life than that.
The signs were all there....
THE SIGNS!!
Signing up for boy's roles in School Plays
"crush" on a boy who looks almost like a boy version of you
Legend of Zelda obsession
Obsess over dude you found online who got this magical sounding thing called top Surgery
Severe depression at the start of and for the duration of Puberty
"This won't awaken anything in me!" -12 year old Lake reading Ranma ½
But the reality is that even when I had the words for myself, it still never really clicked that they were mine, or how much of a part of me they were!
"non-binary" is cool, but I dunno if that's me!
putting on a binder
I just dunno if gender will ever be a big part of my identity.
changing my pronouns on all my social media
idk, am I really trans?? I'm just Lake.
literally doing HRT
I often mourn the loss of my youth - all those years living a life that wasn't fully mine.
The beach is so fun... I've never enjoyed a beach in my whole life till now...
But at the same time my journey is what made me so much of who I am today, and it's hard to say if I'd ever trade that.
Professional queer trainwreck comin' through.
25 years' experience of not knowing what is going on, ever.
A MESS

KAZ FANTONE
(HE/THEY)

Kaz Fantone is a Japanese-Filipino American artist currently living in Los Angeles. He has an extreme soft spot for stories about the mundane. When he's not working, you can find him voraciously reading romance novels and webtoons, or logging too many hours in Mario Kart.

You can find him online at:
kazfantone.myportfolio.com

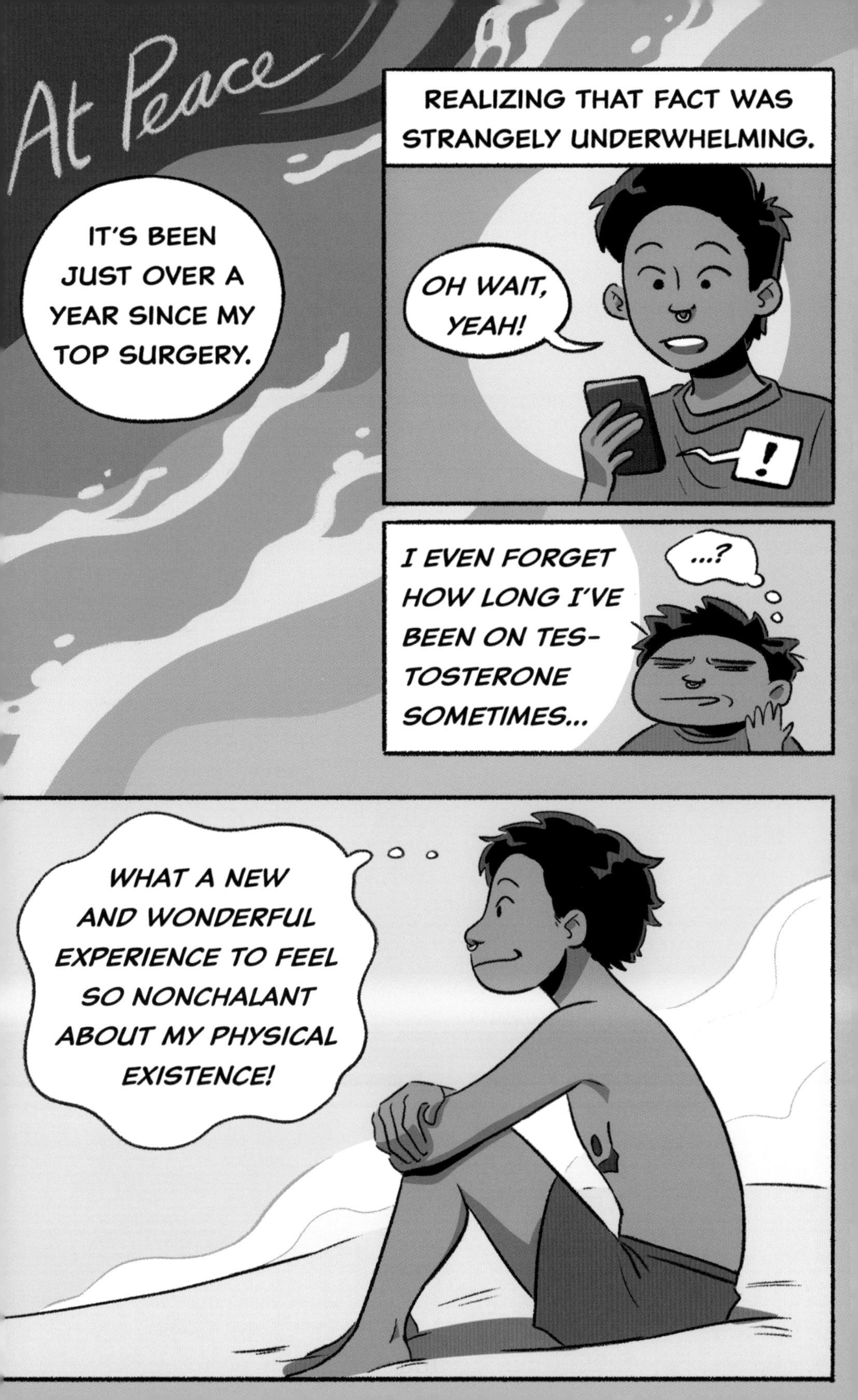
At Peace
IT'S BEEN JUST OVER A YEAR SINCE MY TOP SURGERY.
REALIZING THAT FACT WAS STRANGELY UNDERWHELMING.
OH WAIT, YEAH!
!
I EVEN FORGET HOW LONG I'VE BEEN ON TES-TOSTERONE SOMETIMES...
...?
WHAT A NEW AND WONDERFUL EXPERIENCE TO FEEL SO NONCHALANT ABOUT MY PHYSICAL EXISTENCE!

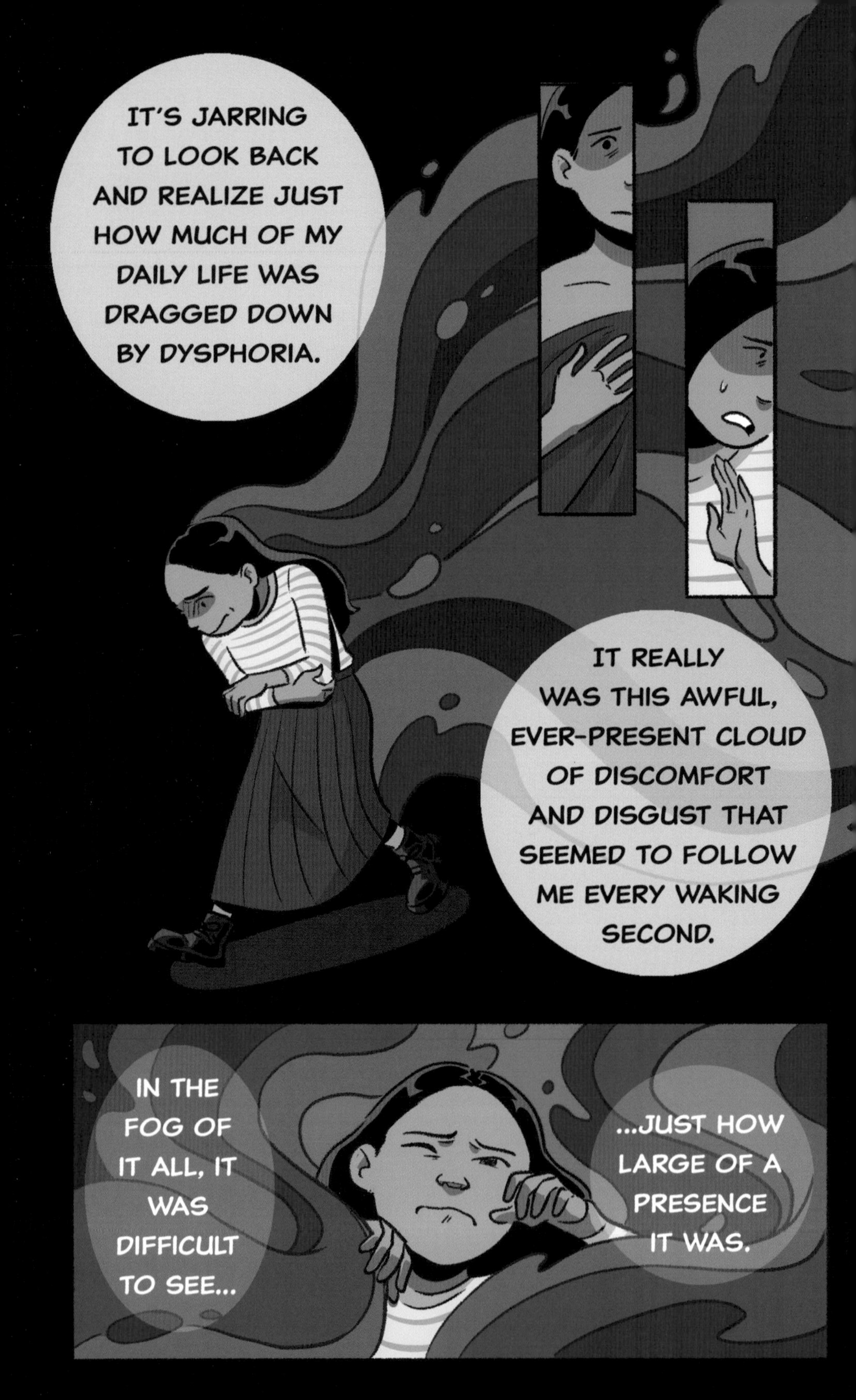
IT'S JARRING TO LOOK BACK AND REALIZE JUST HOW MUCH OF MY DAILY LIFE WAS DRAGGED DOWN BY DYSPHORIA.
IT REALLY WAS THIS AWFUL, EVER-PRESENT CLOUD OF DISCOMFORT AND DISGUST THAT SEEMED TO FOLLOW ME EVERY WAKING SECOND.
IN THE FOG OF IT ALL, IT WAS DIFFICULT TO SEE...
...JUST HOW LARGE OF A PRESENCE IT WAS.

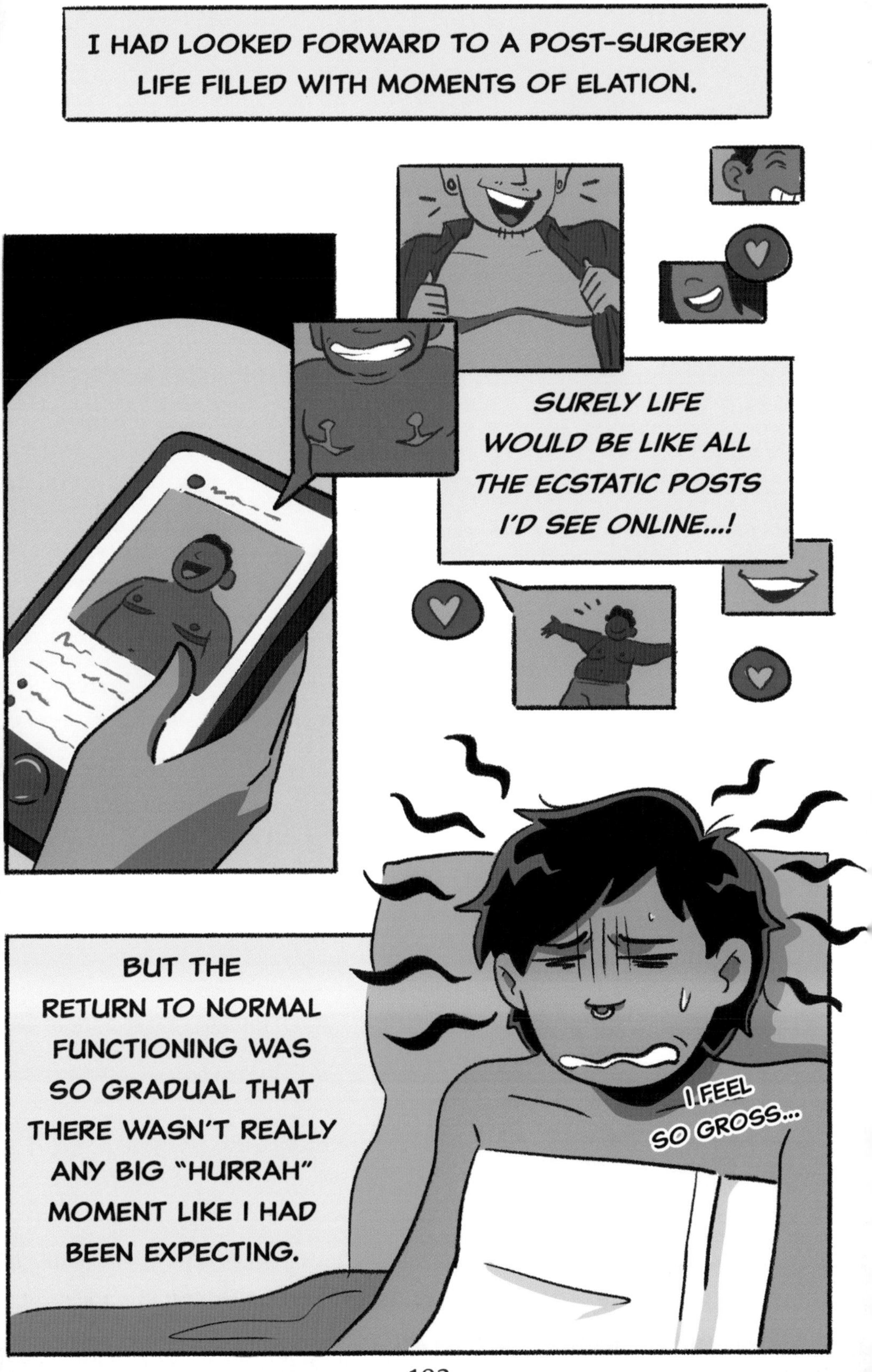
I HAD LOOKED FORWARD TO A POST-SURGERY LIFE FILLED WITH MOMENTS OF ELATION.
SURELY LIFE WOULD BE LIKE ALL THE ECSTATIC POSTS I'D SEE ONLINE...!
BUT THE RETURN TO NORMAL FUNCTIONING WAS SO GRADUAL THAT THERE WASN'T REALLY ANY BIG "HURRAH" MOMENT LIKE I HAD BEEN EXPECTING.
I FEEL SO GROSS...

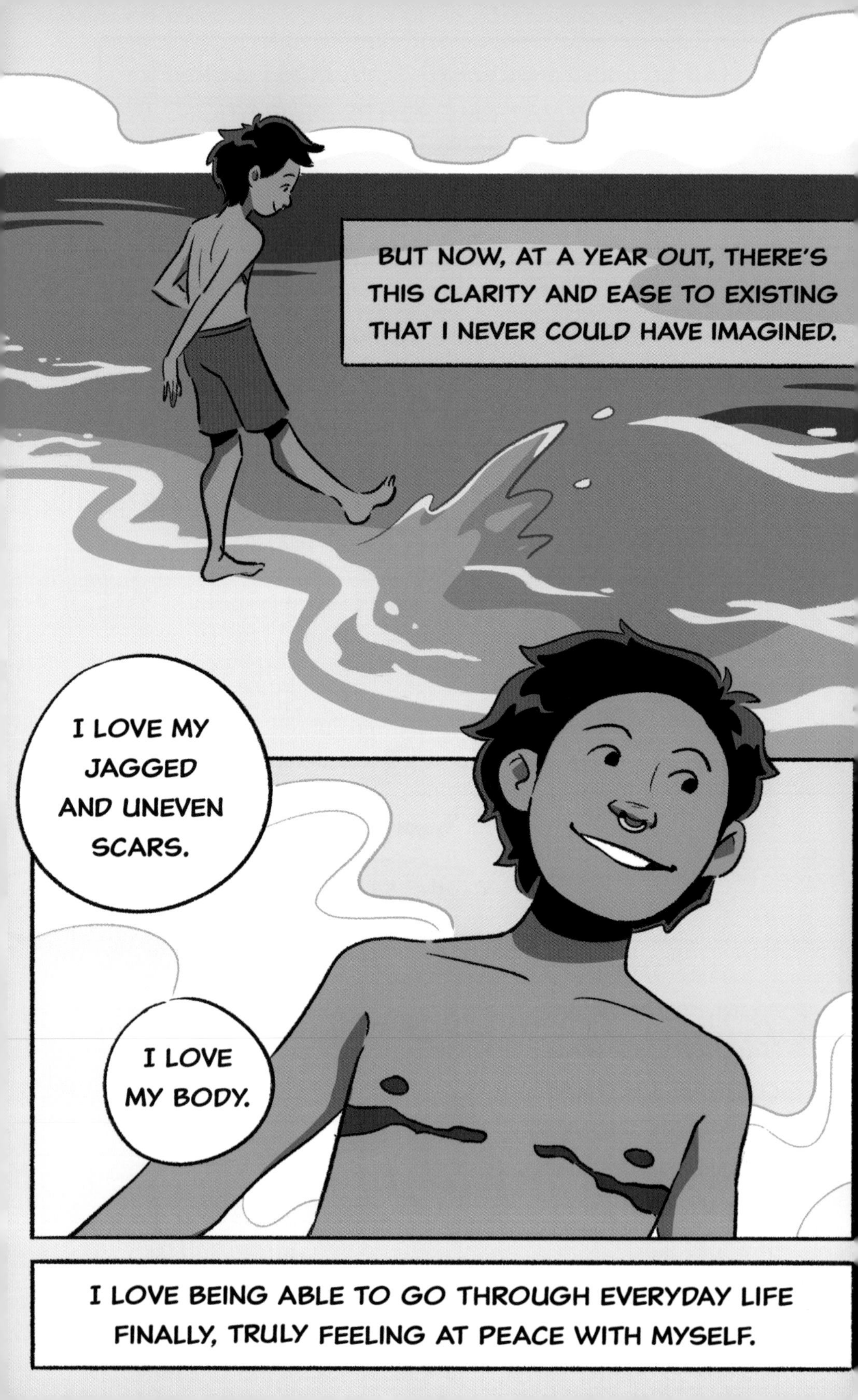
BUT NOW, AT A YEAR OUT, THERE'S THIS CLARITY AND EASE TO EXISTING THAT I NEVER COULD HAVE IMAGINED.
I LOVE MY JAGGED AND UNEVEN SCARS.
I LOVE MY BODY.
I LOVE BEING ABLE TO GO THROUGH EVERYDAY LIFE FINALLY, TRULY FEELING AT PEACE WITH MYSELF.

LUCAS - THE NIFTY FOX
(HE/THEY)

Hey, I'm Lucas! I'm an East Coast Canadian storyteller and designer. I've been drawing silly comic strips on Instagram and Facebook @theNiftyFox since 2017. I love drawing stories about my life experiences, exploring my gender and sexuality, tackling the challenges of ADHD, and generally trying to figure out how adulting works; all with a tongue-in-cheek flair! If you want to see my illustrations for Princess Boo Boo Books, or my graphic design samples, visit my Behance profile.

You can find it at:
behance.net/lucasjamesart

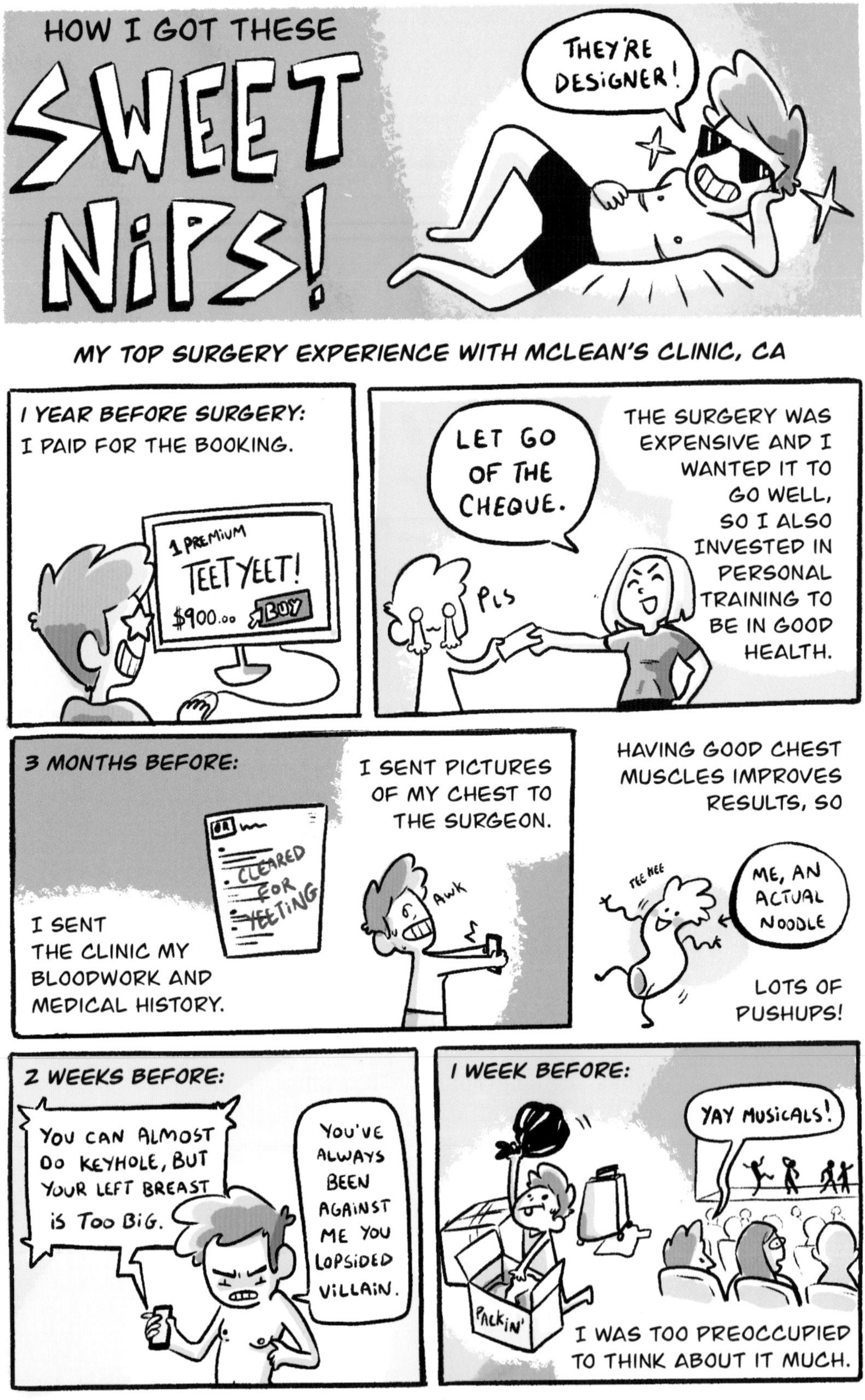
HOW I GOT THESE
SWEET NIPS!
THEY'RE DESIGNER!
MY TOP SURGERY EXPERIENCE WITH MCLEAN'S CLINIC, CA
1 YEAR BEFORE SURGERY:
I PAID FOR THE BOOKING.
1 PREMIUM
TEET YEET!
$900.00
BUY
THE SURGERY WAS EXPENSIVE AND I WANTED IT TO GO WELL, SO I ALSO INVESTED IN PERSONAL TRAINING TO BE IN GOOD HEALTH.
LET GO OF THE CHEQUE.
PLS
3 MONTHS BEFORE:
I SENT THE CLINIC MY BLOODWORK AND MEDICAL HISTORY.
CLEARED FOR YEETING
I SENT PICTURES OF MY CHEST TO THE SURGEON.
AWK
HAVING GOOD CHEST MUSCLES IMPROVES RESULTS, SO
TEE HEE
ME, AN ACTUAL NOODLE
LOTS OF PUSHUPS!
2 WEEKS BEFORE:
YOU CAN ALMOST DO KEYHOLE, BUT YOUR LEFT BREAST IS TOO BIG.
YOU'VE ALWAYS BEEN AGAINST ME YOU LOPSIDED VILLAIN.
1 WEEK BEFORE:
YAY MUSICALS!
PACKIN'
I WAS TOO PREOCCUPIED TO THINK ABOUT IT MUCH.

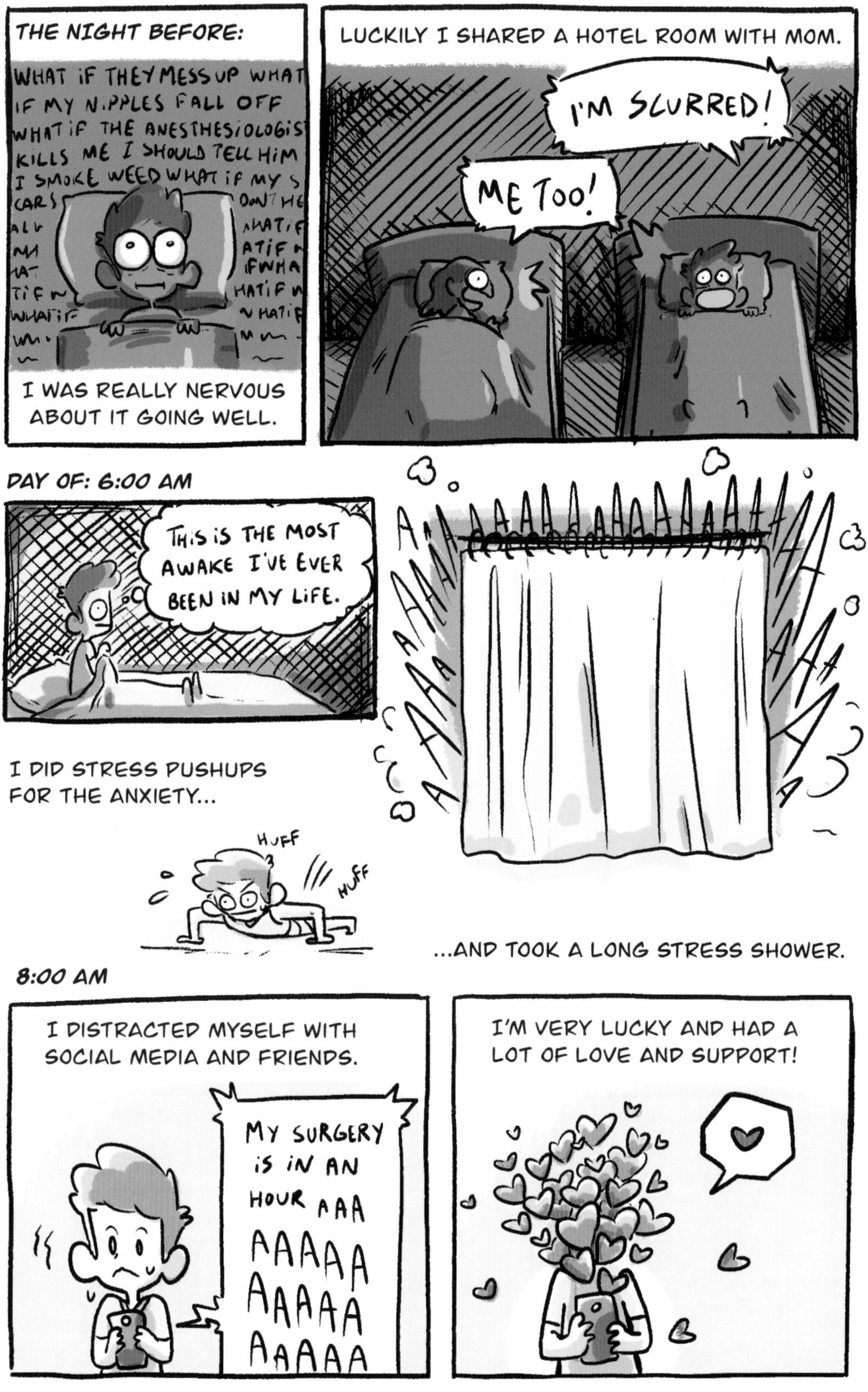

THE NIGHT BEFORE:
WHAT IF THEY MESS UP WHAT
IF MY NIPPLES FALL OFF
WHAT IF THE ANESTHESIOLOGIST
KILLS ME I SHOULD TELL HIM
I SMOKE WEED WHAT IF MY S
CARS
I WAS REALLY NERVOUS ABOUT IT GOING WELL.
LUCKILY I SHARED A HOTEL ROOM WITH MOM.
I'M SCURRED!
ME TOO!
DAY OF: 6:00 AM
THIS IS THE MOST AWAKE I'VE EVER BEEN IN MY LIFE.
I DID STRESS PUSHUPS FOR THE ANXIETY...
HUFF
HUFF
...AND TOOK A LONG STRESS SHOWER.
8:00 AM
I DISTRACTED MYSELF WITH SOCIAL MEDIA AND FRIENDS.
MY SURGERY IS IN AN HOUR AAA AAAAA AAAAA AAAAA
I'M VERY LUCKY AND HAD A LOT OF LOVE AND SUPPORT!

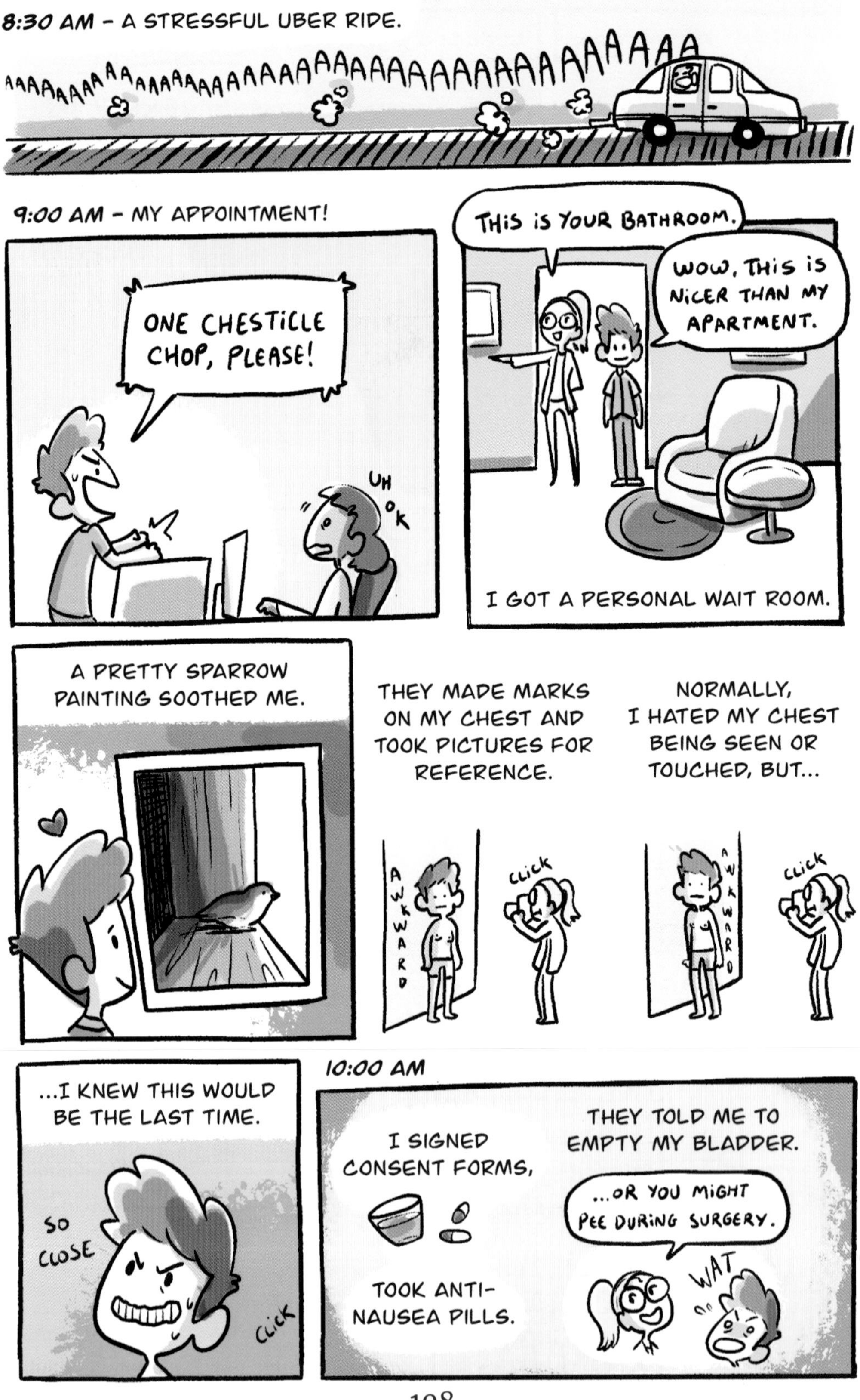
8:30 AM - A STRESSFUL UBER RIDE.
AAAAAAAAAAAAAAAAAAAAAAAAAAAAAAAAAAAAAAAAAAAAAA
9:00 AM - MY APPOINTMENT!
ONE CHESTICLE CHOP, PLEASE!
UH OK
THIS IS YOUR BATHROOM.
WOW, THIS IS NICER THAN MY APARTMENT.
I GOT A PERSONAL WAIT ROOM.
A PRETTY SPARROW PAINTING SOOTHED ME.
THEY MADE MARKS ON MY CHEST AND TOOK PICTURES FOR REFERENCE.
AWKWARD
CLICK
NORMALLY, I HATED MY CHEST BEING SEEN OR TOUCHED, BUT...
AWKWARD
CLICK
...I KNEW THIS WOULD BE THE LAST TIME.
SO CLOSE
CLICK
10:00 AM
I SIGNED CONSENT FORMS,
TOOK ANTI-NAUSEA PILLS.
THEY TOLD ME TO EMPTY MY BLADDER.
...OR YOU MIGHT PEE DURING SURGERY.
WAT

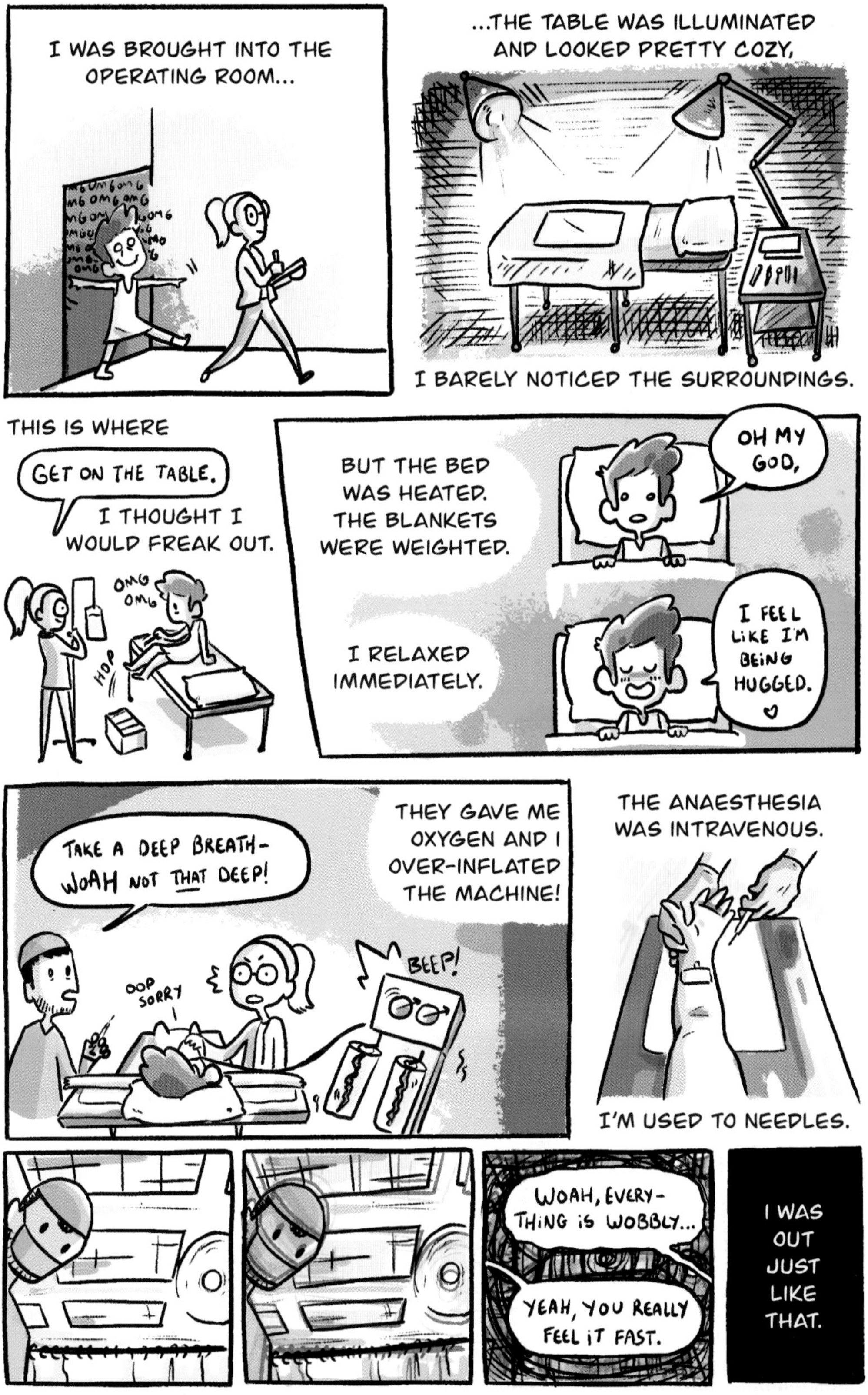
I WAS BROUGHT INTO THE OPERATING ROOM...
...THE TABLE WAS ILLUMINATED AND LOOKED PRETTY COZY,
I BARELY NOTICED THE SURROUNDINGS.
THIS IS WHERE
GET ON THE TABLE.
I THOUGHT I WOULD FREAK OUT.
OMG OMG
HOP
BUT THE BED WAS HEATED. THE BLANKETS WERE WEIGHTED.
OH MY GOD,
I RELAXED IMMEDIATELY.
I FEEL LIKE I'M BEING HUGGED. ♥
TAKE A DEEP BREATH- WOAH NOT THAT DEEP!
THEY GAVE ME OXYGEN AND I OVER-INFLATED THE MACHINE!
OOP SORRY
BEEP!
THE ANAESTHESIA WAS INTRAVENOUS.
I'M USED TO NEEDLES.
WOAH, EVERY-THING IS WOBBLY...
YEAH, YOU REALLY FEEL IT FAST.
I WAS OUT JUST LIKE THAT.

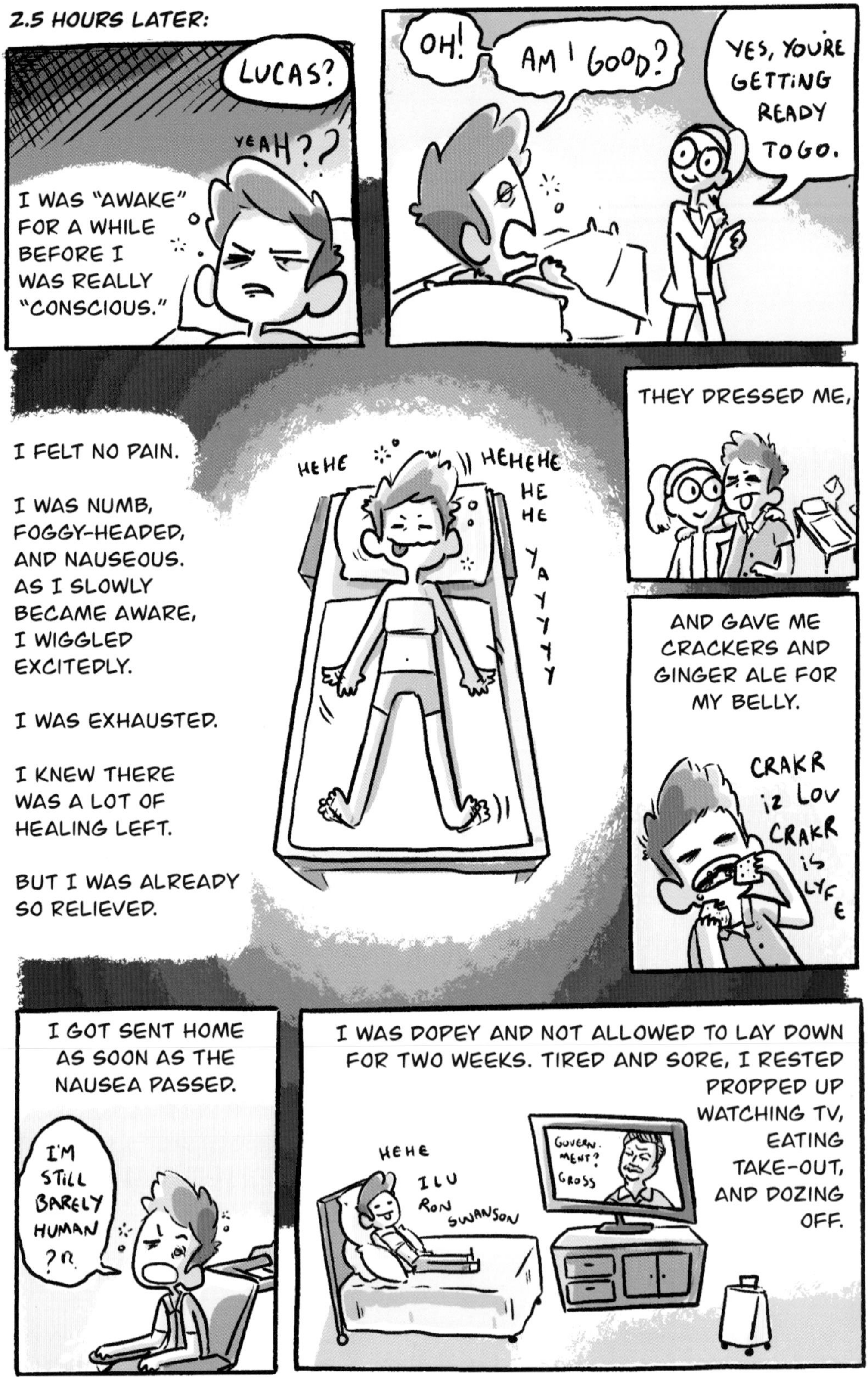
2.5 HOURS LATER:
LUCAS?
YEAH??
I WAS "AWAKE" FOR A WHILE BEFORE I WAS REALLY "CONSCIOUS."
OH!
AM I GOOD?
YES, YOU'RE GETTING READY TO GO.
I FELT NO PAIN.
I WAS NUMB, FOGGY-HEADED, AND NAUSEOUS. AS I SLOWLY BECAME AWARE, I WIGGLED EXCITEDLY.
I WAS EXHAUSTED.
I KNEW THERE WAS A LOT OF HEALING LEFT.
BUT I WAS ALREADY SO RELIEVED.
HEHE
HEHEHE
HE HE
YAYYYYY
THEY DRESSED ME,
AND GAVE ME CRACKERS AND GINGER ALE FOR MY BELLY.
CRAKR iz LOV CRAKR iS LYFE
I GOT SENT HOME AS SOON AS THE NAUSEA PASSED.
I'M STILL BARELY HUMAN ?R
I WAS DOPEY AND NOT ALLOWED TO LAY DOWN FOR TWO WEEKS. TIRED AND SORE, I RESTED PROPPED UP WATCHING TV, EATING TAKE-OUT, AND DOZING OFF.
HEHE
ILU RON SWANSON
GOVERN. MENT? GROSS

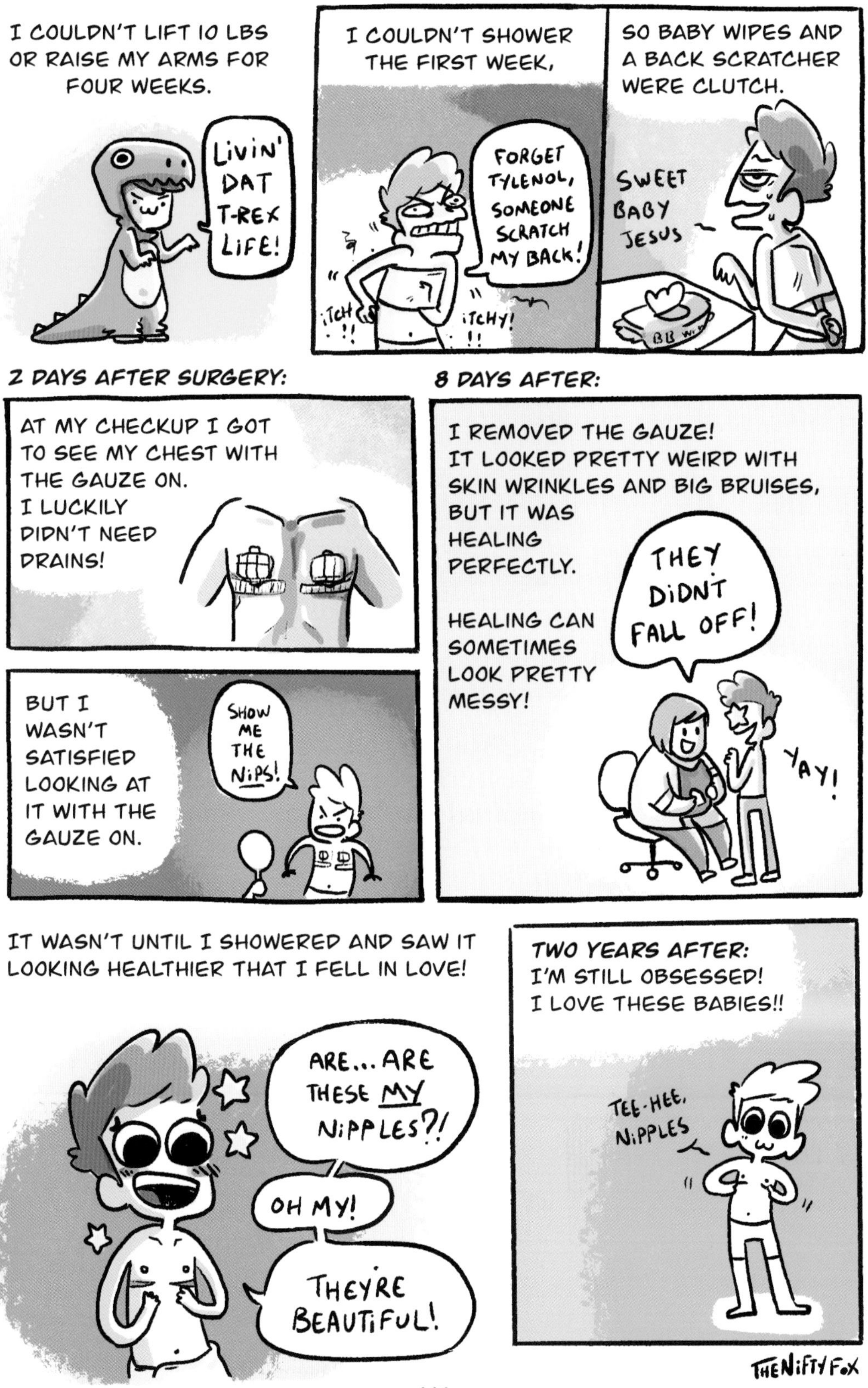
I COULDN'T LIFT 10 LBS OR RAISE MY ARMS FOR FOUR WEEKS.
LIVIN' DAT T-REX LIFE!
I COULDN'T SHOWER THE FIRST WEEK,
FORGET TYLENOL, SOMEONE SCRATCH MY BACK!
ITCH!!
ITCHY!!
SO BABY WIPES AND A BACK SCRATCHER WERE CLUTCH.
SWEET BABY JESUS
2 DAYS AFTER SURGERY:
AT MY CHECKUP I GOT TO SEE MY CHEST WITH THE GAUZE ON. I LUCKILY DIDN'T NEED DRAINS!
BUT I WASN'T SATISFIED LOOKING AT IT WITH THE GAUZE ON.
SHOW ME THE NIPS!
8 DAYS AFTER:
I REMOVED THE GAUZE! IT LOOKED PRETTY WEIRD WITH SKIN WRINKLES AND BIG BRUISES, BUT IT WAS HEALING PERFECTLY.
HEALING CAN SOMETIMES LOOK PRETTY MESSY!
THEY DIDN'T FALL OFF!
YAY!
IT WASN'T UNTIL I SHOWERED AND SAW IT LOOKING HEALTHIER THAT I FELL IN LOVE!
ARE... ARE THESE MY NIPPLES?!
OH MY!
THEY'RE BEAUTIFUL!
TWO YEARS AFTER: I'M STILL OBSESSED! I LOVE THESE BABIES!!
TEE-HEE, NIPPLES
THENIFTYFOX

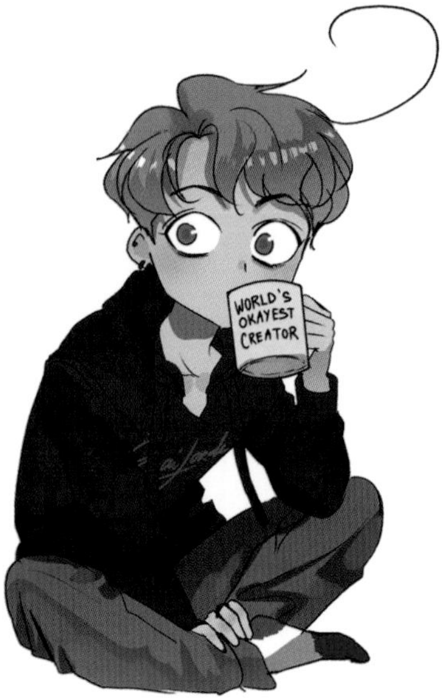
WORLD'S
OKAYEST
CREATOR

AIDYN / SNAILORDS

(HE/HIM)

Two souls accidently got placed into my body. I'm bigender. Took a century for me to accept myself as I am. But I am so much happier now that I've signed a peace treaty with myself.

Find him on Instagram and Twitter:
@Snailords

Never be loved

by Snailords

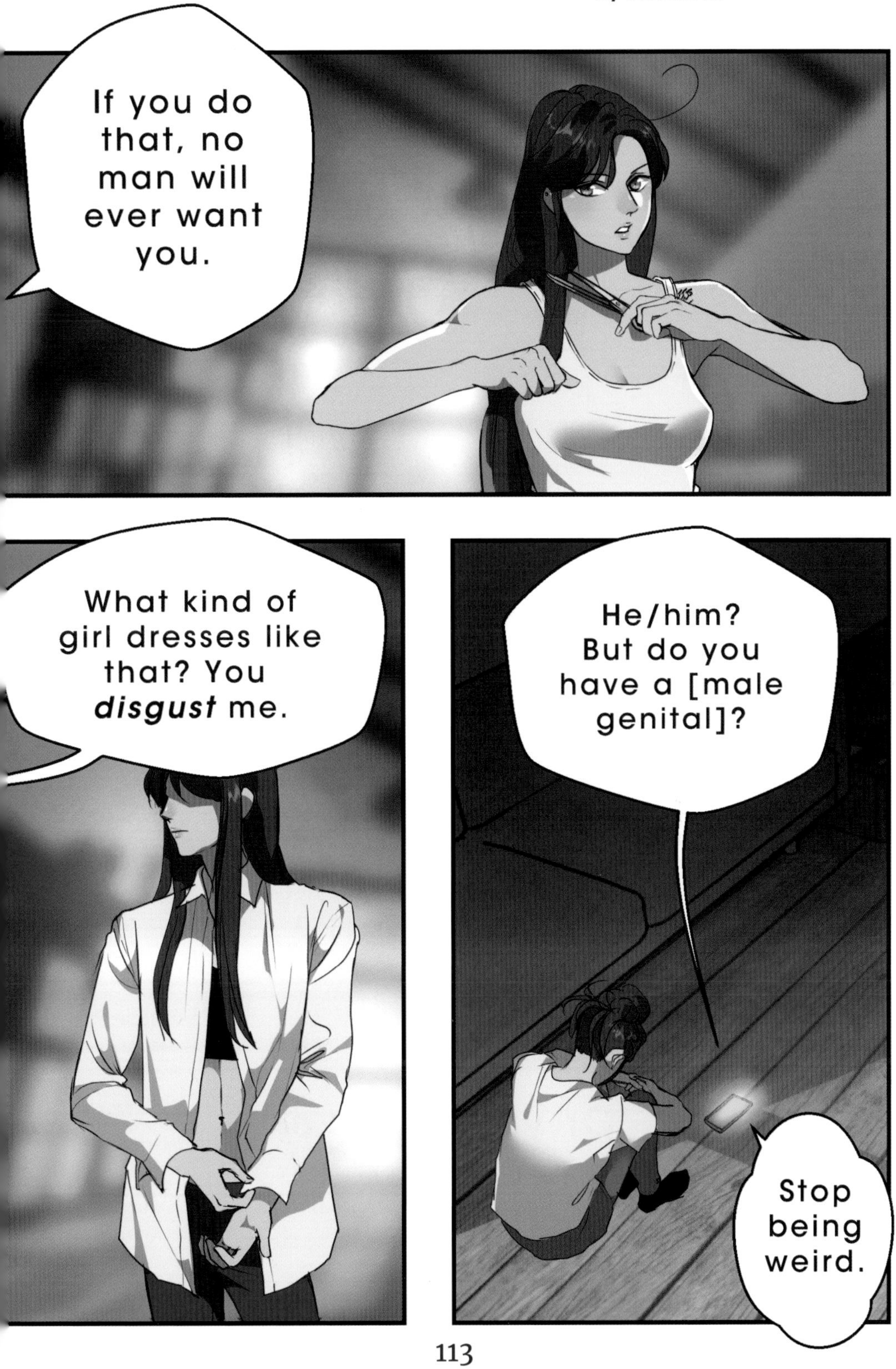
If you do that, no man will ever want you.
What kind of girl dresses like that? You *disgust* me.
He/him? But do you have a [male genital]?
Stop being weird.

Society's message to me
was loud and clear:
"Act ***normal***."

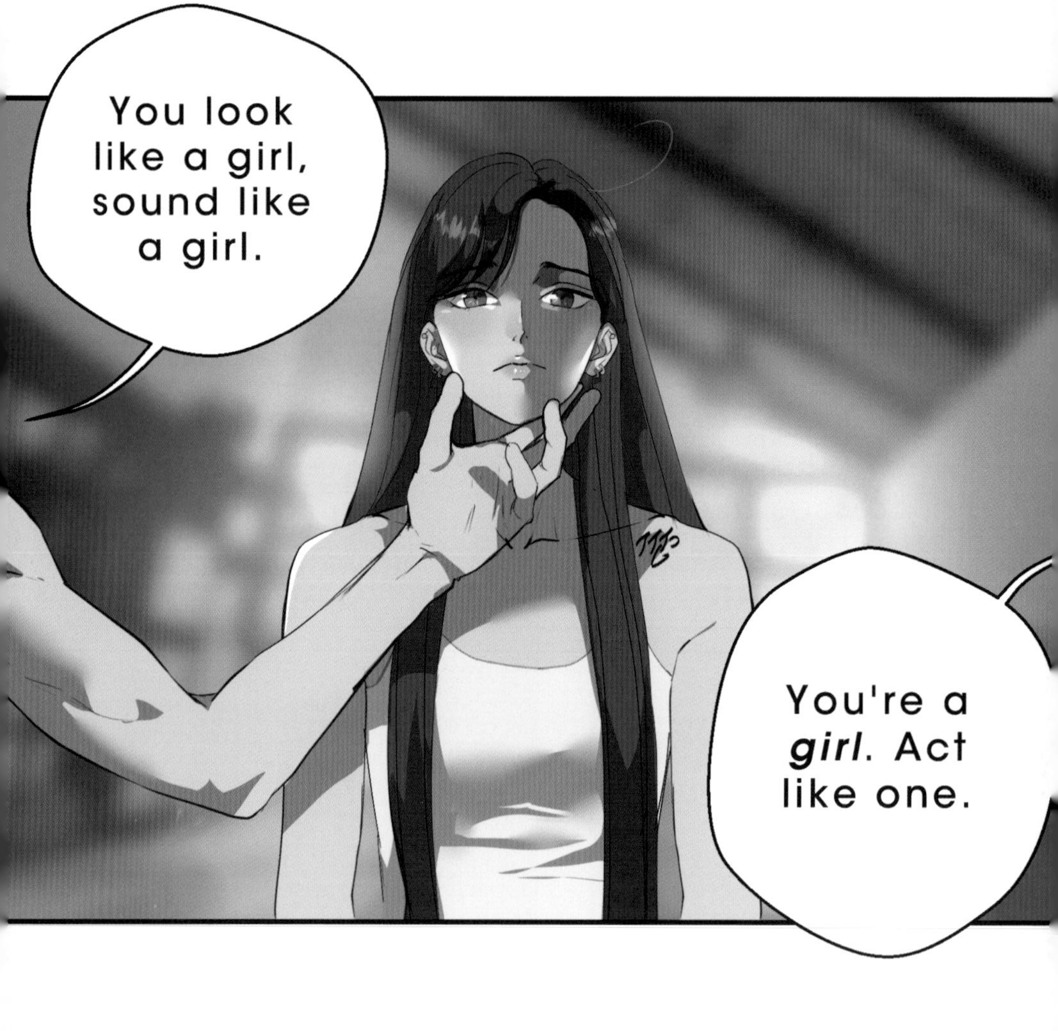
You look like a girl, sound like a girl.
You're a ***girl***. Act like one.

"Or you'll ***never***
be loved,
you ***FREAK***."

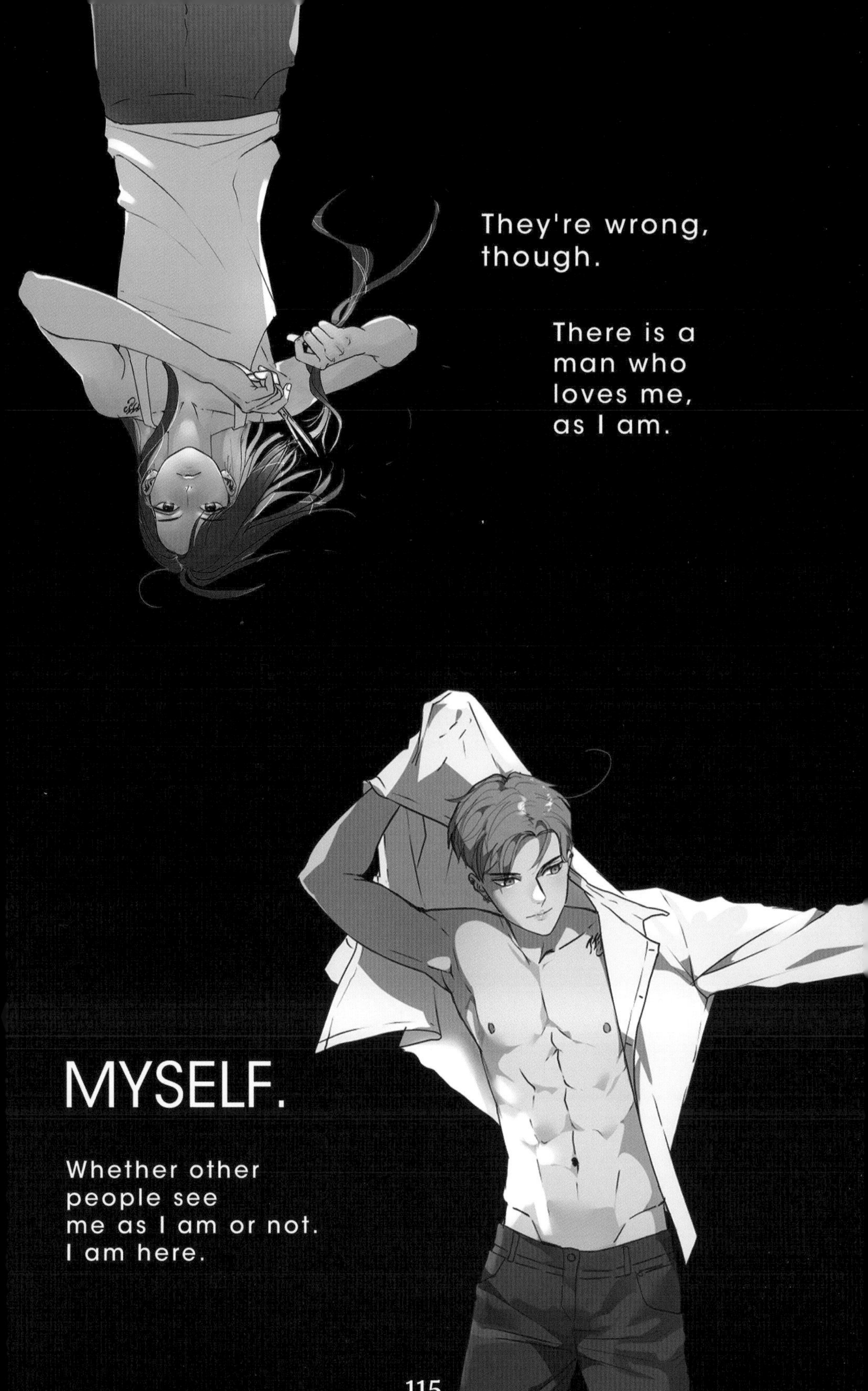
They're wrong, though.
There is a man who loves me, as I am.
MYSELF.
Whether other people see me as I am or not. I am here.

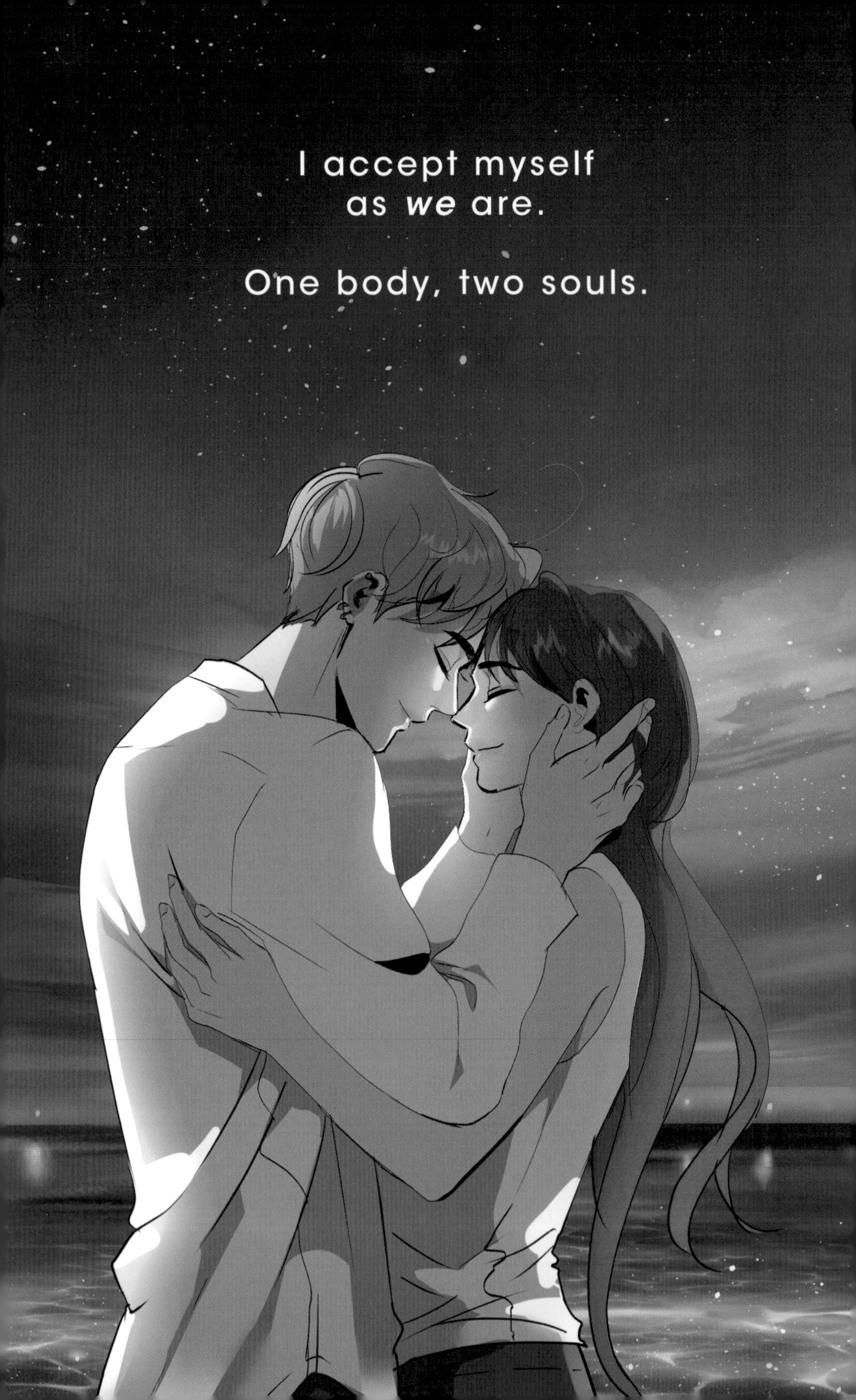
I accept myself
as *we* are.
One body, two souls.

TARA MADISON AVERY
(SHE/HER)

Tara Madison Avery is a cartoonist, the publisher of Stacked Deck Press, and a board member of Prism Comics. She is best known for her bisexual-themed comic, *Gooch*, and as an editor and contributor to the Ignatz Award-winning *We're Still Here: An All-Trans Comics Anthology*. She lives in the California desert with her cat, Sparkles, and still thinks Mary Marvel is the coolest. Colorist Mike Sullivan is a longtime collaborator.

You can find Avery online at:
stackeddeckpress.com

You can find Sullivan's cartooning work at:
virtualinfinitycomics.com

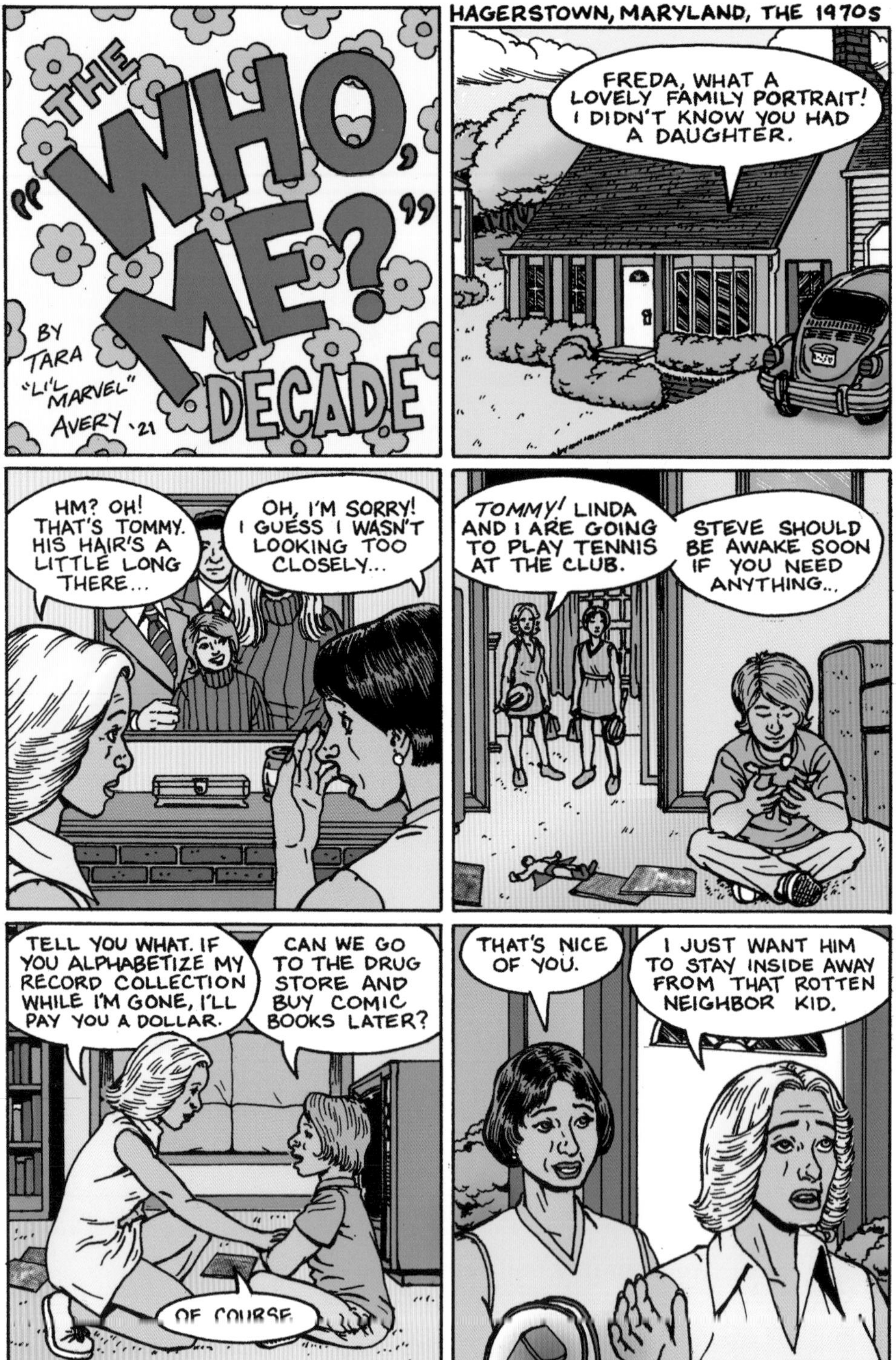
"WHO, ME?" THE DECADE
BY TARA "LI'L MARVEL" AVERY '21
HAGERSTOWN, MARYLAND, THE 1970s
FREDA, WHAT A LOVELY FAMILY PORTRAIT! I DIDN'T KNOW YOU HAD A DAUGHTER.
HM? OH! THAT'S TOMMY. HIS HAIR'S A LITTLE LONG THERE...
OH, I'M SORRY! I GUESS I WASN'T LOOKING TOO CLOSELY...
TOMMY! LINDA AND I ARE GOING TO PLAY TENNIS AT THE CLUB.
STEVE SHOULD BE AWAKE SOON IF YOU NEED ANYTHING...
TELL YOU WHAT. IF YOU ALPHABETIZE MY RECORD COLLECTION WHILE I'M GONE, I'LL PAY YOU A DOLLAR.
CAN WE GO TO THE DRUG STORE AND BUY COMIC BOOKS LATER?
OF COURSE.
THAT'S NICE OF YOU.
I JUST WANT HIM TO STAY INSIDE AWAY FROM THAT ROTTEN NEIGHBOR KID.

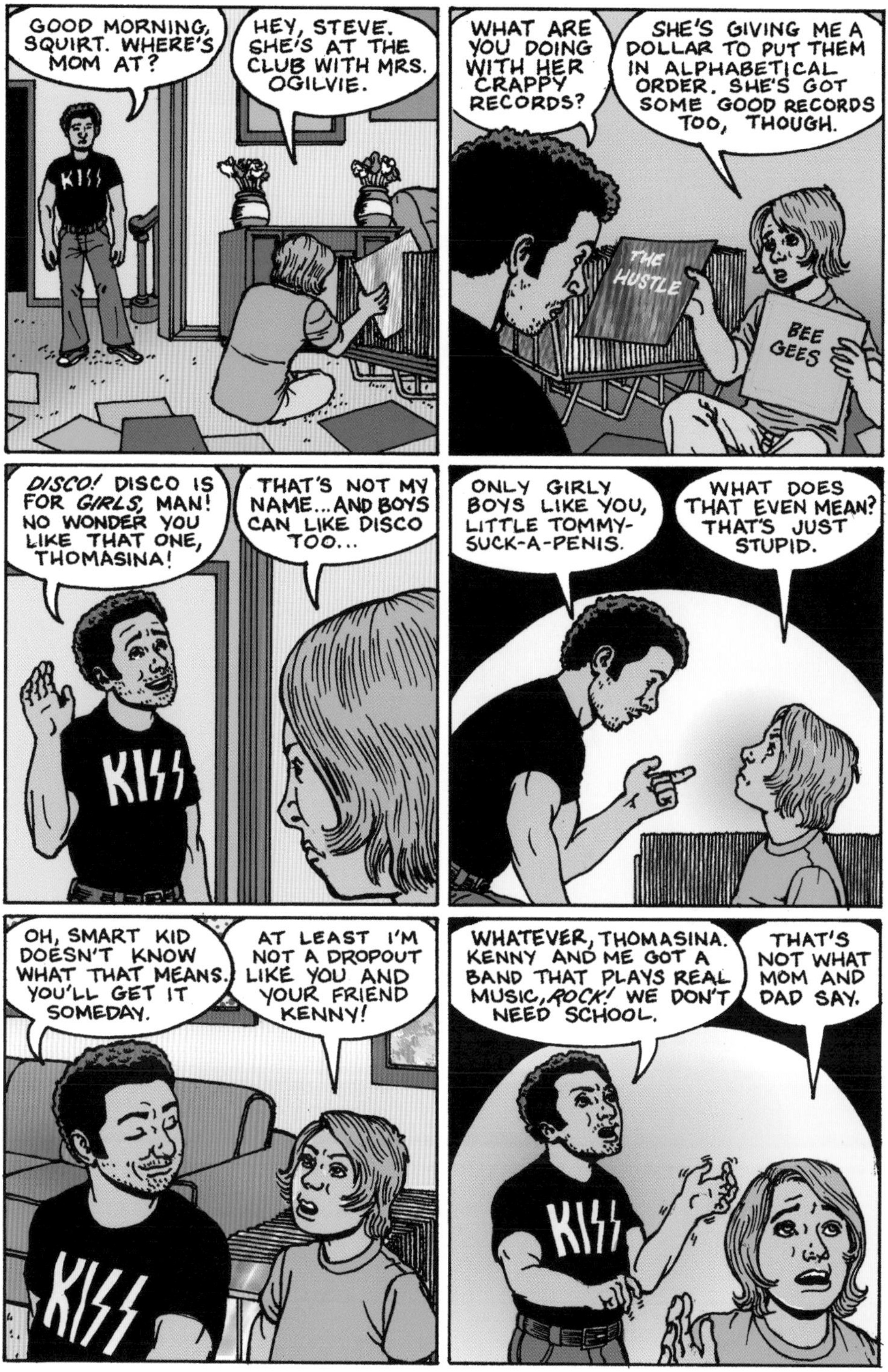
GOOD MORNING, SQUIRT. WHERE'S MOM AT?
HEY, STEVE. SHE'S AT THE CLUB WITH MRS. OGILVIE.
WHAT ARE YOU DOING WITH HER CRAPPY RECORDS?
SHE'S GIVING ME A DOLLAR TO PUT THEM IN ALPHABETICAL ORDER. SHE'S GOT SOME GOOD RECORDS TOO, THOUGH.
THE HUSTLE
BEE GEES
DISCO! DISCO IS FOR *GIRLS,* MAN! NO WONDER YOU LIKE THAT ONE, THOMASINA!
THAT'S NOT MY NAME...AND BOYS CAN LIKE DISCO TOO...
ONLY GIRLY BOYS LIKE YOU, LITTLE TOMMY-SUCK-A-PENIS.
WHAT DOES THAT EVEN MEAN? THAT'S JUST STUPID.
OH, SMART KID DOESN'T KNOW WHAT THAT MEANS. YOU'LL GET IT SOMEDAY.
AT LEAST I'M NOT A DROPOUT LIKE YOU AND YOUR FRIEND KENNY!
WHATEVER, THOMASINA. KENNY AND ME GOT A BAND THAT PLAYS REAL MUSIC, *ROCK!* WE DON'T NEED SCHOOL.
THAT'S NOT WHAT MOM AND DAD SAY.

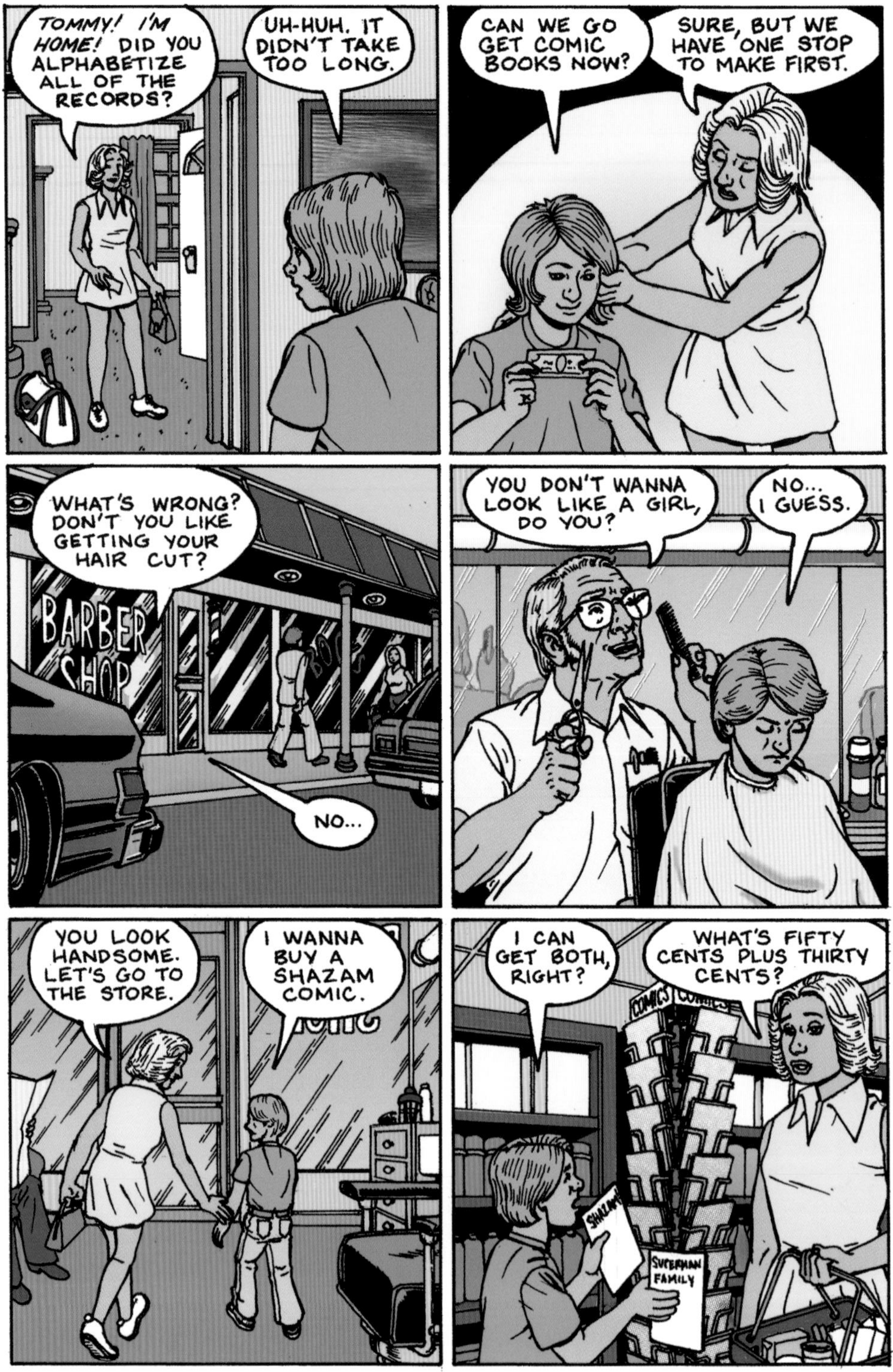
TOMMY! I'M HOME! DID YOU ALPHABETIZE ALL OF THE RECORDS?
UH-HUH. IT DIDN'T TAKE TOO LONG.
CAN WE GO GET COMIC BOOKS NOW?
SURE, BUT WE HAVE ONE STOP TO MAKE FIRST.
WHAT'S WRONG? DON'T YOU LIKE GETTING YOUR HAIR CUT?
BARBER SHOP
NO...
YOU DON'T WANNA LOOK LIKE A GIRL, DO YOU?
NO... I GUESS.
YOU LOOK HANDSOME. LET'S GO TO THE STORE.
I WANNA BUY A SHAZAM COMIC.
I CAN GET BOTH, RIGHT?
WHAT'S FIFTY CENTS PLUS THIRTY CENTS?
COMICS
SUPERMAN FAMILY

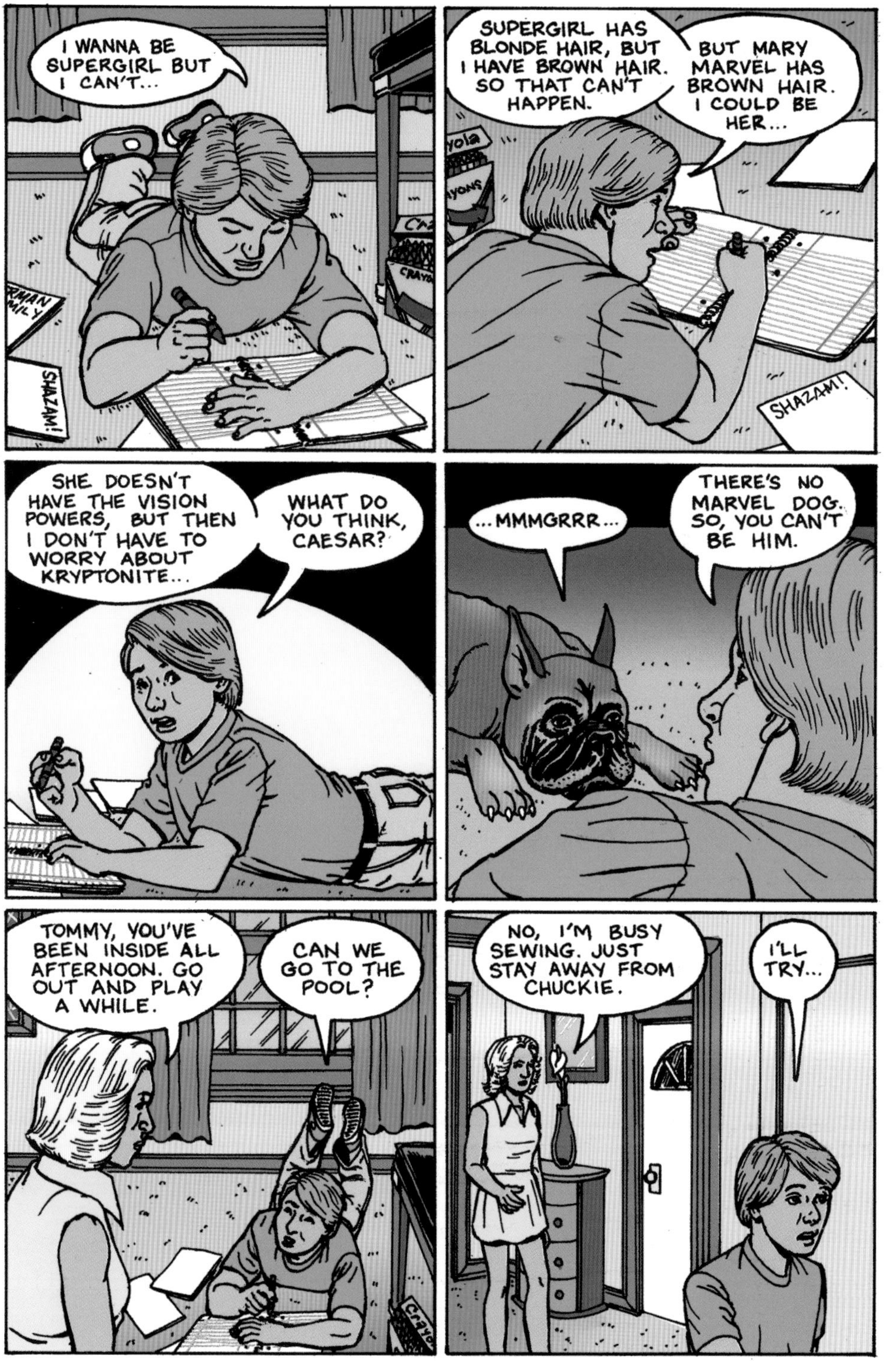
I WANNA BE SUPERGIRL BUT I CAN'T...
SHAZAM!
SUPERGIRL HAS BLONDE HAIR, BUT I HAVE BROWN HAIR. SO THAT CAN'T HAPPEN.
BUT MARY MARVEL HAS BROWN HAIR. I COULD BE HER...
SHAZAM!
SHE DOESN'T HAVE THE VISION POWERS, BUT THEN I DON'T HAVE TO WORRY ABOUT KRYPTONITE...
WHAT DO YOU THINK, CAESAR?
...MMMGRRR...
THERE'S NO MARVEL DOG. SO, YOU CAN'T BE HIM.
TOMMY, YOU'VE BEEN INSIDE ALL AFTERNOON. GO OUT AND PLAY A WHILE.
CAN WE GO TO THE POOL?
NO, I'M BUSY SEWING. JUST STAY AWAY FROM CHUCKIE.
I'LL TRY...

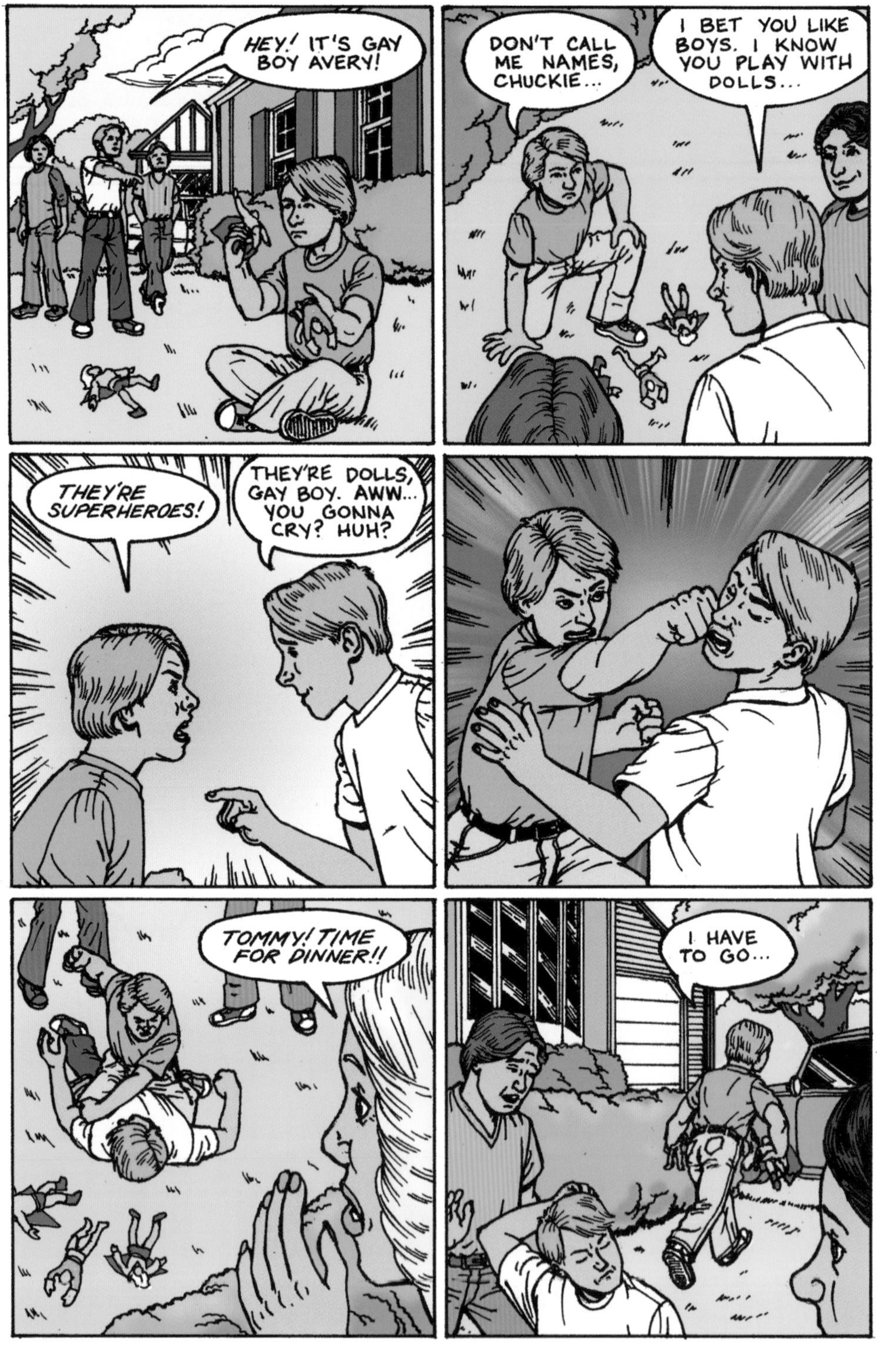
HEY! IT'S GAY BOY AVERY!
DON'T CALL ME NAMES, CHUCKIE...
I BET YOU LIKE BOYS. I KNOW YOU PLAY WITH DOLLS...
THEY'RE SUPERHEROES!
THEY'RE DOLLS, GAY BOY. AWW... YOU GONNA CRY? HUH?
TOMMY! TIME FOR DINNER!!
I HAVE TO GO...

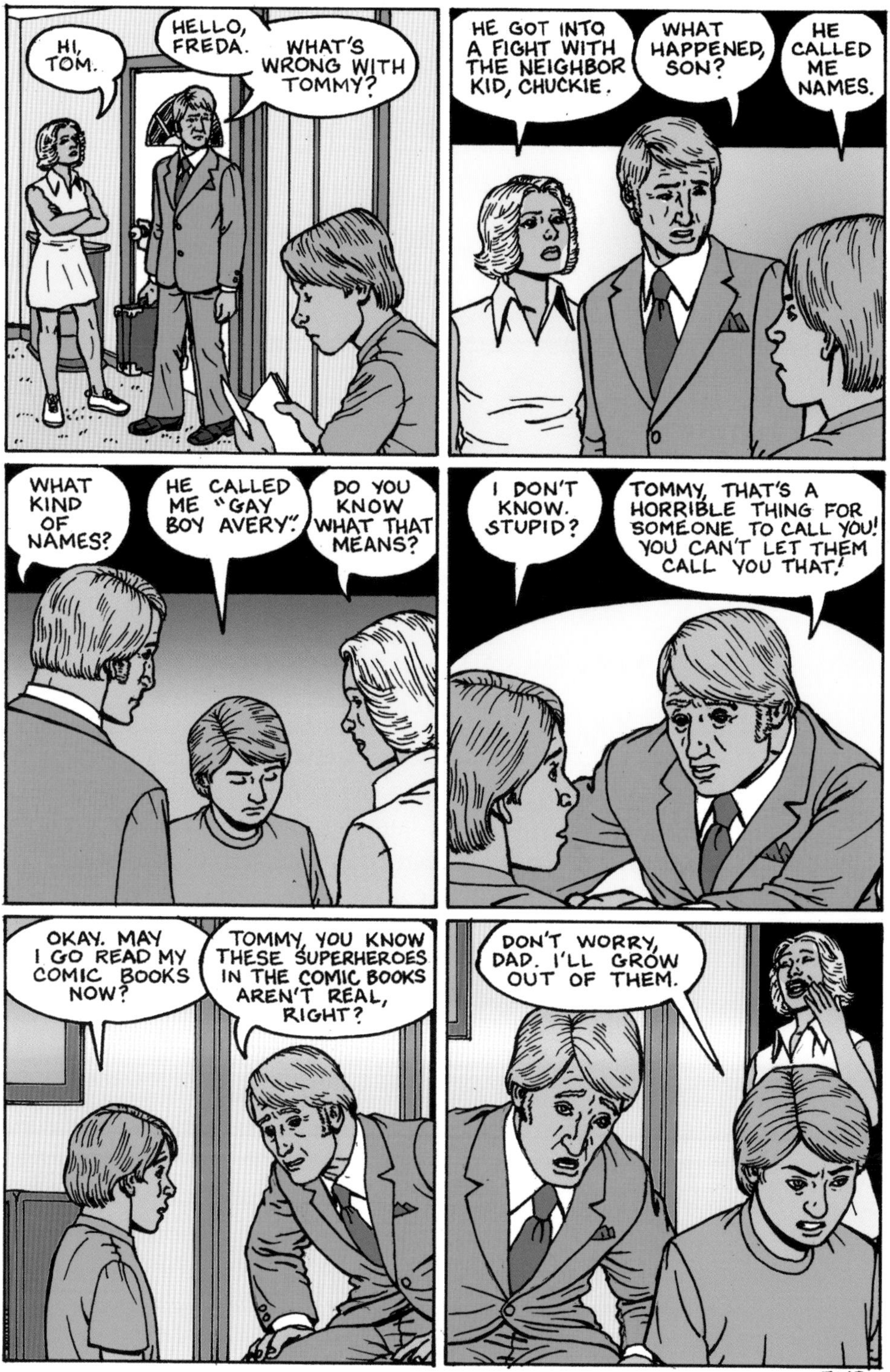
HI, TOM.
HELLO, FREDA.
WHAT'S WRONG WITH TOMMY?
HE GOT INTO A FIGHT WITH THE NEIGHBOR KID, CHUCKIE.
WHAT HAPPENED, SON?
HE CALLED ME NAMES.
WHAT KIND OF NAMES?
HE CALLED ME "GAY BOY AVERY".
DO YOU KNOW WHAT THAT MEANS?
I DON'T KNOW. STUPID?
TOMMY, THAT'S A HORRIBLE THING FOR SOMEONE TO CALL YOU! YOU CAN'T LET THEM CALL YOU THAT!
OKAY. MAY I GO READ MY COMIC BOOKS NOW?
TOMMY, YOU KNOW THESE SUPERHEROES IN THE COMIC BOOKS AREN'T REAL, RIGHT?
DON'T WORRY, DAD. I'LL GROW OUT OF THEM.

END

DANA SIMPSON
(SHE/HER)

Dana Claire Simpson has been making comics a long time. When her comic strip, *Phoebe and Her Unicorn*, launched in papers in 2015, it made her the first out transgender person in syndicated comics. (She's now one of several.)

You can find her strip on GoComics.com, and really anywhere they sell books. She lives in Santa Barbara, California, with her nonbinary spouse and her very fluffy cat.

You can find her online at:
danasimpson.com

JUNE 20, 2005 *by dana*

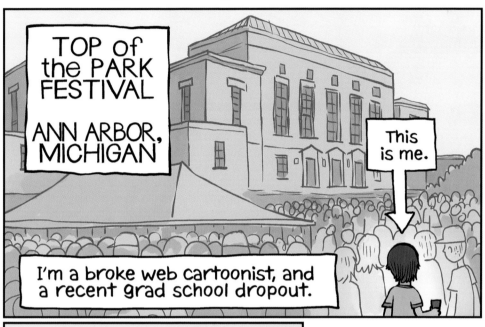

TOP of the PARK FESTIVAL

ANN ARBOR, MICHIGAN

This is me.

I'm a broke web cartoonist, and a recent grad school dropout.

I don't know it, but I'm about to have a life-changing conversation.

Hey.

We need to talk.

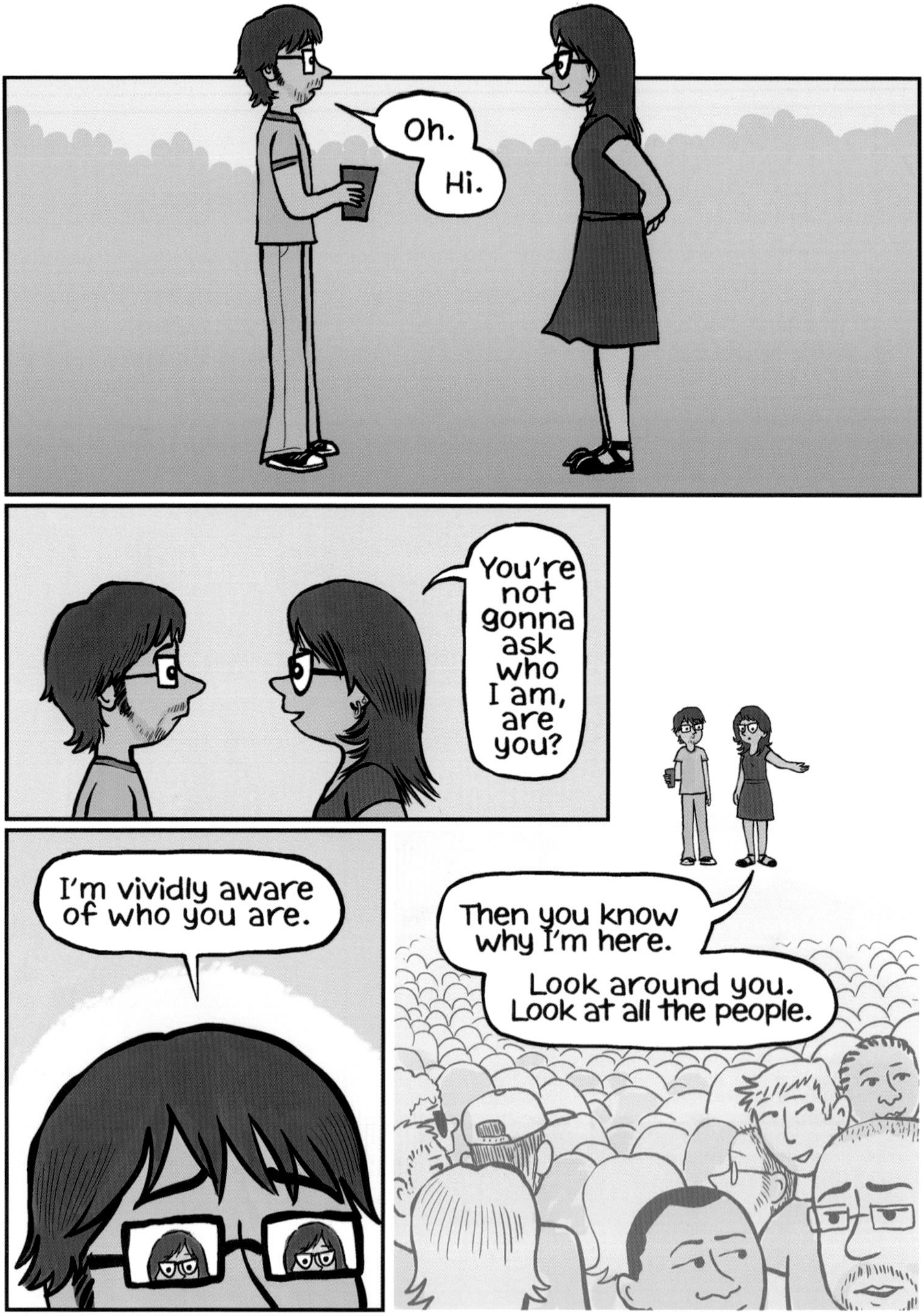
Oh.
Hi.
You're not gonna ask who I am, are you?
I'm vividly aware of who you are.
Then you know why I'm here.
Look around you. Look at all the people.

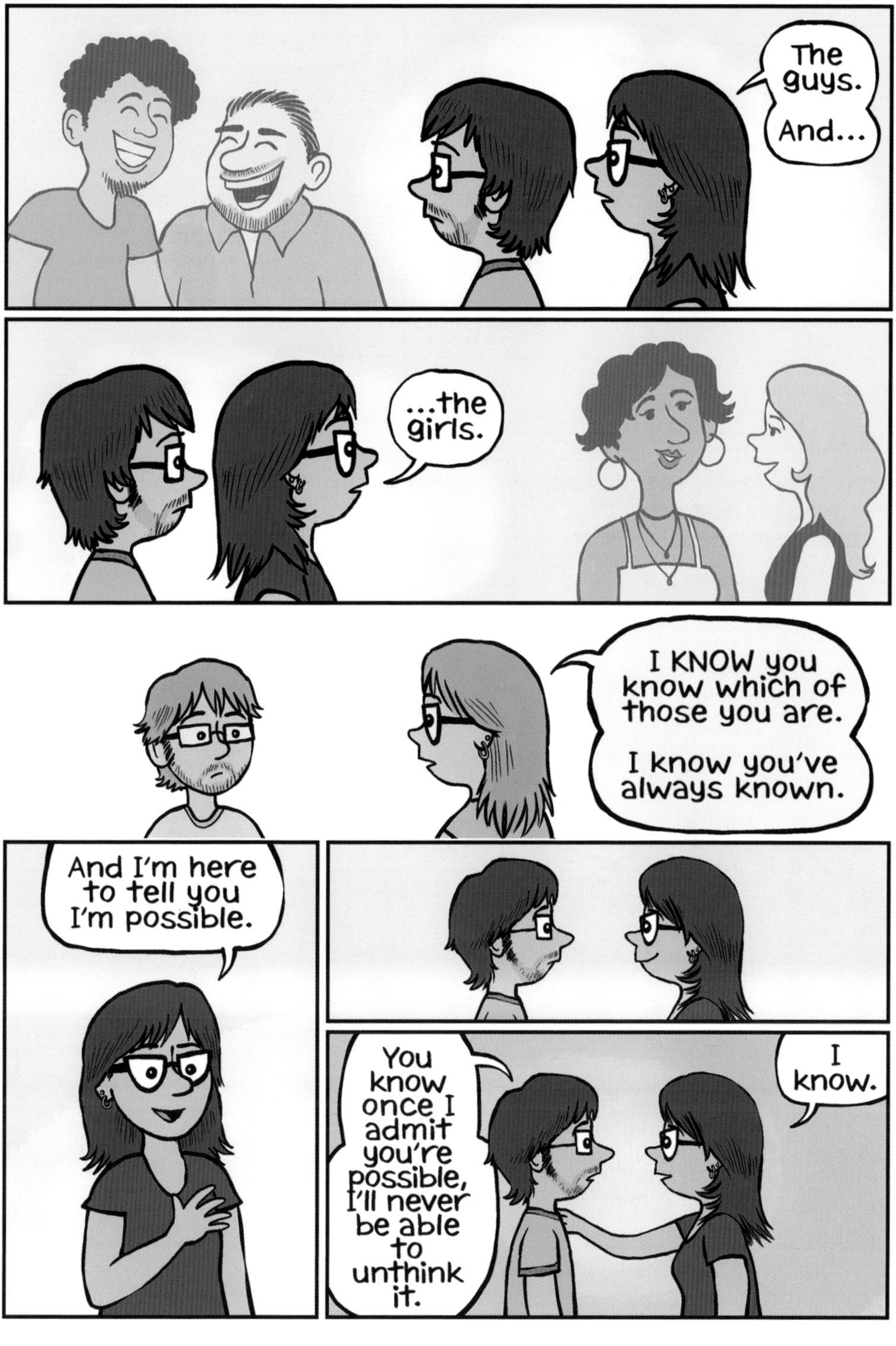
The guys.
And...
...the girls.
I KNOW you know which of those you are.
I know you've always known.
And I'm here to tell you I'm possible.
You know once I admit you're possible, I'll never be able to unthink it.
I know.

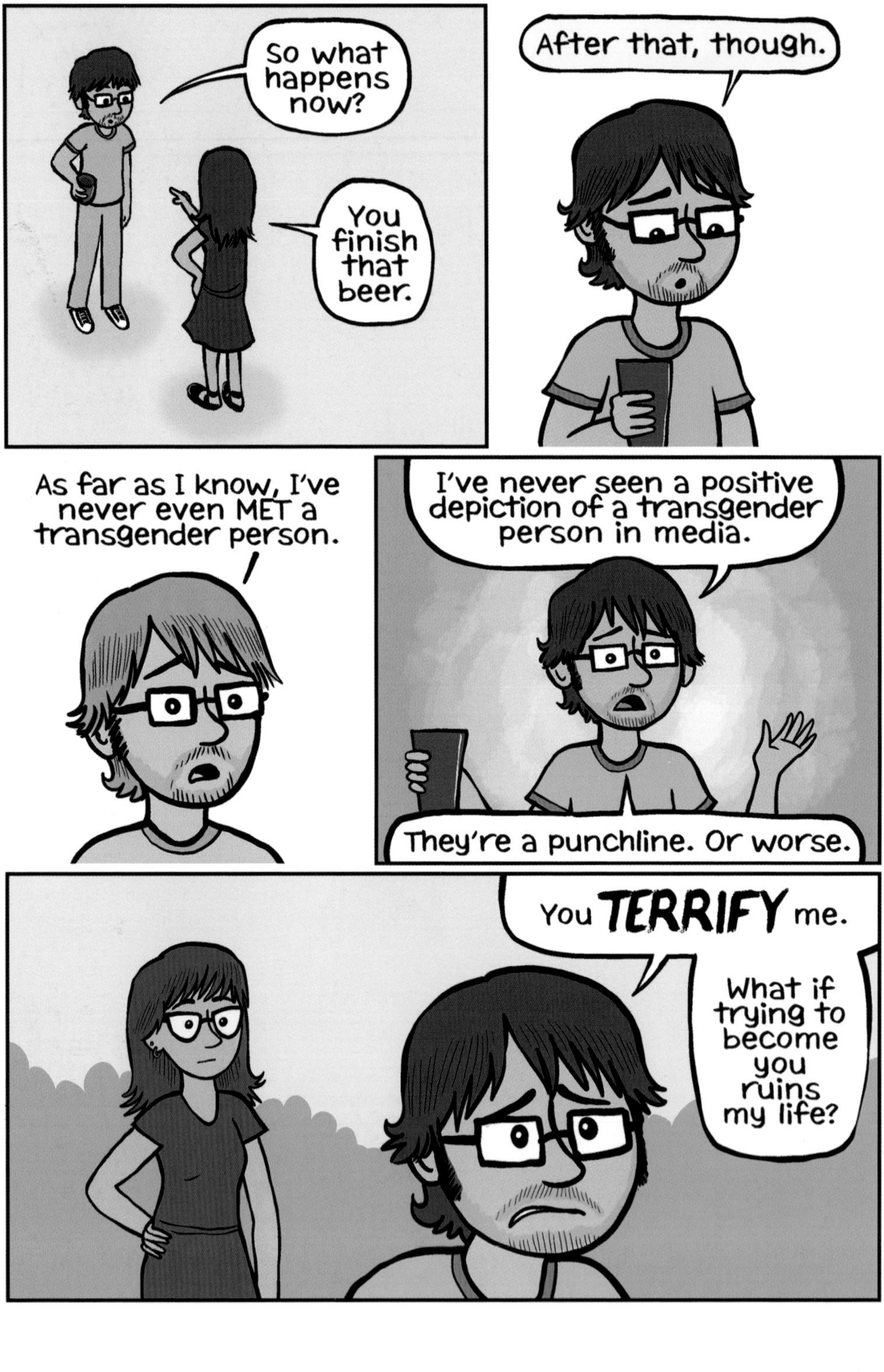
So what happens now?
You finish that beer.
After that, though.
As far as I know, I've never even MET a transgender person.
I've never seen a positive depiction of a transgender person in media.
They're a punchline. Or worse.
You TERRIFY me.
What if trying to become you ruins my life?

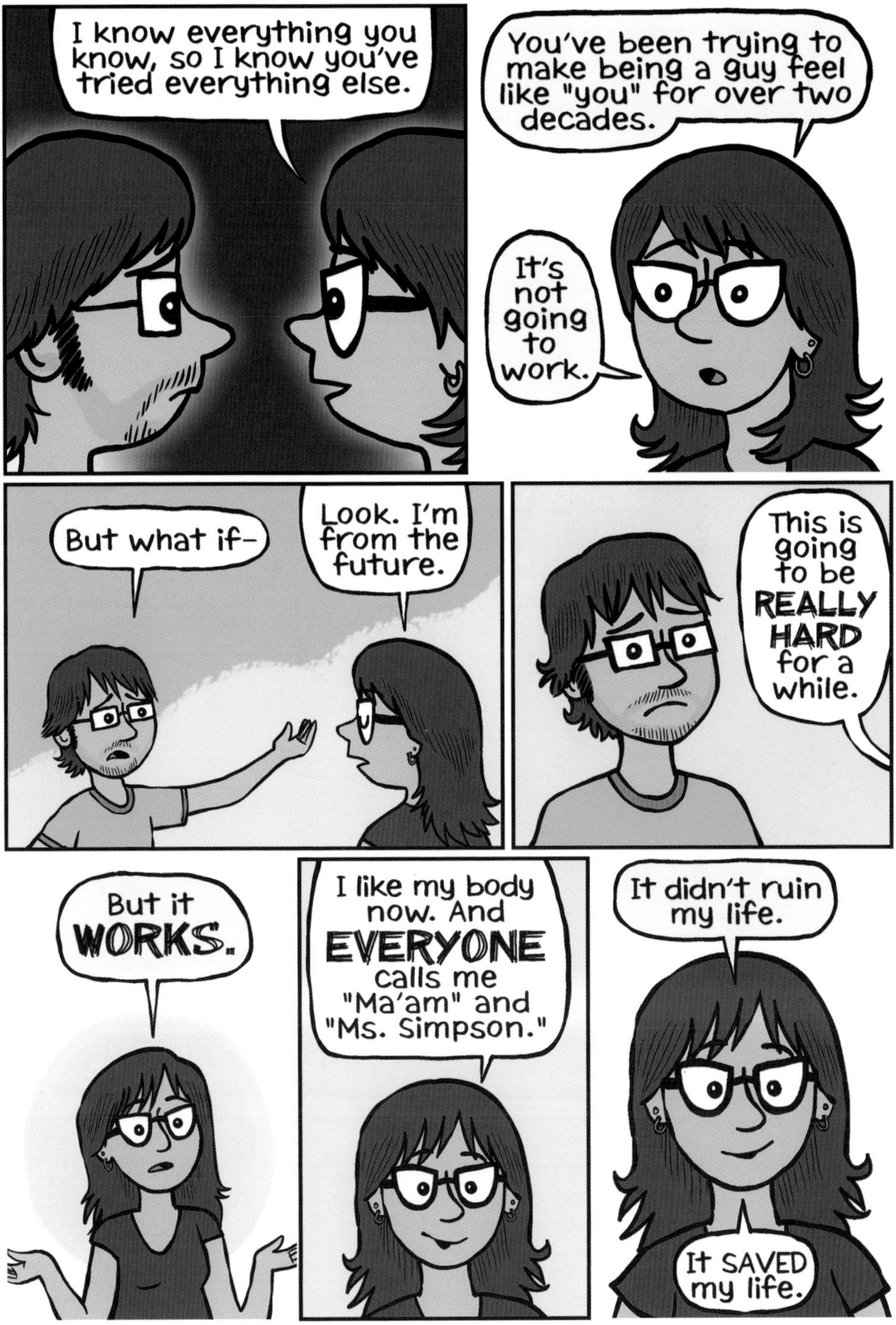
I know everything you know, so I know you've tried everything else.
You've been trying to make being a guy feel like "you" for over two decades.
It's not going to work.
But what if-
Look. I'm from the future.
This is going to be REALLY HARD for a while.
But it WORKS.
I like my body now. And EVERYONE calls me "Ma'am" and "Ms. Simpson."
It didn't ruin my life.
It SAVED my life.

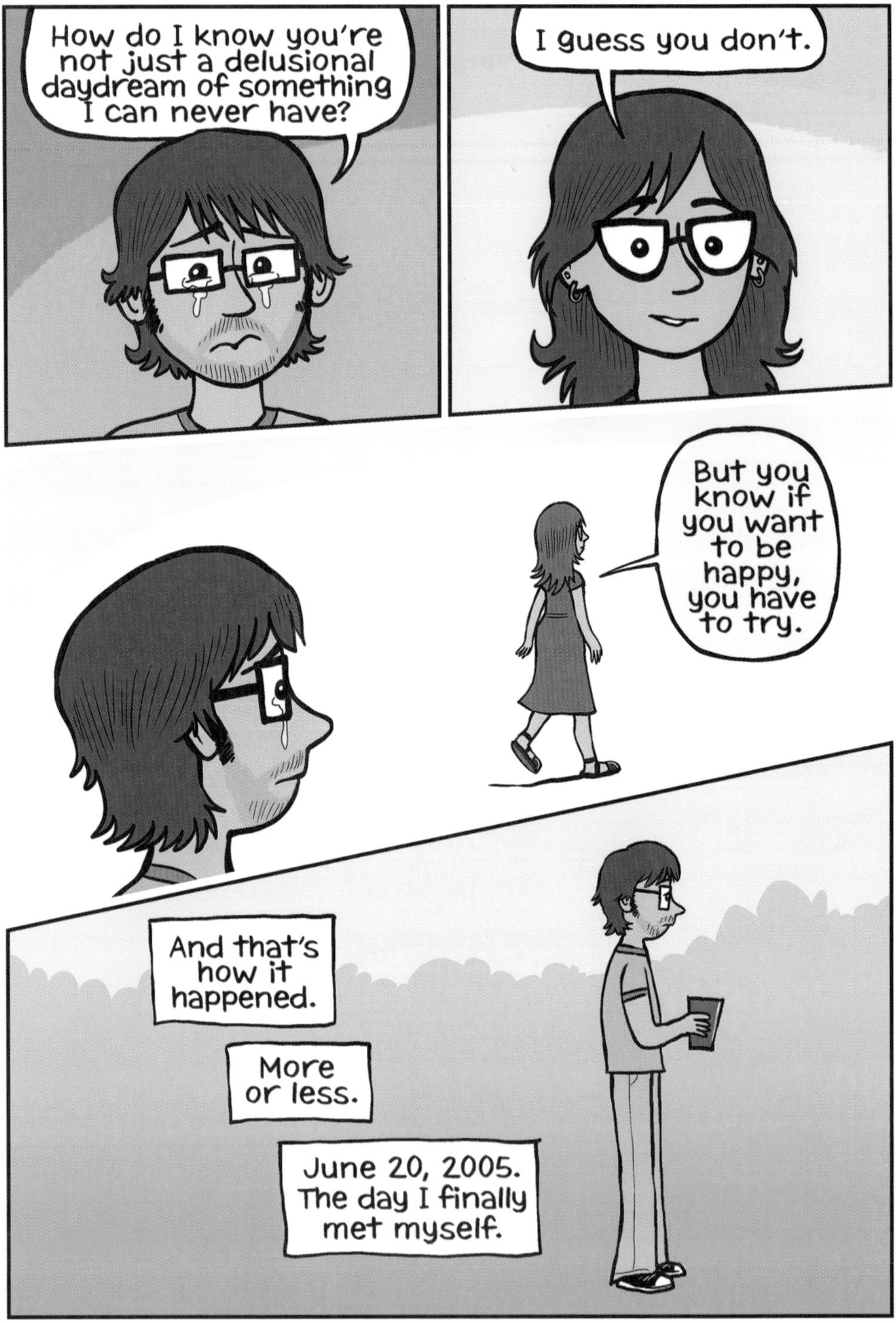
How do I know you're not just a delusional daydream of something I can never have?
I guess you don't.
But you know if you want to be happy, you have to try.
And that's how it happened.
More or less.
June 20, 2005. The day I finally met myself.

CYRUS
(HE/HIM)

Cyrus is a Hispanic-Asian transmasc individual and self-taught artist located in the southwestern United States. He enjoys expressing himself through drawings for fun and hopes to also inspire others. Aside from art, Cyrus loves listening to music, taking care of his plants, playing video games, and snowboarding in the wintertime.

Find him on Instagram and Twitter:
@VukoBird

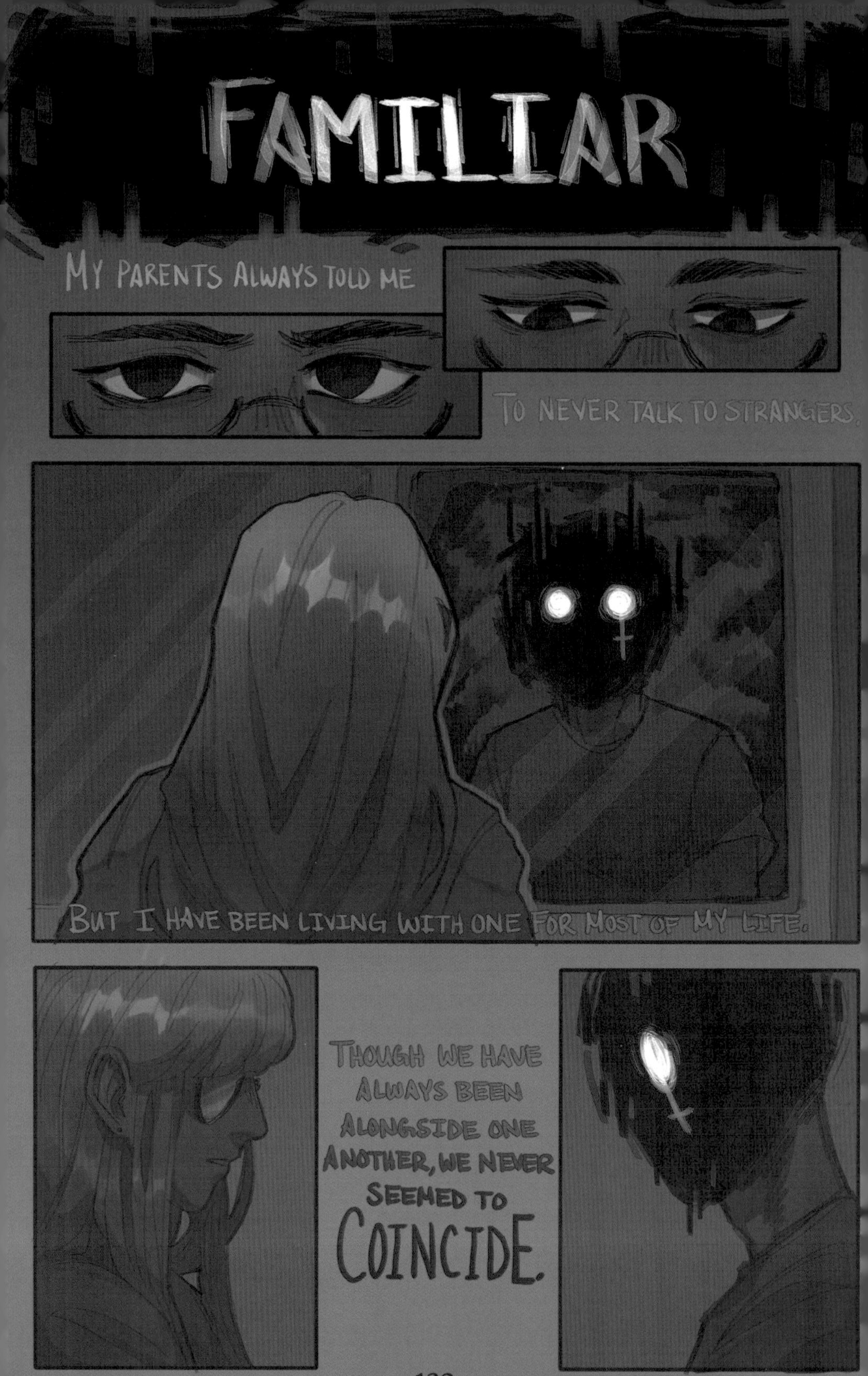
FAMILIAR
MY PARENTS ALWAYS TOLD ME
TO NEVER TALK TO STRANGERS.
BUT I HAVE BEEN LIVING WITH ONE FOR MOST OF MY LIFE.
THOUGH WE HAVE ALWAYS BEEN ALONGSIDE ONE ANOTHER, WE NEVER SEEMED TO COINCIDE.

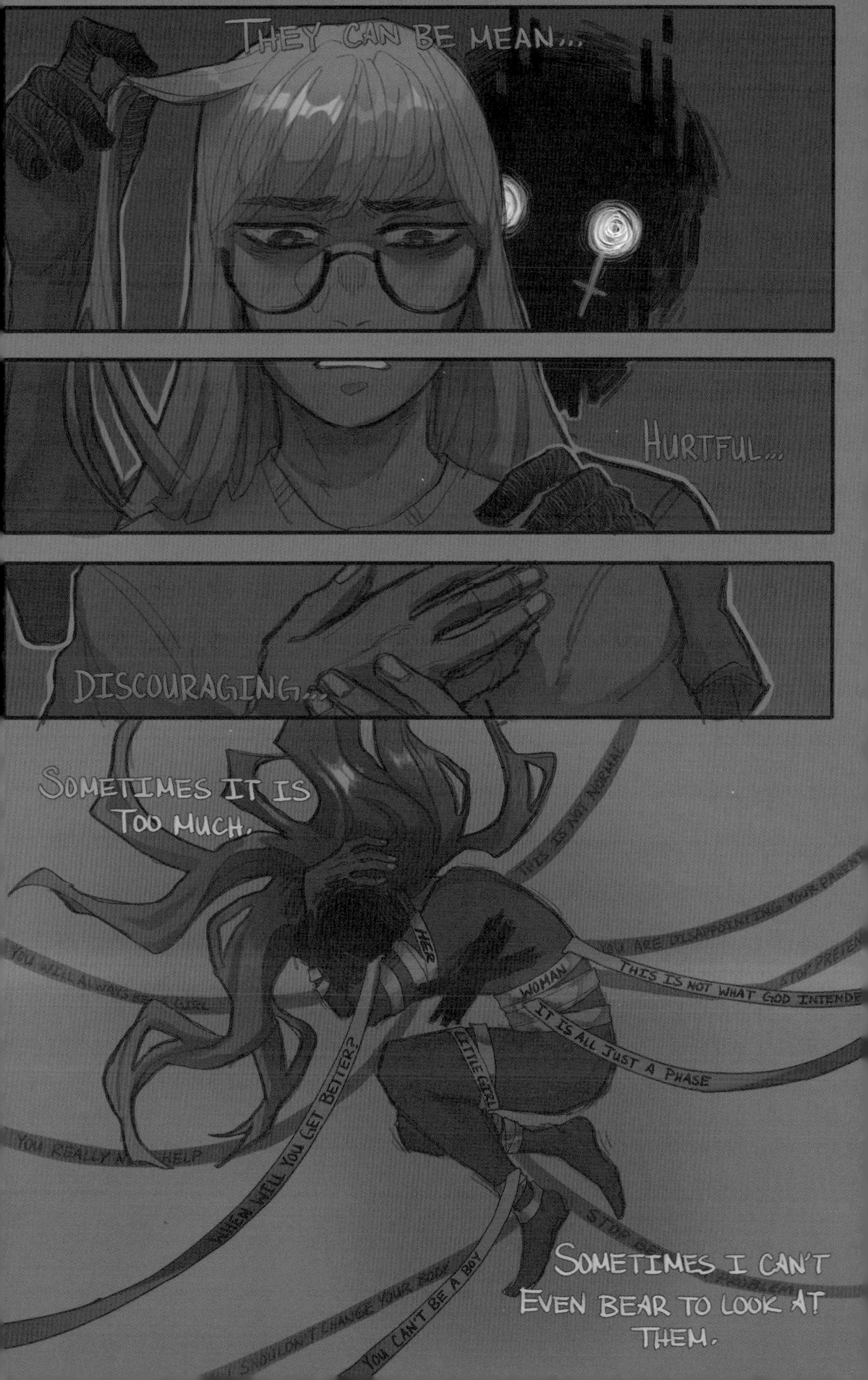
THEY CAN BE MEAN...
HURTFUL...
DISCOURAGING...
SOMETIMES IT IS TOO MUCH.
THIS IS NOT NORMAL
HER
WOMAN
THIS IS NOT WHAT GOD INTENDE
IT IS ALL JUST A PHASE
LITTLE GIRL
WHEN WILL YOU GET BETTER?
YOU CAN'T BE A BOY
SOMETIMES I CAN'T EVEN BEAR TO LOOK AT THEM.

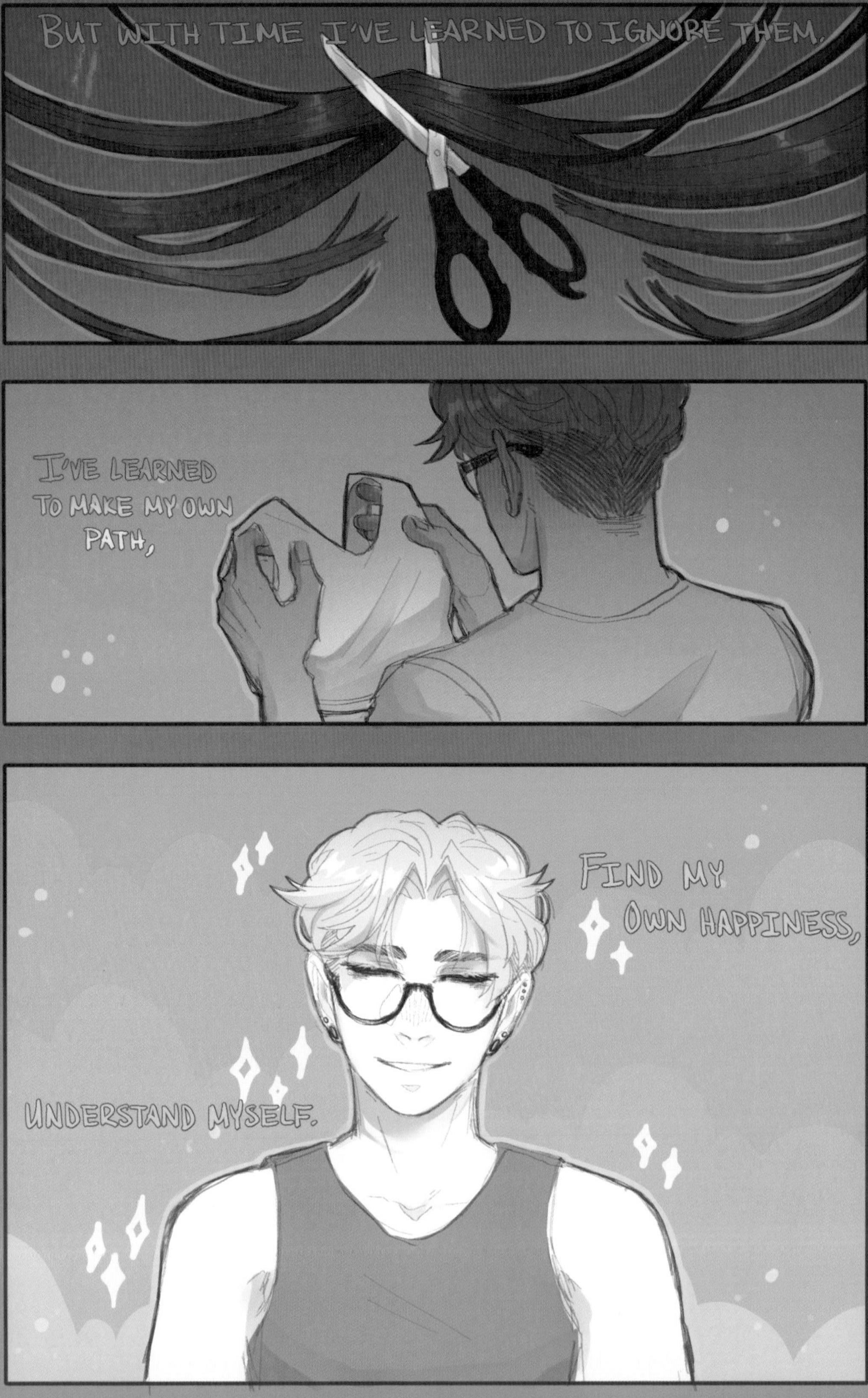
But with time I've learned to ignore them.
I've learned to make my own path,
Find my own happiness,
Understand myself.

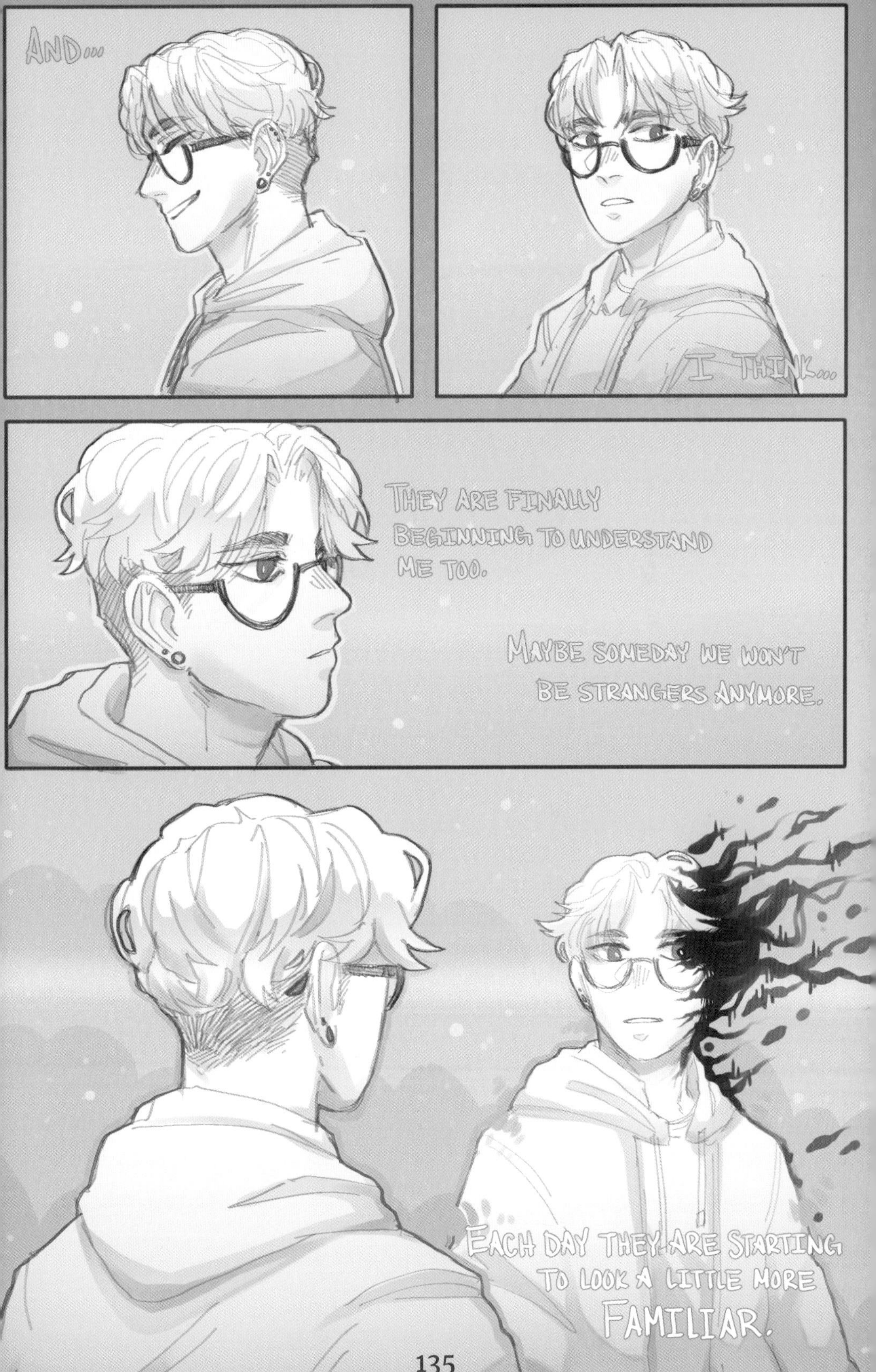
And...
I think...
They are finally beginning to understand me too.
Maybe someday we won't be strangers anymore.
Each day they are starting to look a little more Familiar.

NASR BIN SAFWAN
(HE/THEY)

I am an Emirati-Honduran concept artist and storyteller from the UAE, based in Chicago. I consider myself a jack of some trades, as I like to dabble in different visual media. I find joy in expressing myself through the melding and meshing of what I can do to make something new. Stories hold incredible importance, and I believe they create something new out of us as well. Besides freelancing for games and ruminating, I spend my time engaging in my various interests, which include astronomy, marine biology, horror, sci-fi, and fashion.

They can be found online at:
temporaryvoid.weebly.com

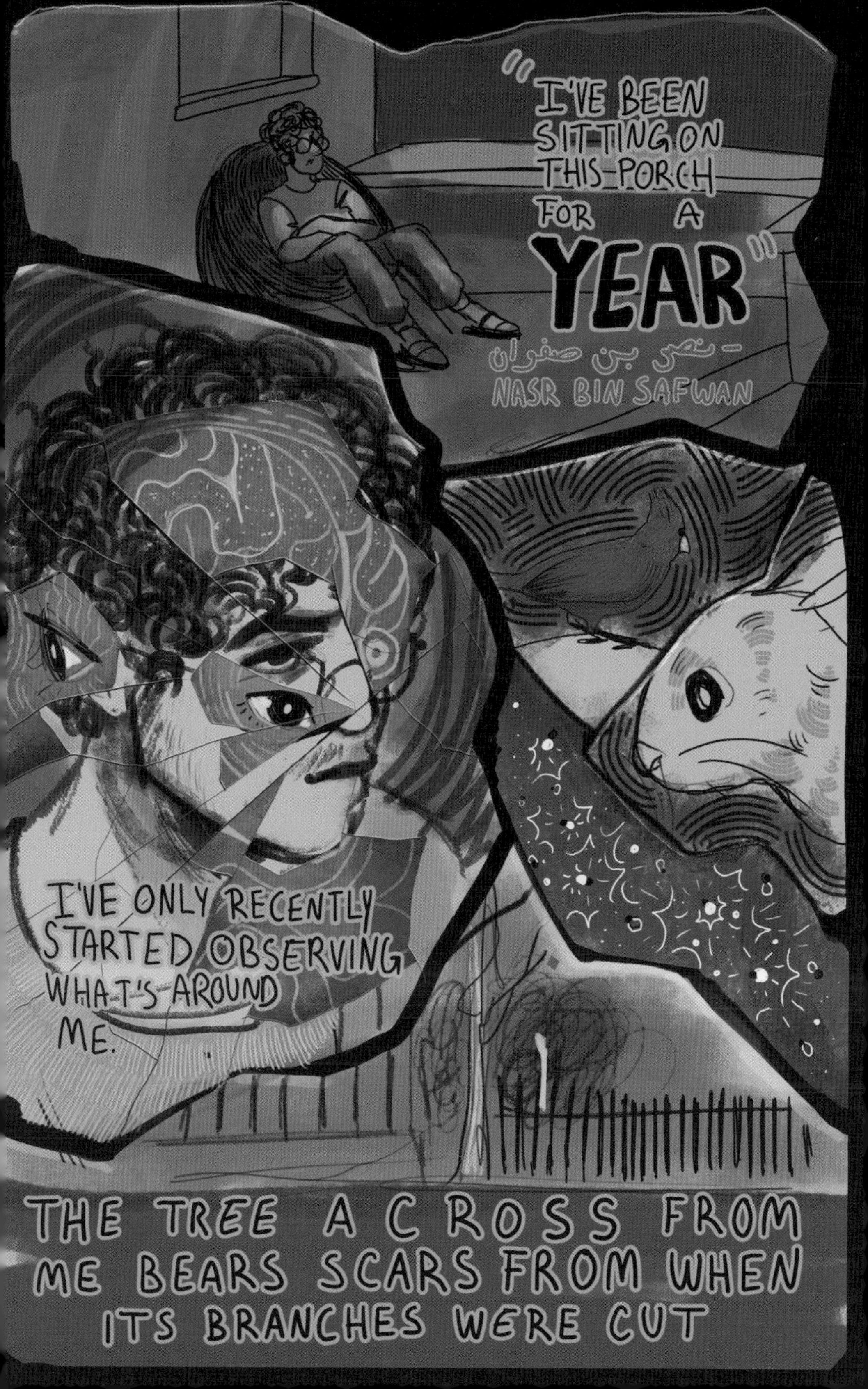
"I'VE BEEN SITTING ON THIS PORCH FOR A YEAR"
- نصر بن صفوان
NASR BIN SAFWAN
I'VE ONLY RECENTLY STARTED OBSERVING WHAT'S AROUND ME.
THE TREE ACROSS FROM ME BEARS SCARS FROM WHEN ITS BRANCHES WERE CUT

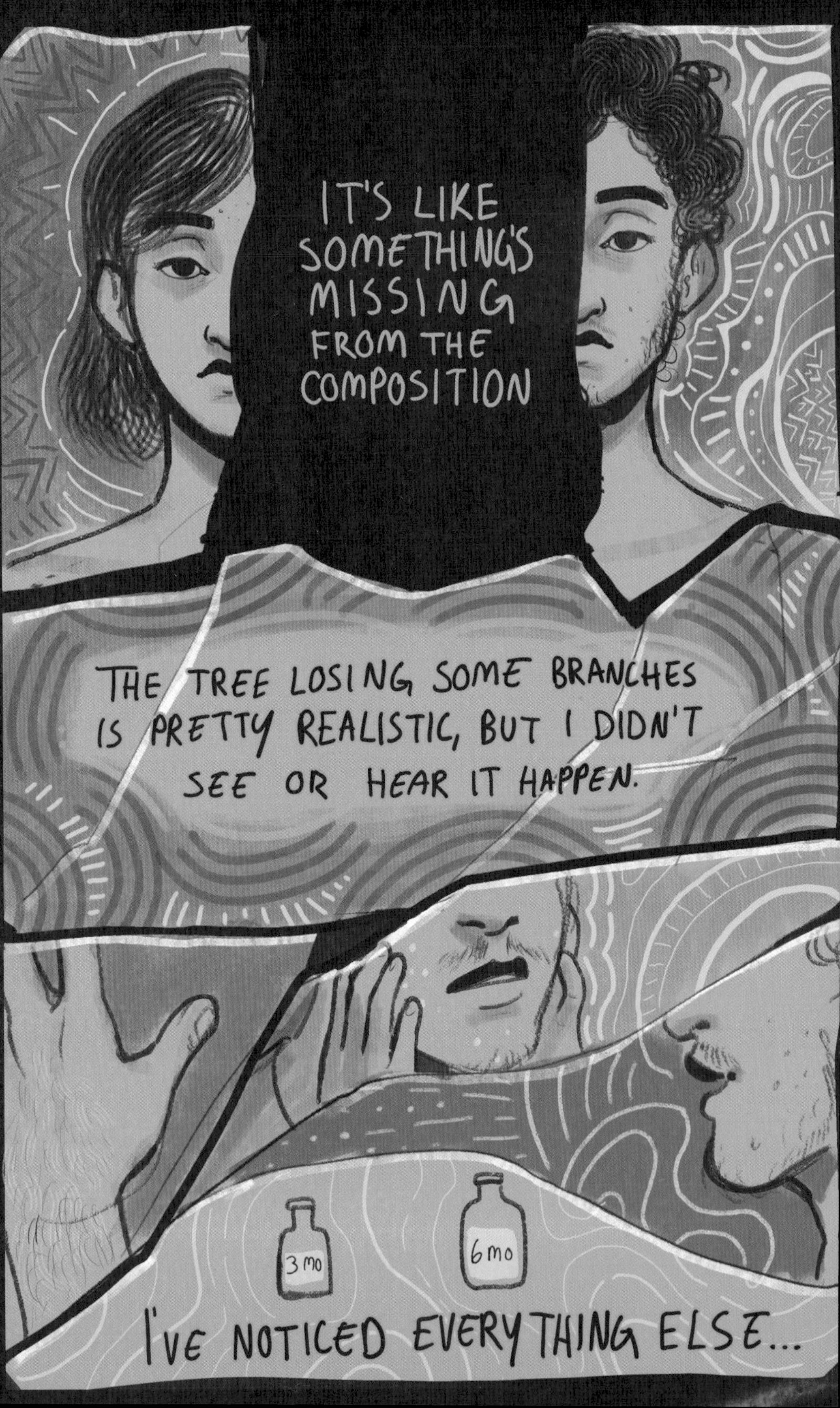
IT'S LIKE SOMETHING'S MISSING FROM THE COMPOSITION
THE TREE LOSING SOME BRANCHES IS PRETTY REALISTIC, BUT I DIDN'T SEE OR HEAR IT HAPPEN.
3mo
6mo
I'VE NOTICED EVERYTHING ELSE...

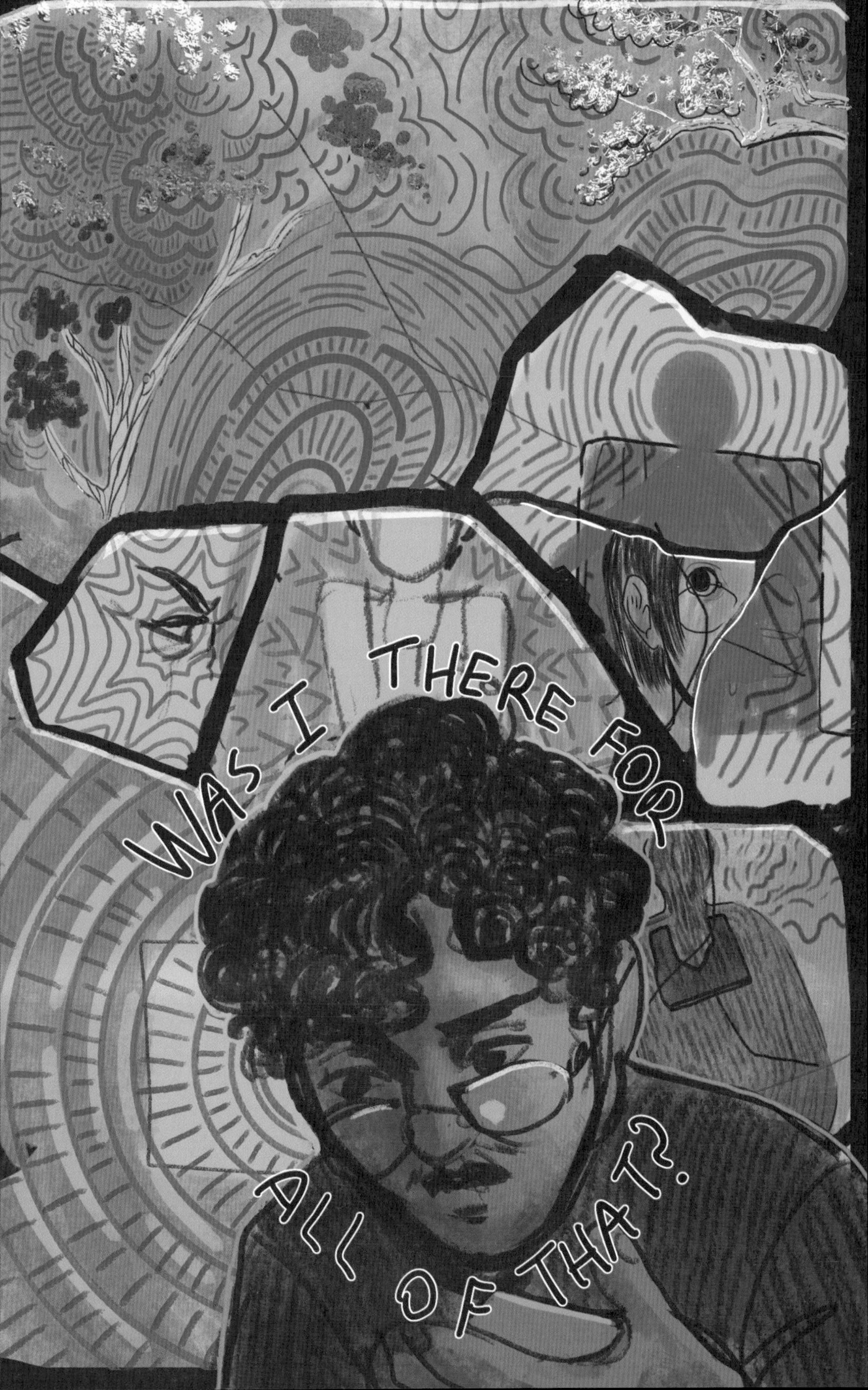
WAS I THERE FOR ALL OF THAT?.

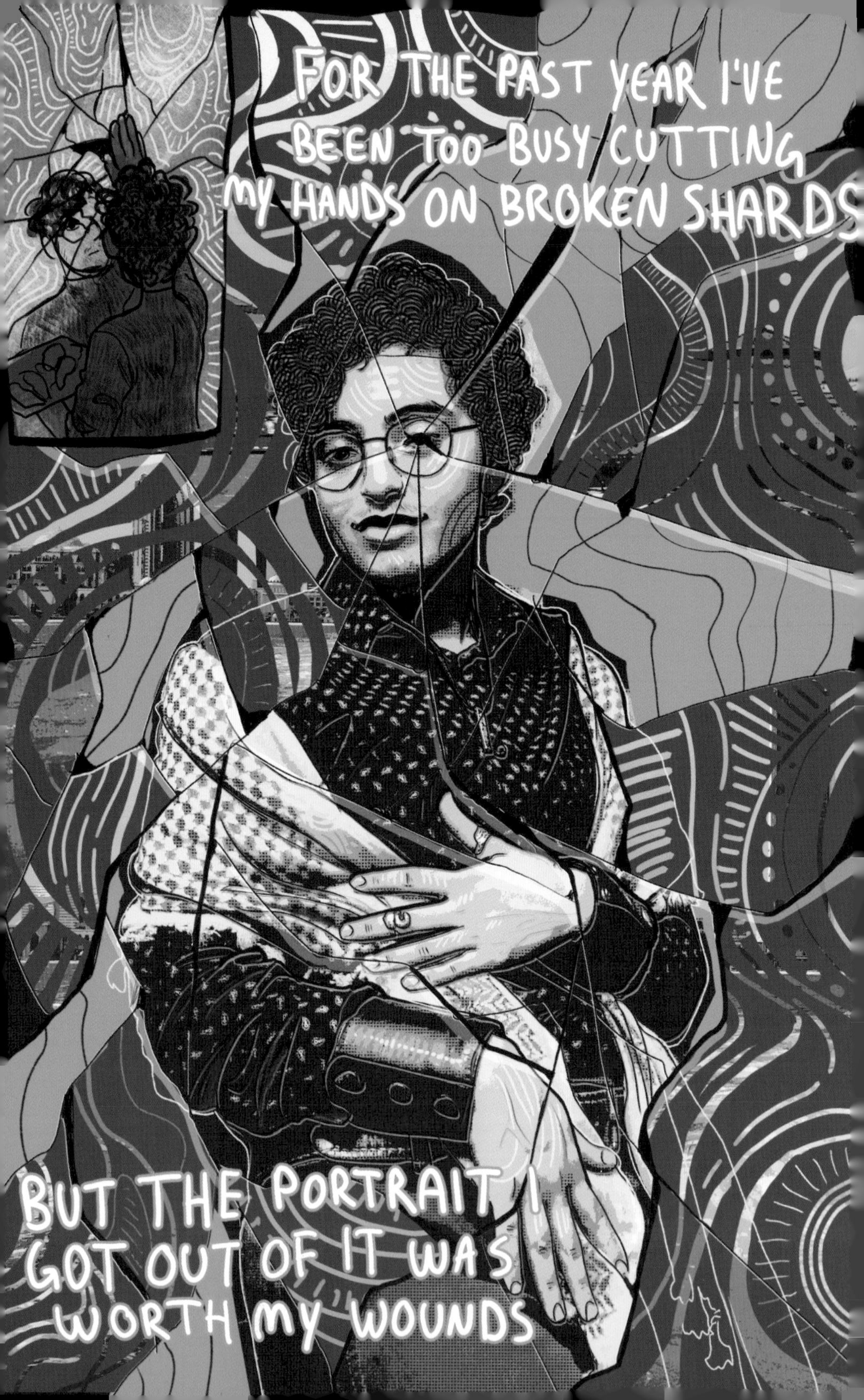
FOR THE PAST YEAR I'VE
BEEN TOO BUSY CUTTING
MY HANDS ON BROKEN SHARDS
BUT THE PORTRAIT I
GOT OUT OF IT WAS
WORTH MY WOUNDS

MEL VALENTINE VARGAS
(THEY/THEM)

Mel is a queer Cuban-American graphic novelist located in Chicago. They hope to draw the kind of illustrations that their younger self, and others like them, could have seen to feel less alone. Mel loves singing in Spanish, playing farming video games, and eating gyoza with friends.

You can find them on Twitter:
@MelValentineV

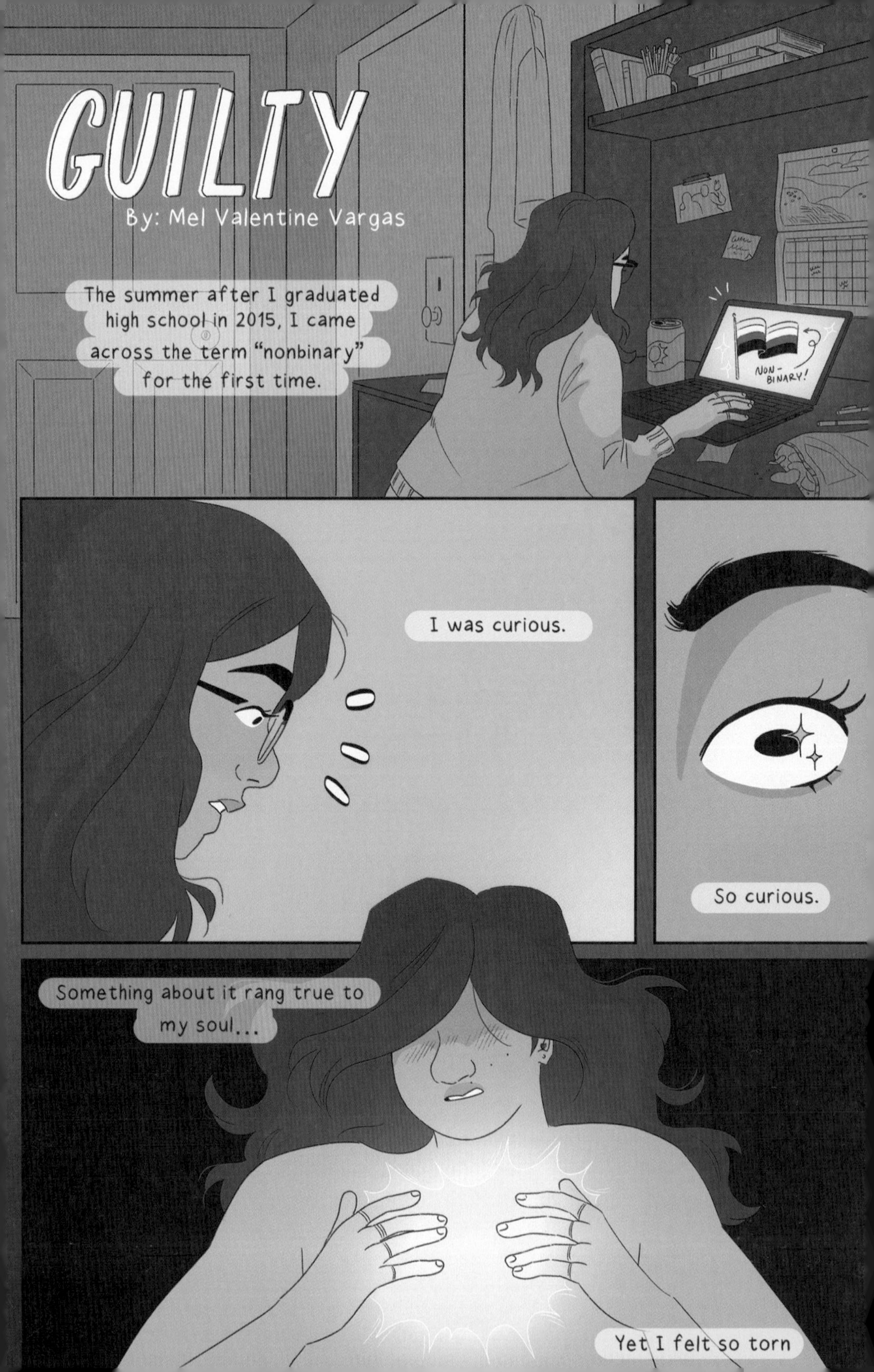
GUILTY
By: Mel Valentine Vargas
The summer after I graduated high school in 2015, I came across the term "nonbinary" for the first time.
NON-BINARY!
I was curious.
So curious.
Something about it rang true to my soul...
Yet I felt so torn

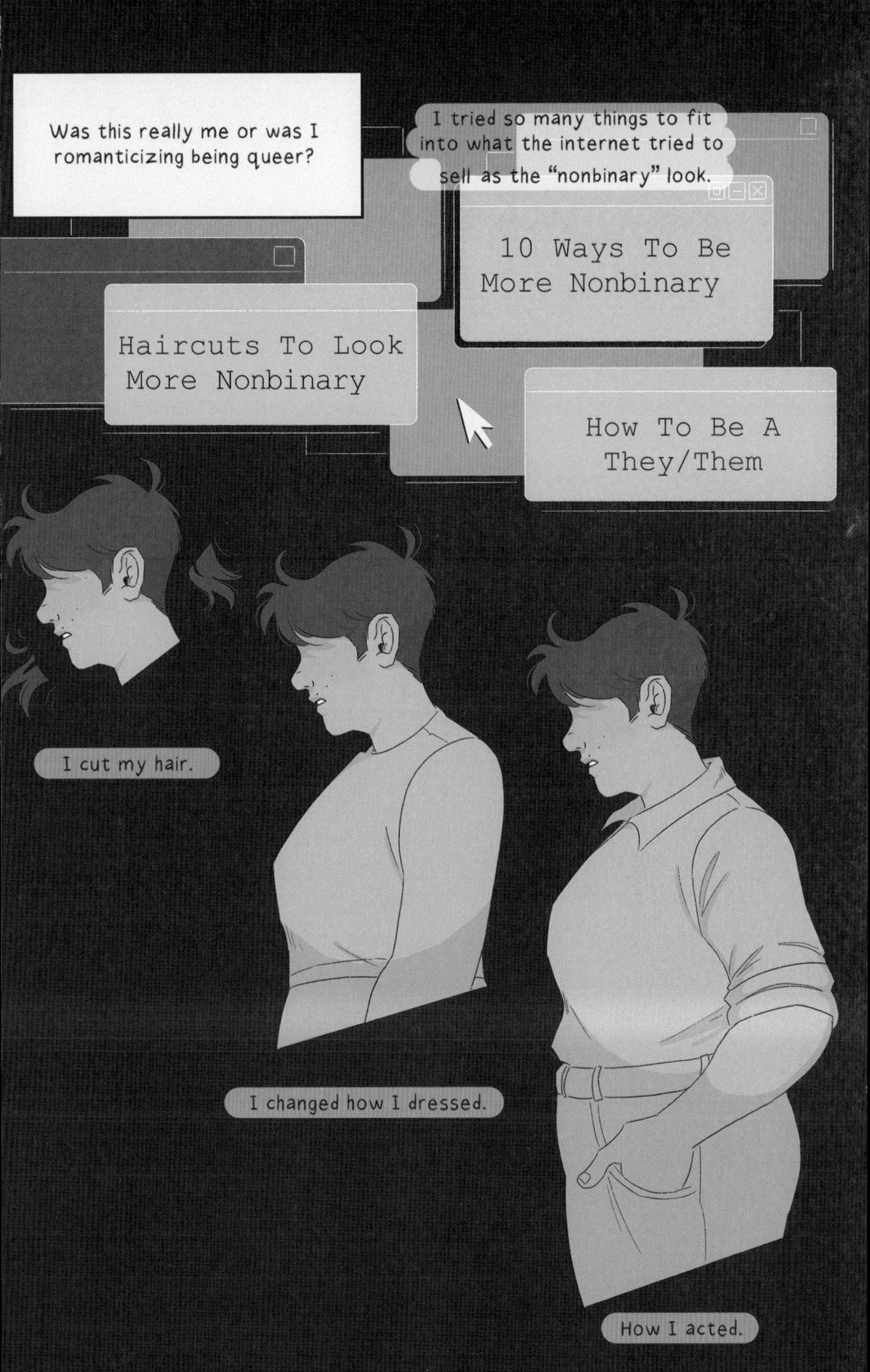
Was this really me or was I romanticizing being queer?
I tried so many things to fit into what the internet tried to sell as the "nonbinary" look.
10 Ways To Be More Nonbinary
Haircuts To Look More Nonbinary
How To Be A They/Them
I cut my hair.
I changed how I dressed.
How I acted.

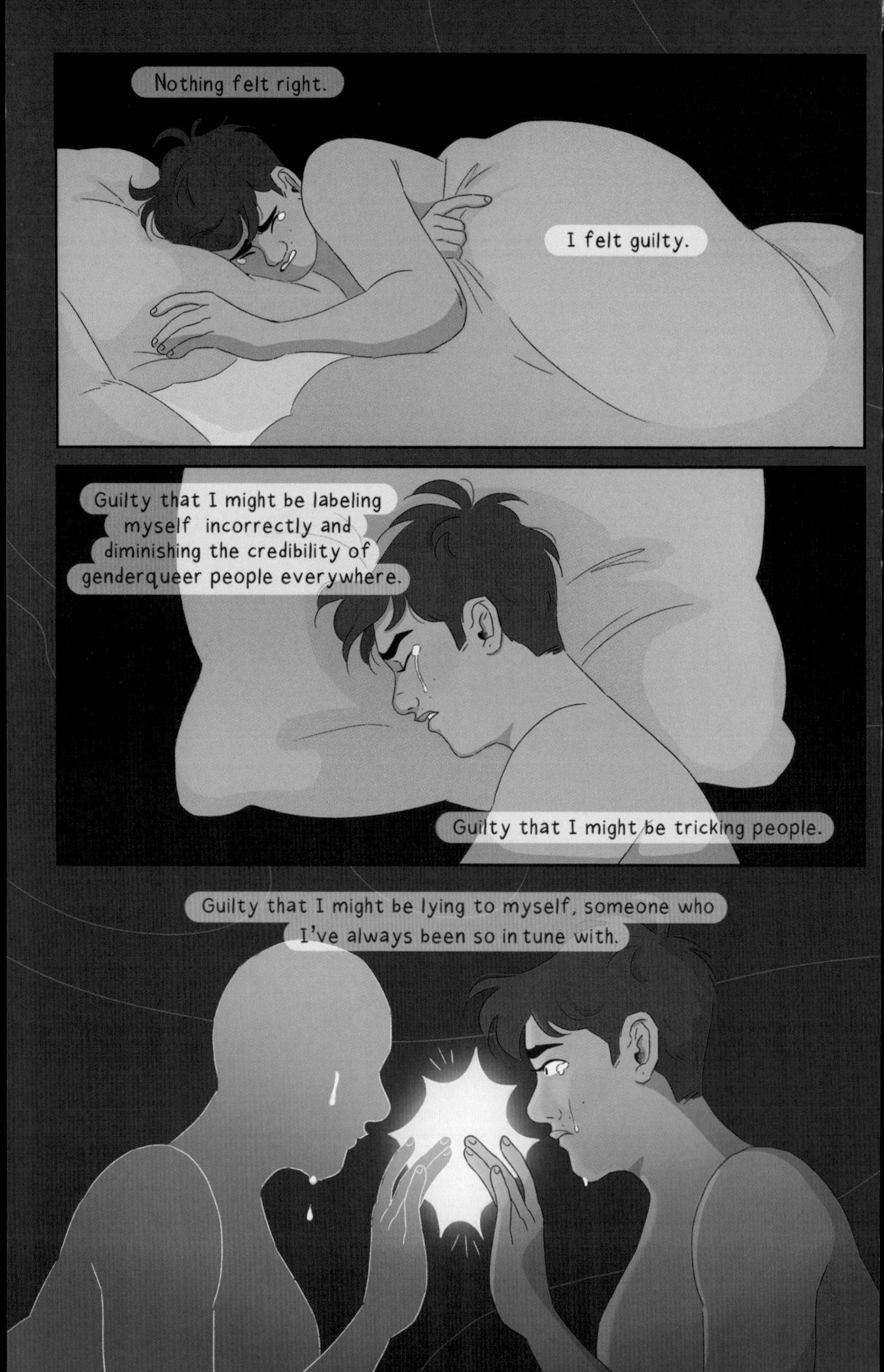
Nothing felt right.
I felt guilty.
Guilty that I might be labeling myself incorrectly and diminishing the credibility of genderqueer people everywhere.
Guilty that I might be tricking people.
Guilty that I might be lying to myself, someone who I've always been so in tune with.

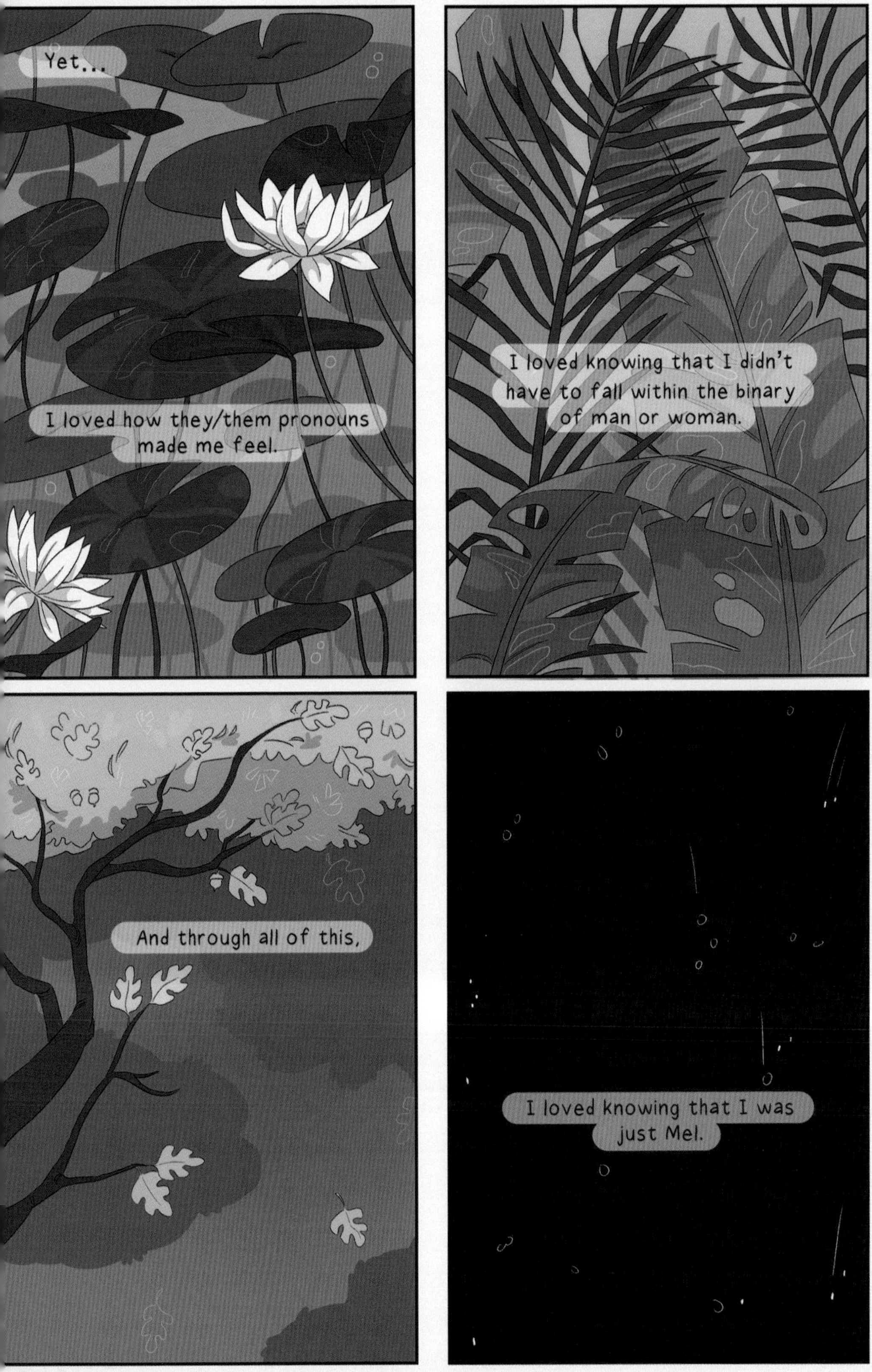
Yet...
I loved how they/them pronouns made me feel.
I loved knowing that I didn't have to fall within the binary of man or woman.
And through all of this,
I loved knowing that I was just Mel.

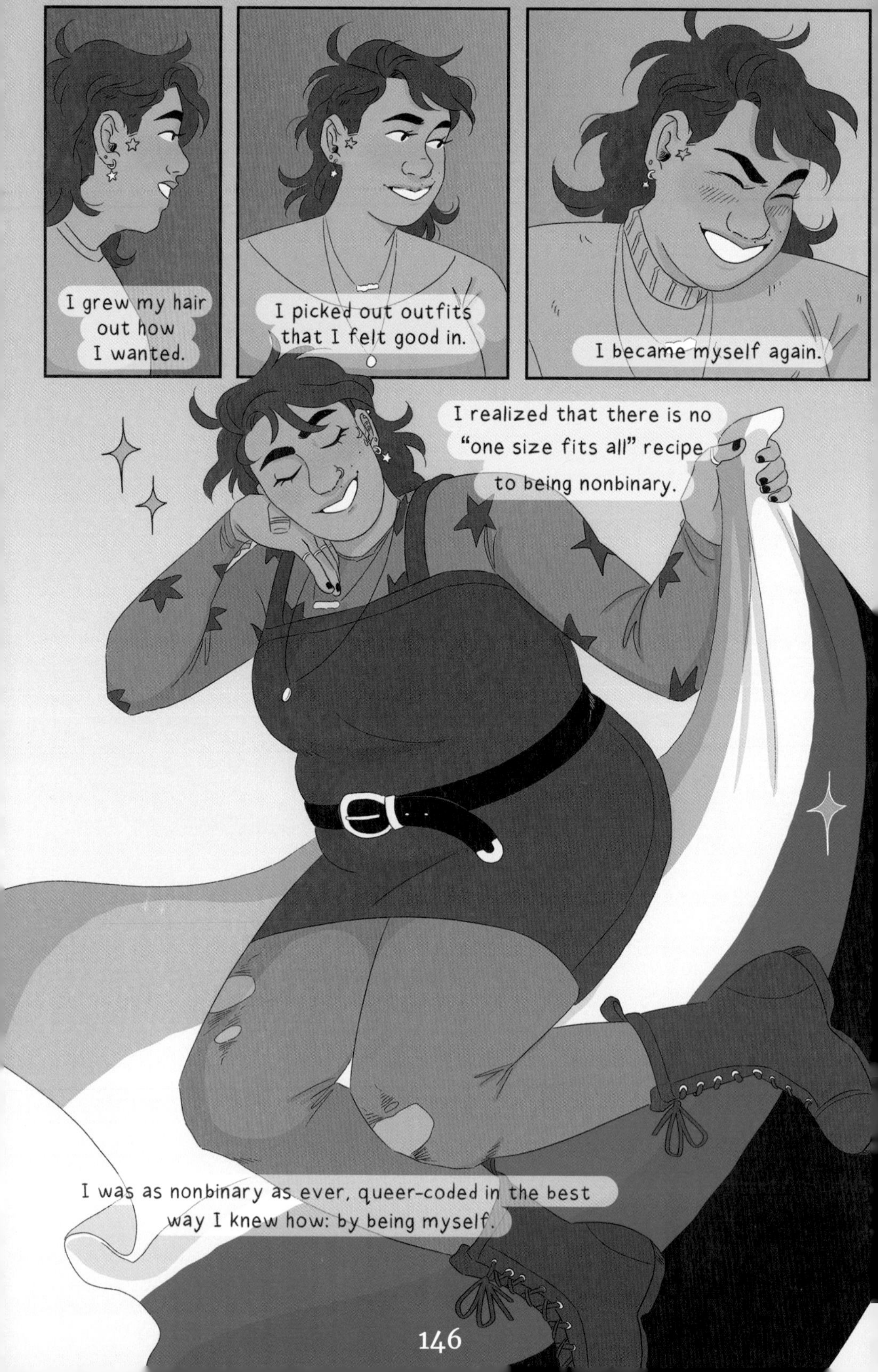
I grew my hair out how I wanted.
I picked out outfits that I felt good in.
I became myself again.
I realized that there is no "one size fits all" recipe to being nonbinary.
I was as nonbinary as ever, queer-coded in the best way I knew how: by being myself.

AL ACEVEDO
(THEY/THEM)

Al is a nonbinary, asexual Chicanx artist born and raised in Southern California. They are a product designer currently living in Los Angeles with their partner and cats, and they make a comic called *HUSK* in their free time. When they aren't glued to their computer, they enjoy playing video games and taking the cats for walks.

You can find them on Twitter:
@RaisingIcarus

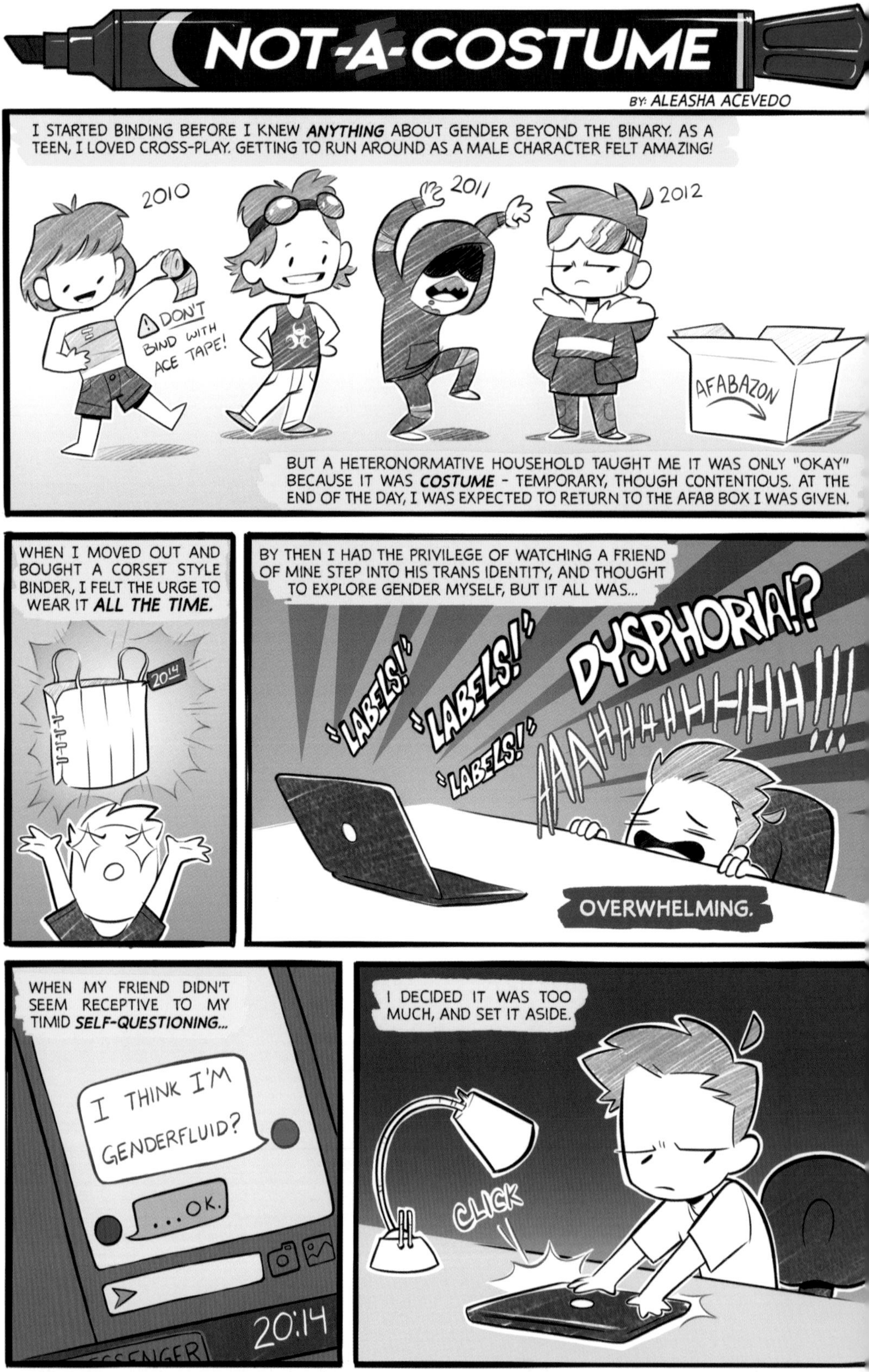
NOT-A-COSTUME
BY: ALEASHA ACEVEDO
I STARTED BINDING BEFORE I KNEW ANYTHING ABOUT GENDER BEYOND THE BINARY. AS A TEEN, I LOVED CROSS-PLAY. GETTING TO RUN AROUND AS A MALE CHARACTER FELT AMAZING!
2010
DON'T BIND WITH ACE TAPE!
2011
2012
AFABAZON
BUT A HETERONORMATIVE HOUSEHOLD TAUGHT ME IT WAS ONLY "OKAY" BECAUSE IT WAS COSTUME - TEMPORARY, THOUGH CONTENTIOUS. AT THE END OF THE DAY, I WAS EXPECTED TO RETURN TO THE AFAB BOX I WAS GIVEN.
WHEN I MOVED OUT AND BOUGHT A CORSET STYLE BINDER, I FELT THE URGE TO WEAR IT ALL THE TIME.
2014
BY THEN I HAD THE PRIVILEGE OF WATCHING A FRIEND OF MINE STEP INTO HIS TRANS IDENTITY, AND THOUGHT TO EXPLORE GENDER MYSELF, BUT IT ALL WAS...
LABELS!
LABELS!
LABELS!
DYSPHORIA!?
AAAHHHHHHHHHH!!!
OVERWHELMING.
WHEN MY FRIEND DIDN'T SEEM RECEPTIVE TO MY TIMID SELF-QUESTIONING...
I THINK I'M GENDERFLUID?
...OK.
20:14
I DECIDED IT WAS TOO MUCH, AND SET IT ASIDE.
CLICK

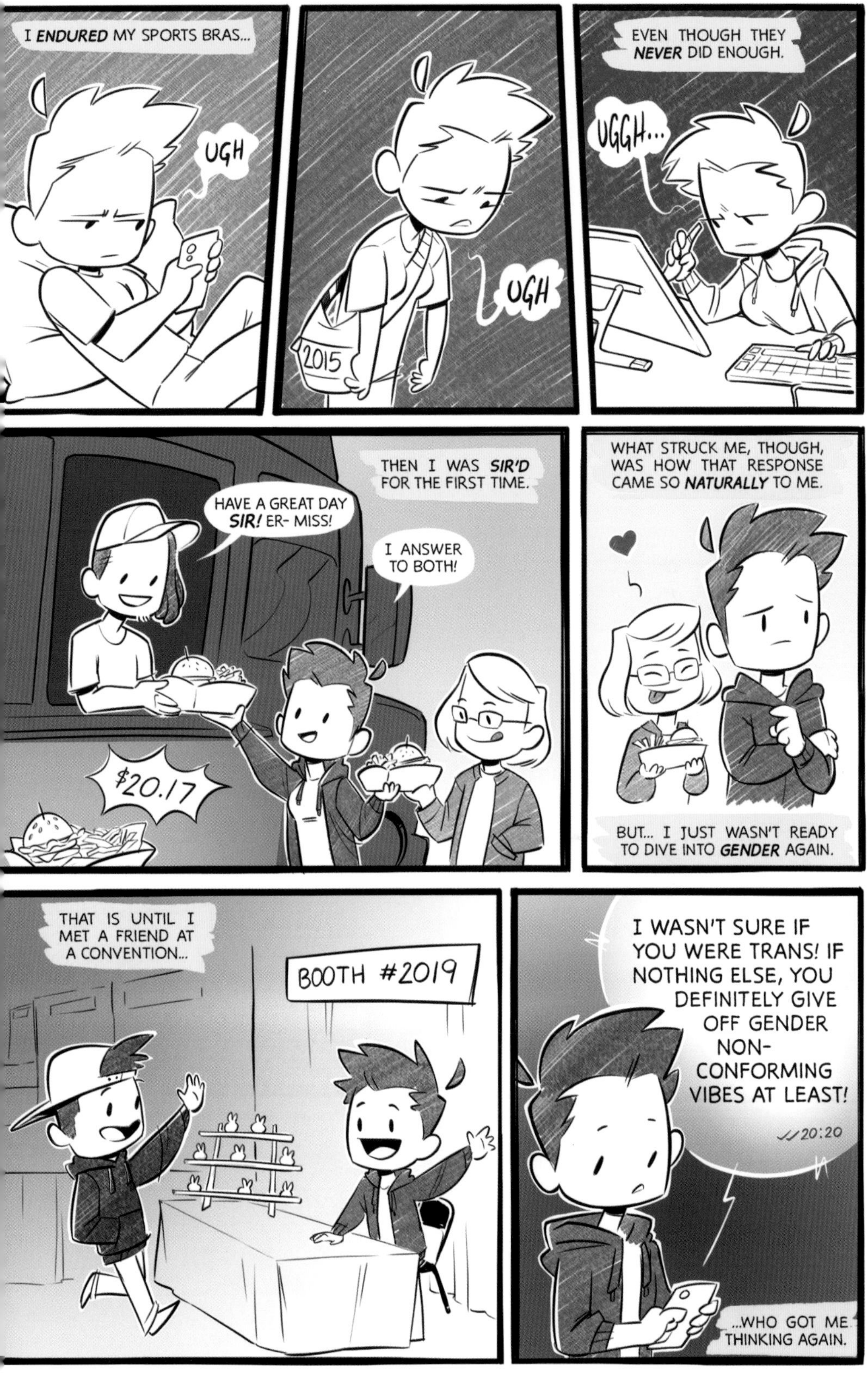
I *ENDURED* MY SPORTS BRAS...
UGH
2015
UGH
EVEN THOUGH THEY *NEVER* DID ENOUGH.
UGGH...
THEN I WAS *SIR'D* FOR THE FIRST TIME.
HAVE A GREAT DAY *SIR!* ER- MISS!
I ANSWER TO BOTH!
$20.17
WHAT STRUCK ME, THOUGH, WAS HOW THAT RESPONSE CAME SO *NATURALLY* TO ME.
BUT... I JUST WASN'T READY TO DIVE INTO *GENDER* AGAIN.
THAT IS UNTIL I MET A FRIEND AT A CONVENTION...
BOOTH #2019
I WASN'T SURE IF YOU WERE TRANS! IF NOTHING ELSE, YOU DEFINITELY GIVE OFF GENDER NON-CONFORMING VIBES AT LEAST!
20:20
...WHO GOT ME THINKING AGAIN.

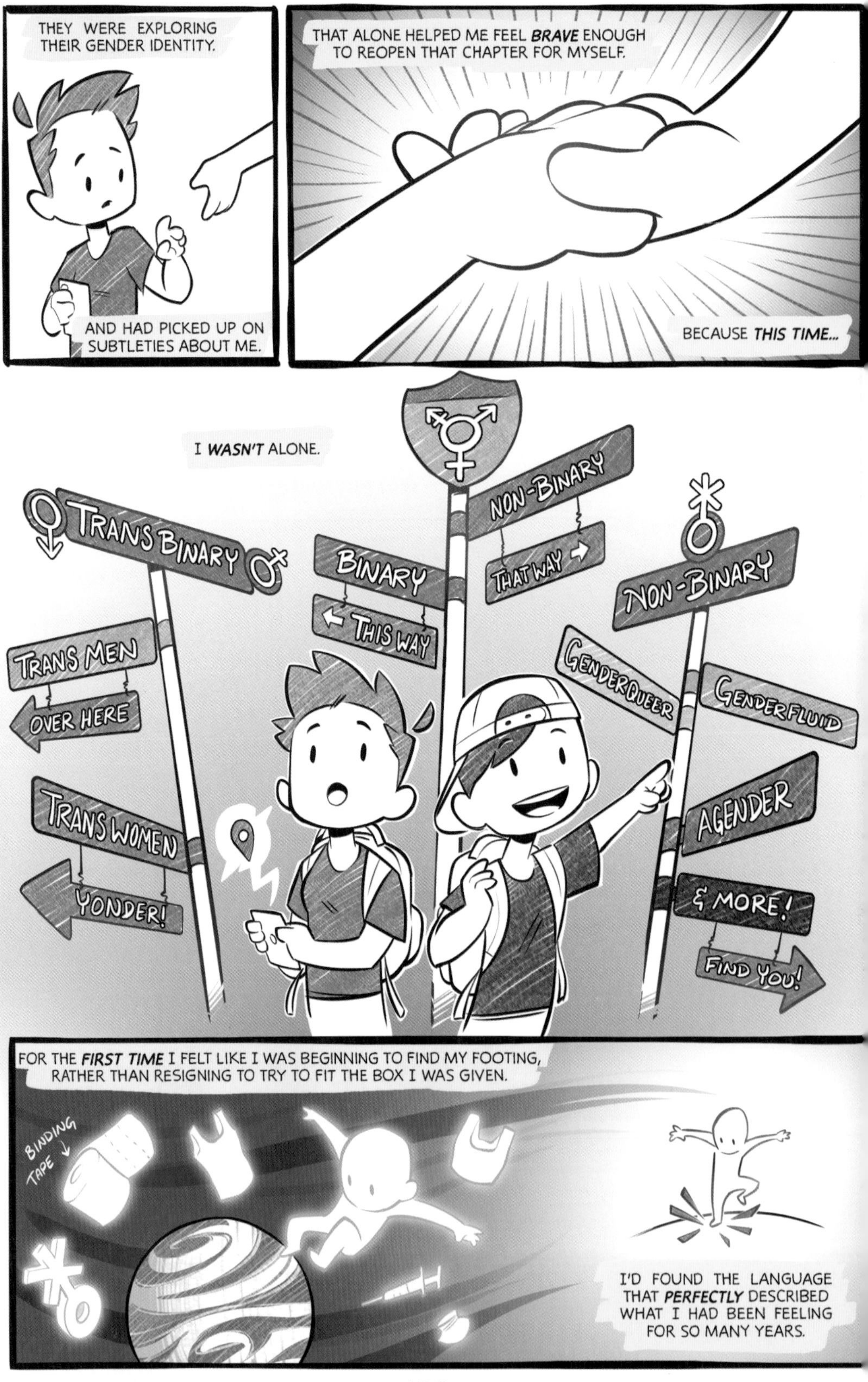
THEY WERE EXPLORING THEIR GENDER IDENTITY.
AND HAD PICKED UP ON SUBTLETIES ABOUT ME.
THAT ALONE HELPED ME FEEL BRAVE ENOUGH TO REOPEN THAT CHAPTER FOR MYSELF.
BECAUSE THIS TIME...
I WASN'T ALONE.
TRANS BINARY
TRANS MEN
OVER HERE
TRANS WOMEN
YONDER!
BINARY
THIS WAY
NON-BINARY
THAT WAY
NON-BINARY
GENDERQUEER
GENDERFLUID
AGENDER
& MORE!
FIND YOU!
FOR THE FIRST TIME I FELT LIKE I WAS BEGINNING TO FIND MY FOOTING, RATHER THAN RESIGNING TO TRY TO FIT THE BOX I WAS GIVEN.
BINDING TAPE
I'D FOUND THE LANGUAGE THAT PERFECTLY DESCRIBED WHAT I HAD BEEN FEELING FOR SO MANY YEARS.

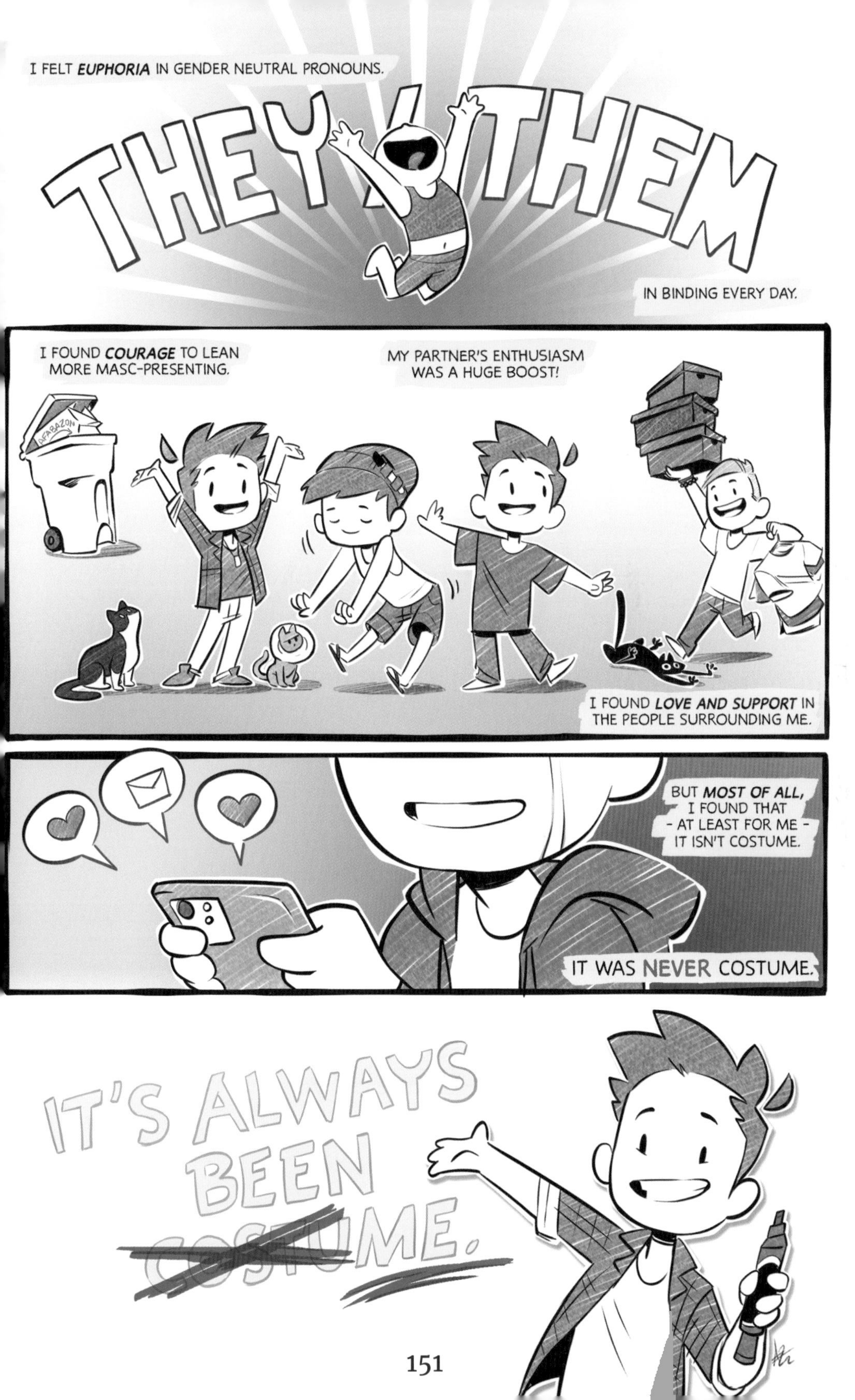

I FELT EUPHORIA IN GENDER NEUTRAL PRONOUNS.
THEY / THEM
IN BINDING EVERY DAY.
I FOUND COURAGE TO LEAN MORE MASC-PRESENTING.
AFABAZON
MY PARTNER'S ENTHUSIASM WAS A HUGE BOOST!
I FOUND LOVE AND SUPPORT IN THE PEOPLE SURROUNDING ME.
BUT MOST OF ALL, I FOUND THAT - AT LEAST FOR ME - IT ISN'T COSTUME.
IT WAS NEVER COSTUME.
IT'S ALWAYS BEEN COSTUME.

SAGE COFFEY
(THEY/THEM)

Sage Coffey is a trans nonbinary artist living in Chicago. They've done comic work with *The New Yorker*, *The Washington Post*, and *The Nib*. In addition, they are known for editing the comic collection *Sweaty Palms: The Anthology About Anxiety*. They also recently created the illustrations for the GLAAD award-nominated video game BUGSNAX, and one of *Vulture*'s funniest books of 2021, *I AM NOT A WOLF*. In their free time, they play (probably too many) indie games, drink orange blossom tea, and cuddle with their cat, Zipper.

You can find them online at:
sagecoffey.com

TEN MORE SECONDS

A STORY BY
SAGE COFFEY

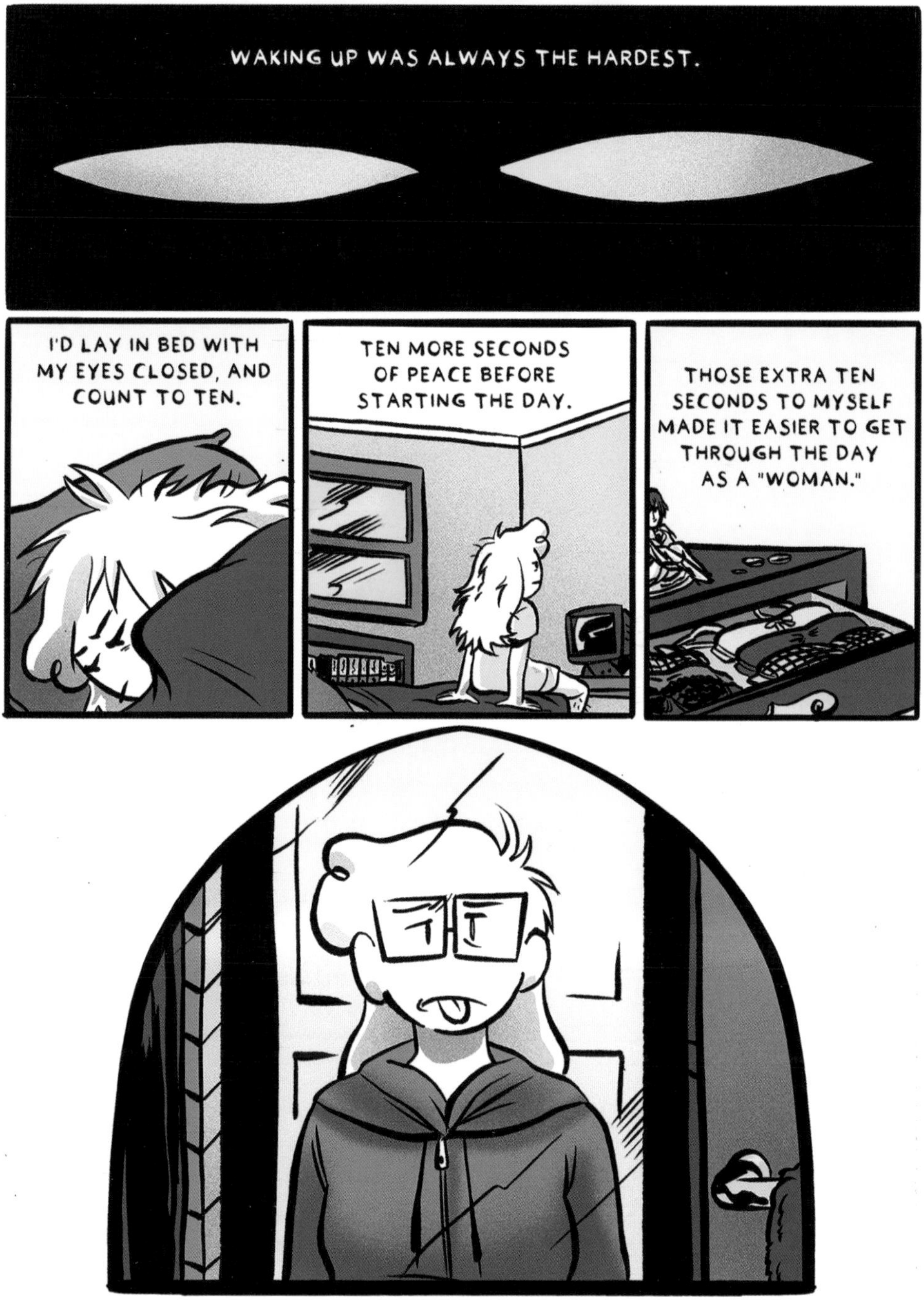
WAKING UP WAS ALWAYS THE HARDEST.
I'D LAY IN BED WITH MY EYES CLOSED, AND COUNT TO TEN.
TEN MORE SECONDS OF PEACE BEFORE STARTING THE DAY.
THOSE EXTRA TEN SECONDS TO MYSELF MADE IT EASIER TO GET THROUGH THE DAY AS A "WOMAN."

I WAS TOLD I WAS A WOMAN. BUT I CERTAINLY DIDN'T FEEL LIKE ONE.

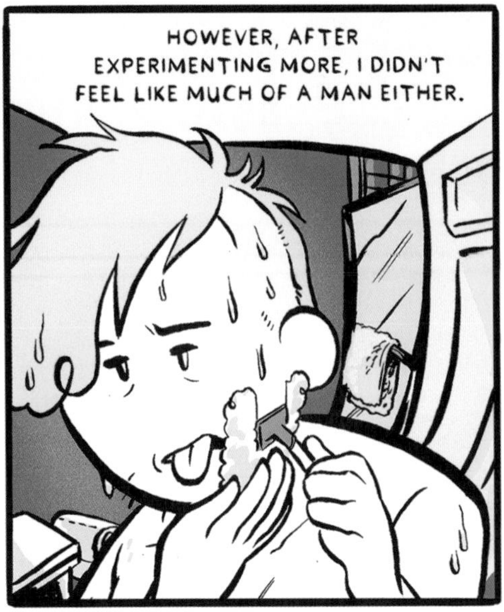
HOWEVER, AFTER EXPERIMENTING MORE, I DIDN'T FEEL LIKE MUCH OF A MAN EITHER.

IT WAS CLEAR THAT PRESENTING WITHOUT A CHEST MADE ME MUCH, MUCH HAPPIER.

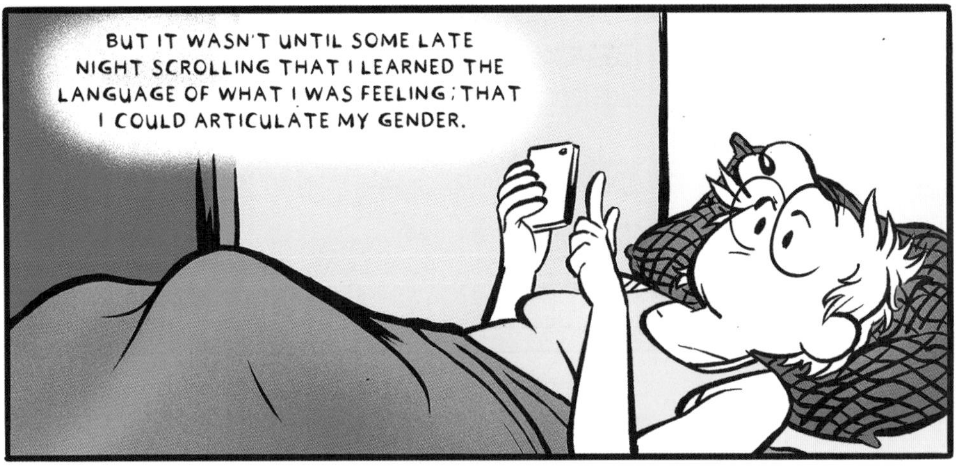
BUT IT WASN'T UNTIL SOME LATE NIGHT SCROLLING THAT I LEARNED THE LANGUAGE OF WHAT I WAS FEELING; THAT I COULD ARTICULATE MY GENDER.

I'VE BEEN A WOMAN.

I'VE BEEN A MAN.

I'VE BEEN A MILLION DIFFERENT VERSIONS OF MYSELF TO PLEASE A BINARY WE'RE FORCED TO ASCRIBE TO.

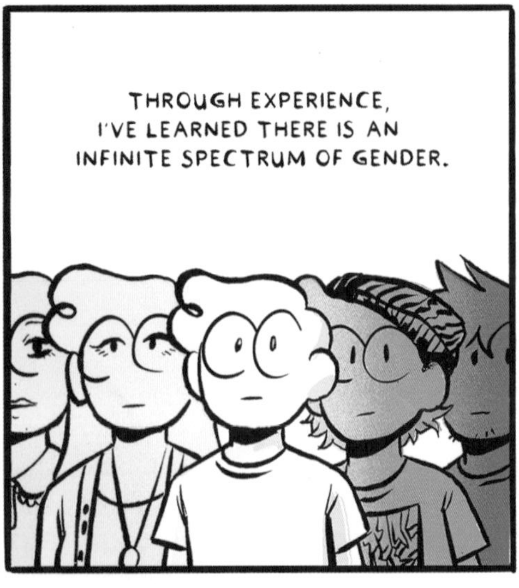
THROUGH EXPERIENCE, I'VE LEARNED THERE IS AN INFINITE SPECTRUM OF GENDER.

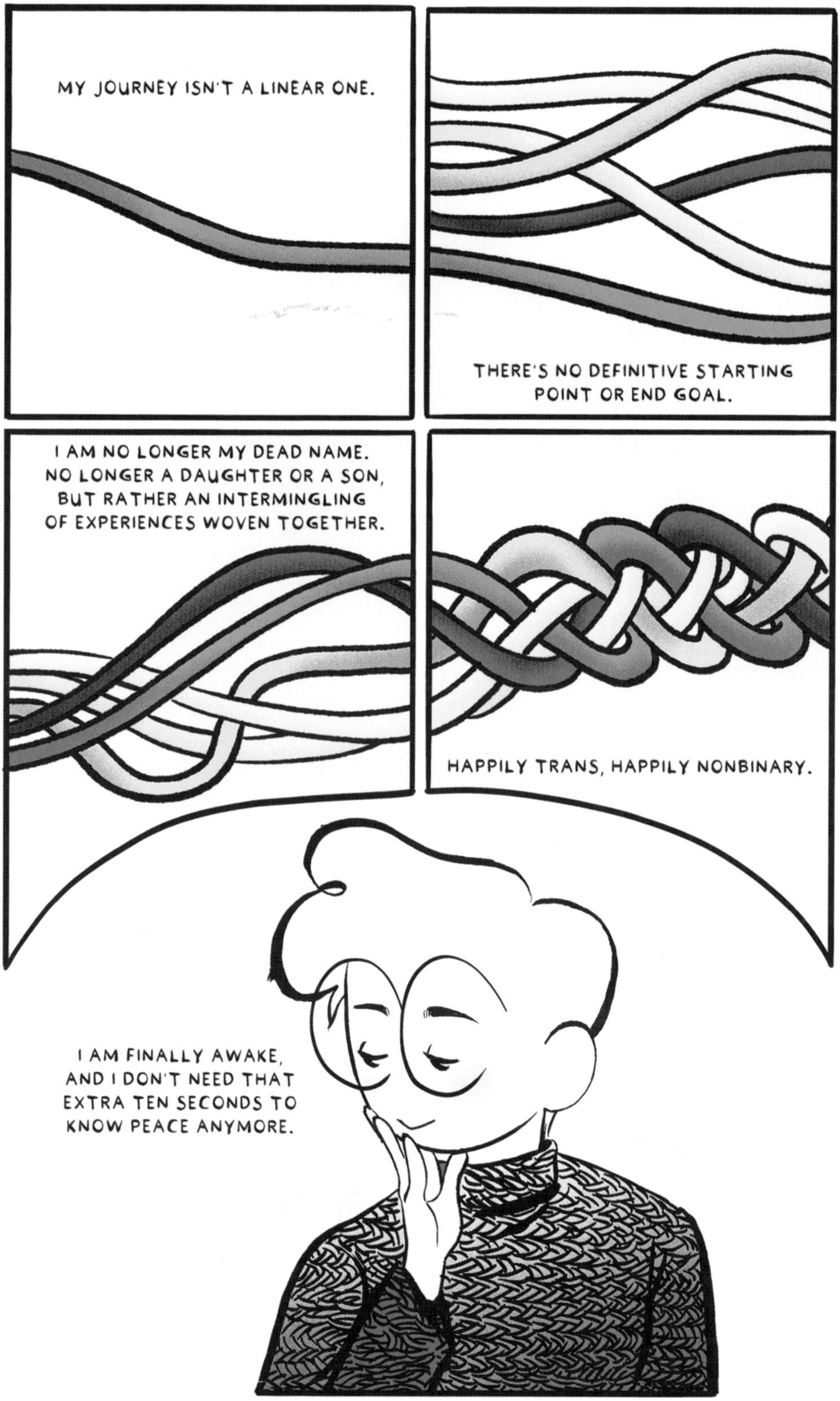
MY JOURNEY ISN'T A LINEAR ONE.
THERE'S NO DEFINITIVE STARTING POINT OR END GOAL.
I AM NO LONGER MY DEAD NAME. NO LONGER A DAUGHTER OR A SON, BUT RATHER AN INTERMINGLING OF EXPERIENCES WOVEN TOGETHER.
HAPPILY TRANS, HAPPILY NONBINARY.
I AM FINALLY AWAKE, AND I DON'T NEED THAT EXTRA TEN SECONDS TO KNOW PEACE ANYMORE.

WREN!
(SHE/HER/HE/HIM)

Wren is a cartoonist and illustrator from the great state of Maryland! Best known for her diary comics on Instagram, Wren loves to overshare (on the internet). Creating comics that marginalized people can identify with is her lifetime goal. When she's not hunched over her iPad, you can find Wren walking her dog (Jaykee!) or playing a heavily modded version of the Sims 4.

You can find Wren online at:
wren.best

GIRL!

by Wren

For a long time
I felt like
I was a . . .

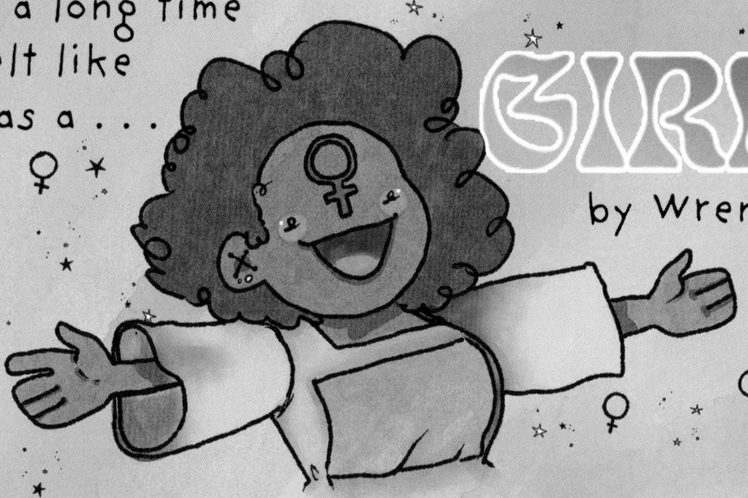

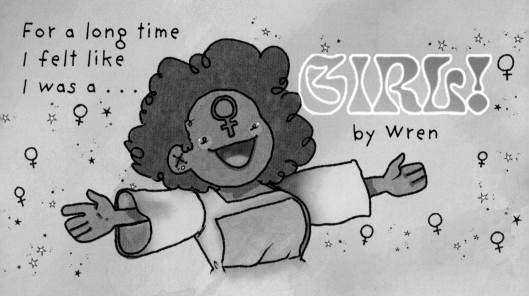

All my life I've loved "girly" things.

I collected vintage porcelain
dolls and rare Barbies

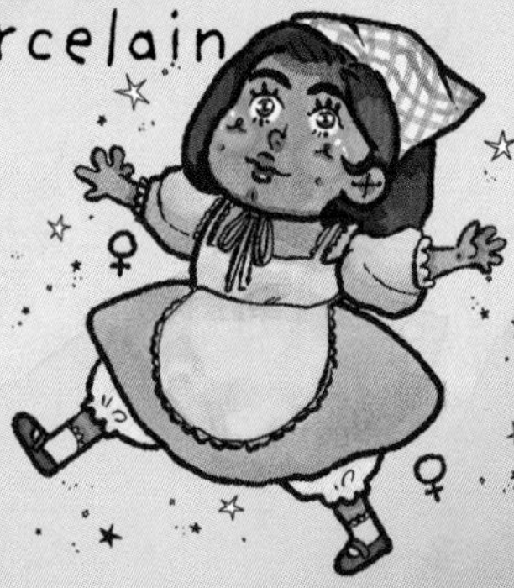

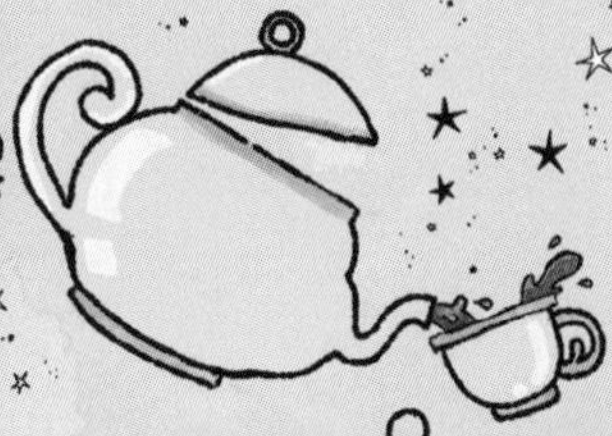

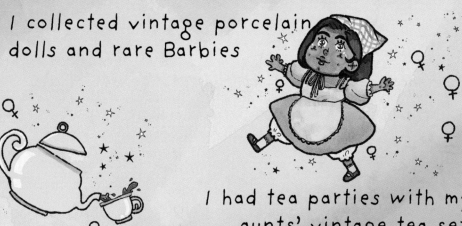

I had tea parties with my
aunts' vintage tea sets

And even now, I have a love
of big poofy glittery dresses

Granted, I was also
an avid gamer but...
that didn't feel
like it counted.

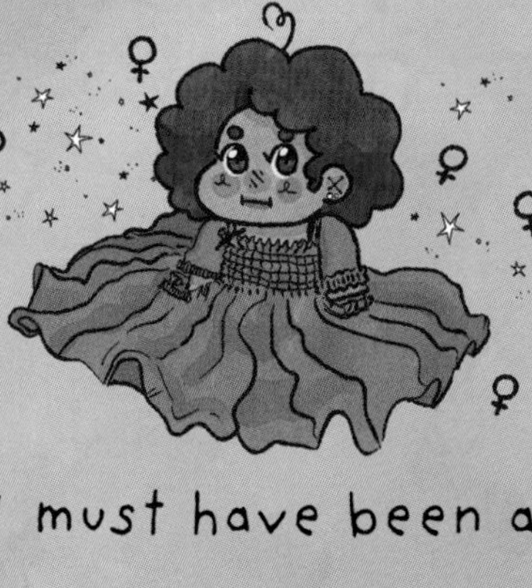

I liked girly things, so I must have been a girl.

Growing up I had long, flowing hair that made me feel like I was a princess. It was a badge of my femininity. It took a lot of chemicals to keep it to my parents' liking and one day, it all went bad.

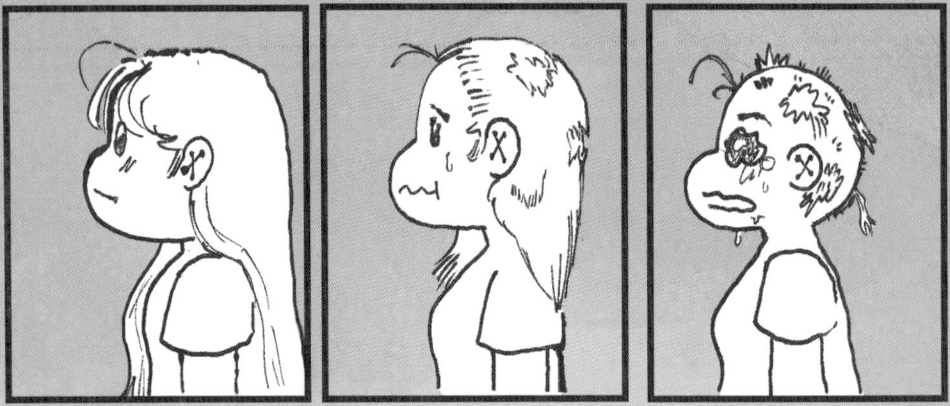

My hair was falling out in chunks.
My scalp was burned.
My mom had to take me to get a buzz cut.

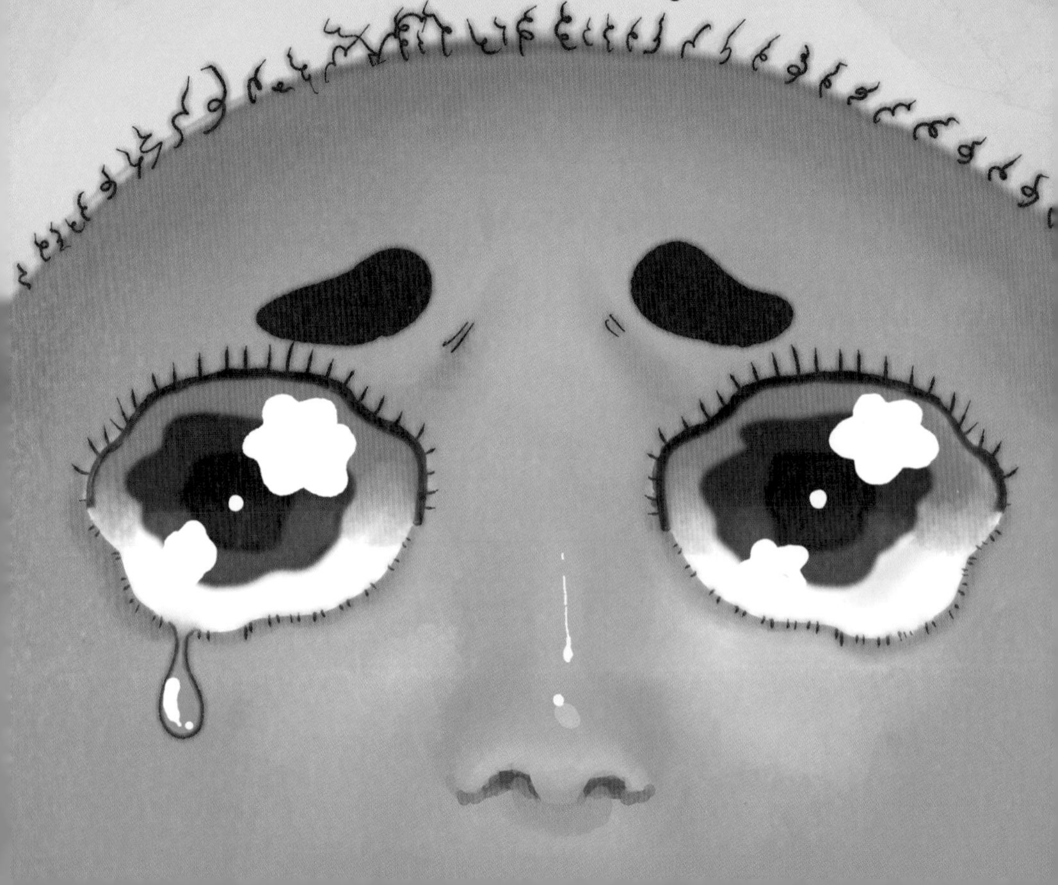

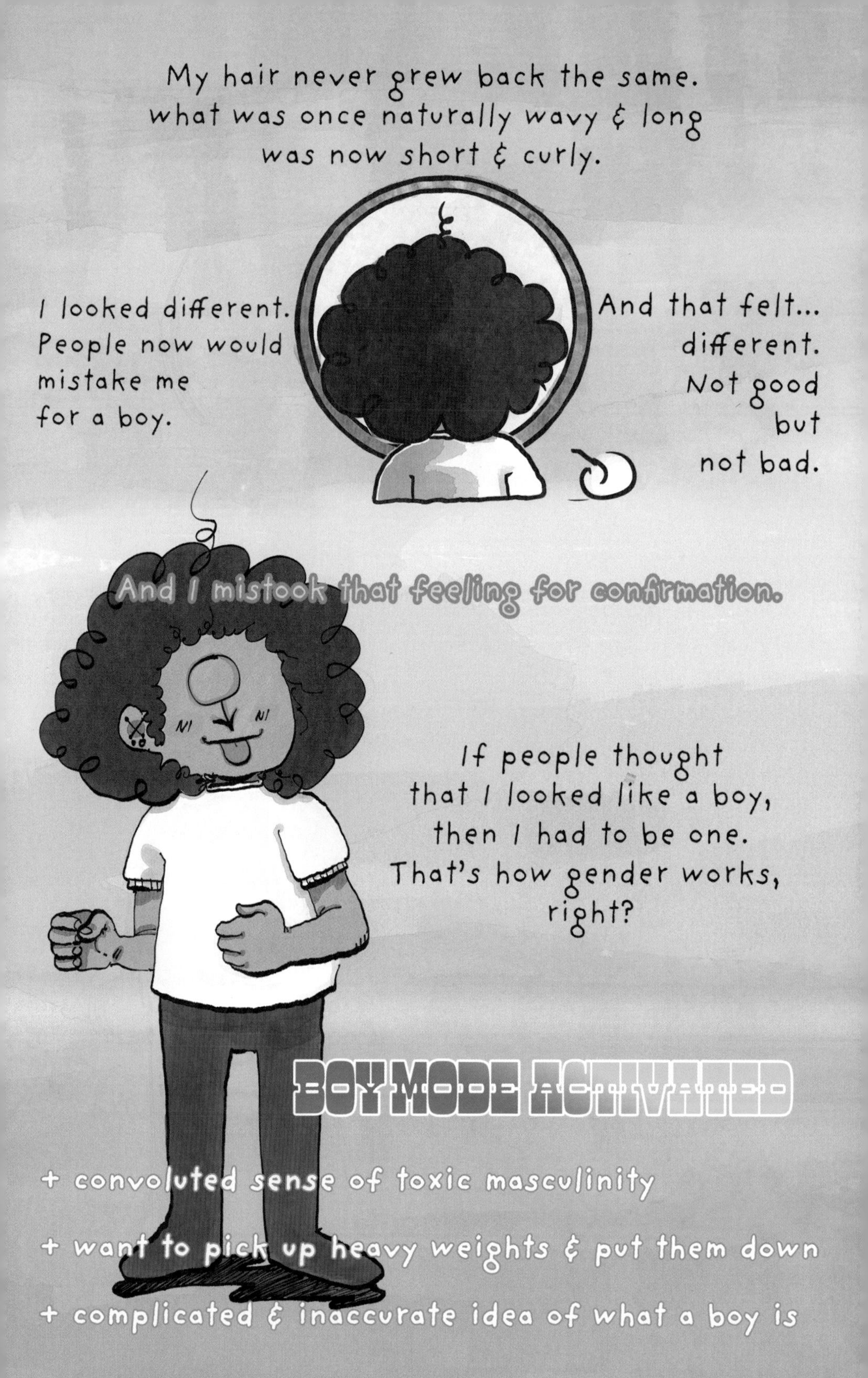
My hair never grew back the same. what was once naturally wavy & long was now short & curly.
I looked different. People now would mistake me for a boy.
And that felt... different. Not good but not bad.
And I mistook that feeling for confirmation.
If people thought that I looked like a boy, then I had to be one. That's how gender works, right?
BOY MODE ACTIVATED
+ convoluted sense of toxic masculinity
+ want to pick up heavy weights & put them down
+ complicated & inaccurate idea of what a boy is

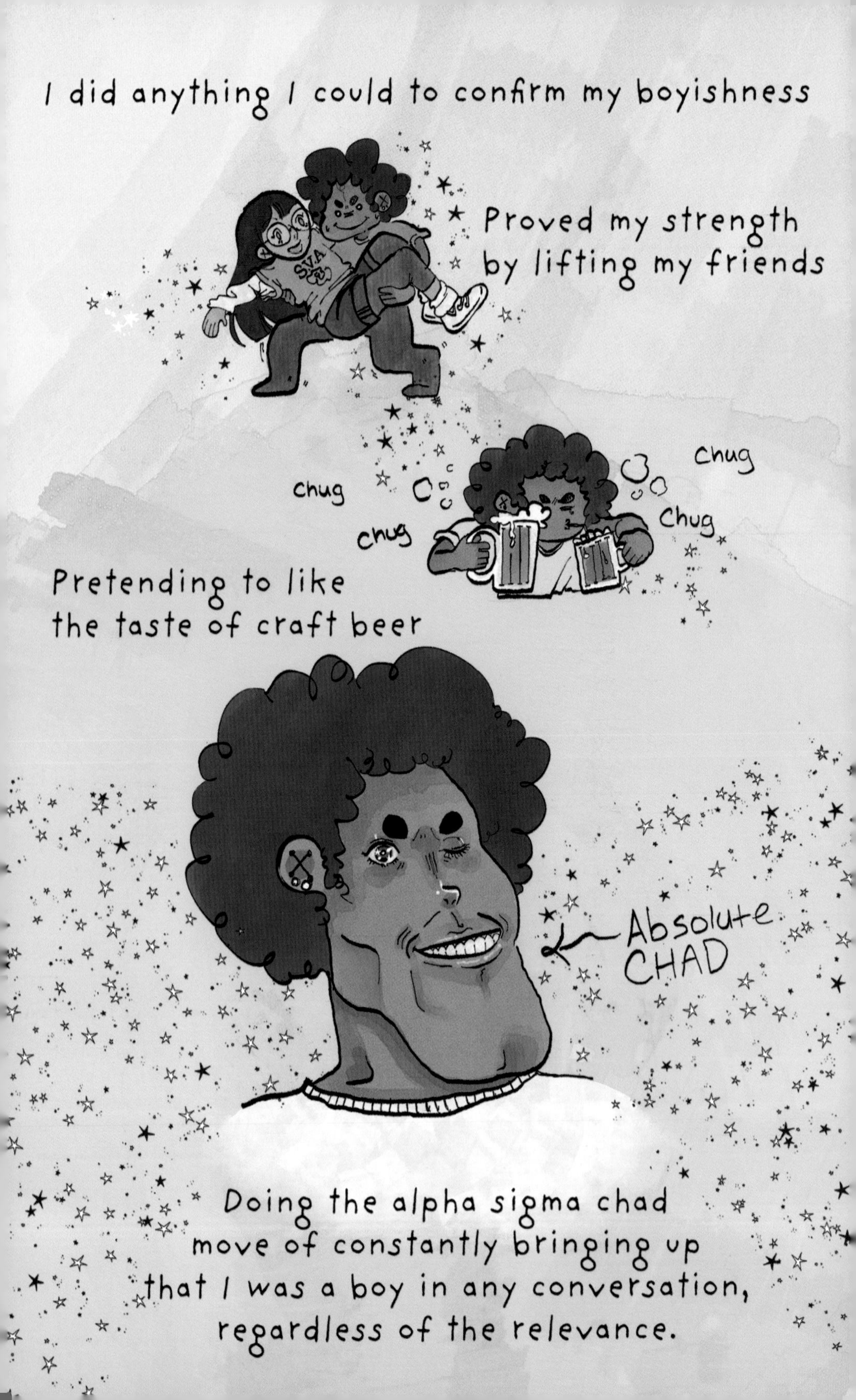
I did anything I could to confirm my boyishness
Proved my strength by lifting my friends
SVA
Chug
Chug
Chug
Chug
Pretending to like the taste of craft beer
Absolute CHAD
Doing the alpha sigma chad move of constantly bringing up that I was a boy in any conversation, regardless of the relevance.

I was overwhelmed with the concept of gender, I just didn't understand why neither girl nor boy felt right.

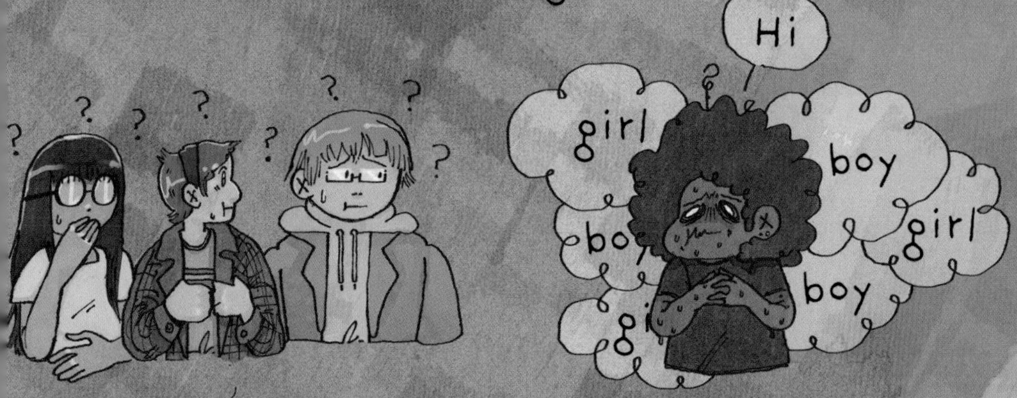
Hi
girl
boy
girl
boy

My friends picked up on my gender distress and we all sat down to piece together who I was.

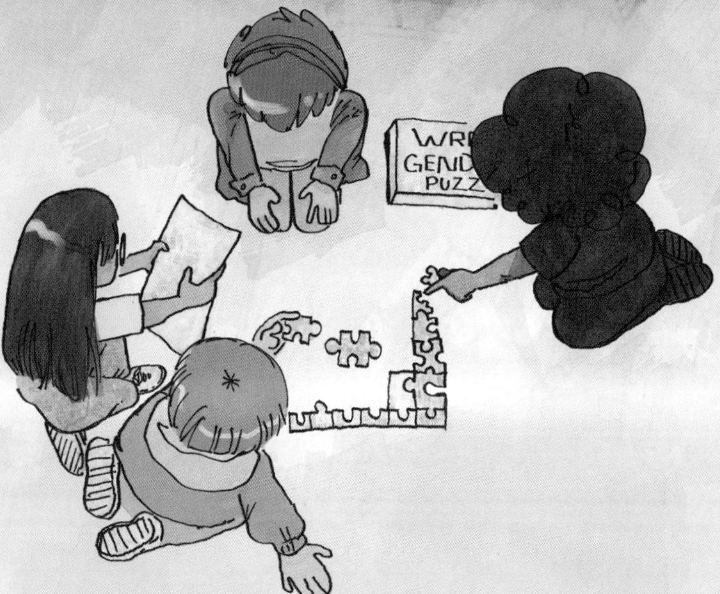

"Many hands help the plant grow."
An old saying I just made up.

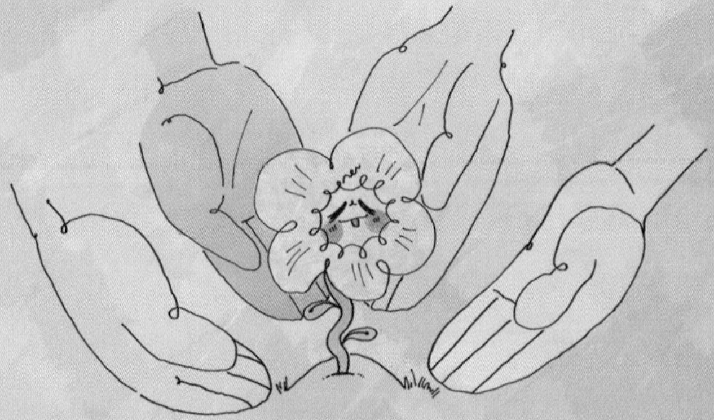

So much of my gender identity was lonely. I struggled by myself because honestly...

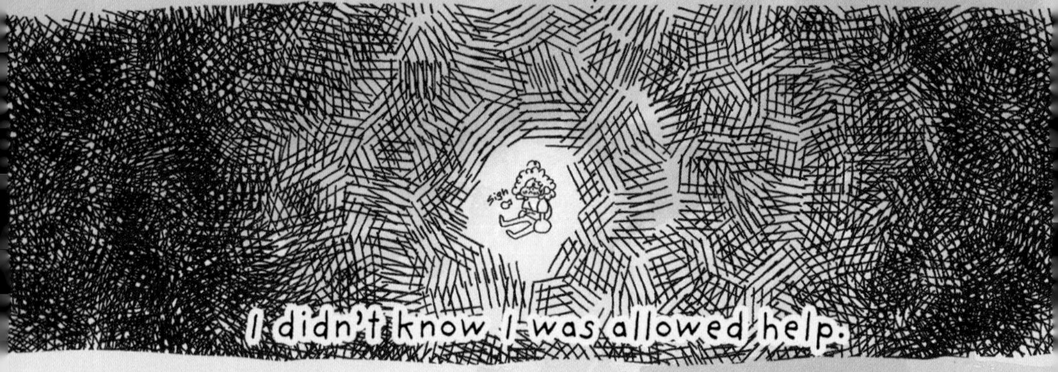
Sigh
I didn't know I was allowed help.

But being able to talk to my friends gave me something real to build my gender on.

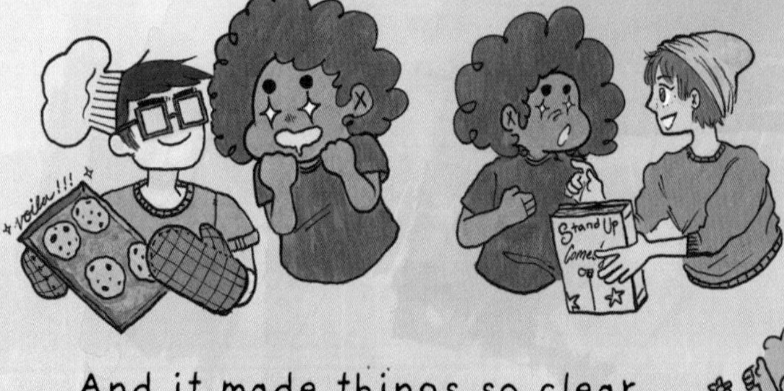
voila!!!
Stand Up

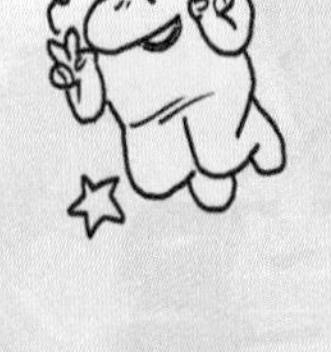

And it made things so clear...

I finally feel right as a nonbinary queer!

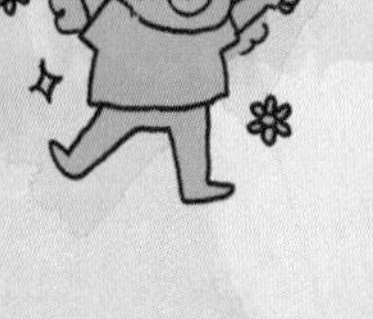

SALWA - DATOONIE
(THEY/THEM)

Hello! I'm a nonbinary digital artist who loves goofy, cartoony styles! Sharing my experience this way is something I never expected to be doing. I hope I can make a positive impact on those who read my small story, so they know they don't have to feel so alone.

You can find them online at:
datoonie.carrd.co

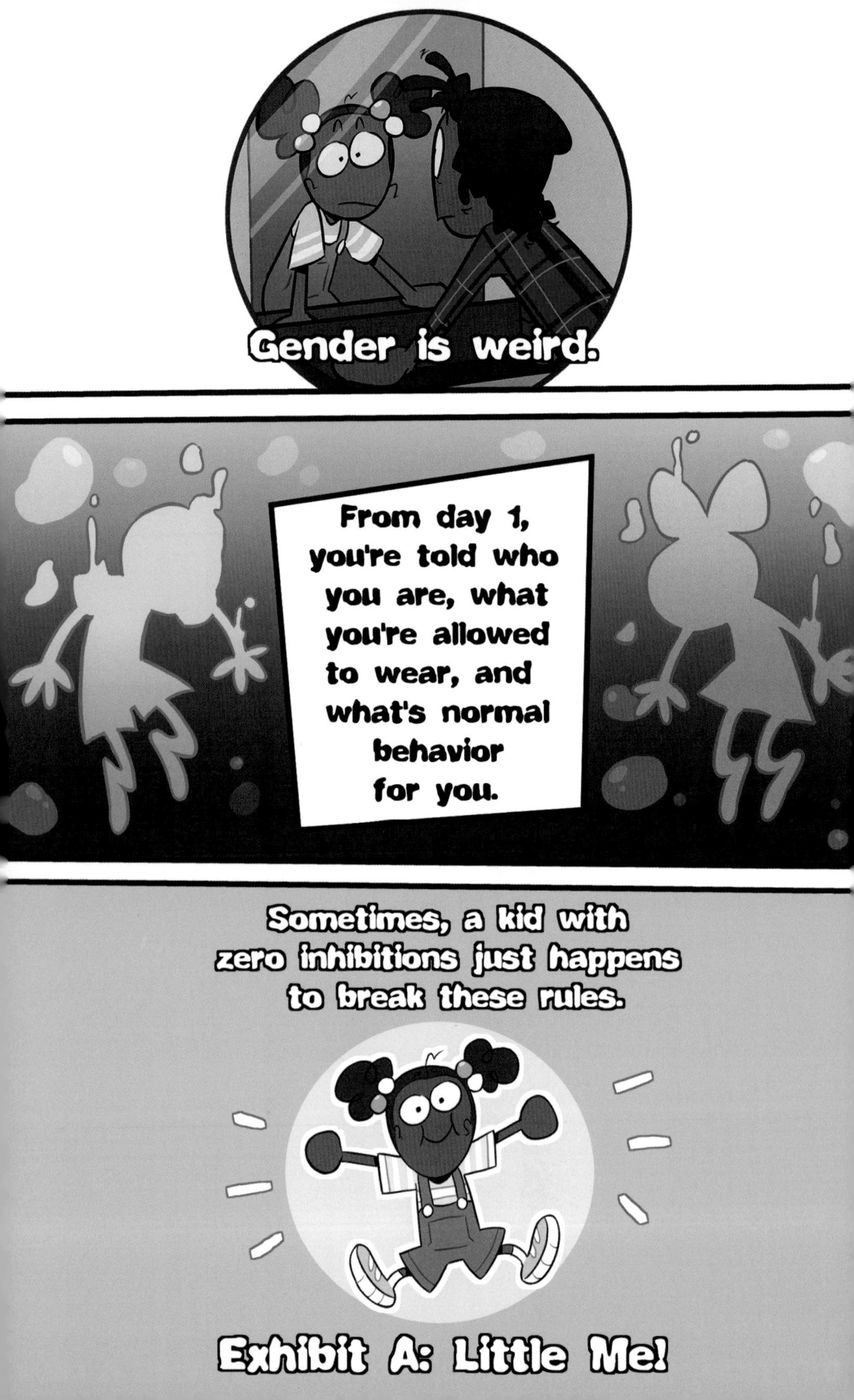
Gender is weird.
From day 1, you're told who you are, what you're allowed to wear, and what's normal behavior for you.
Sometimes, a kid with zero inhibitions just happens to break these rules.
Exhibit A: Little Me!

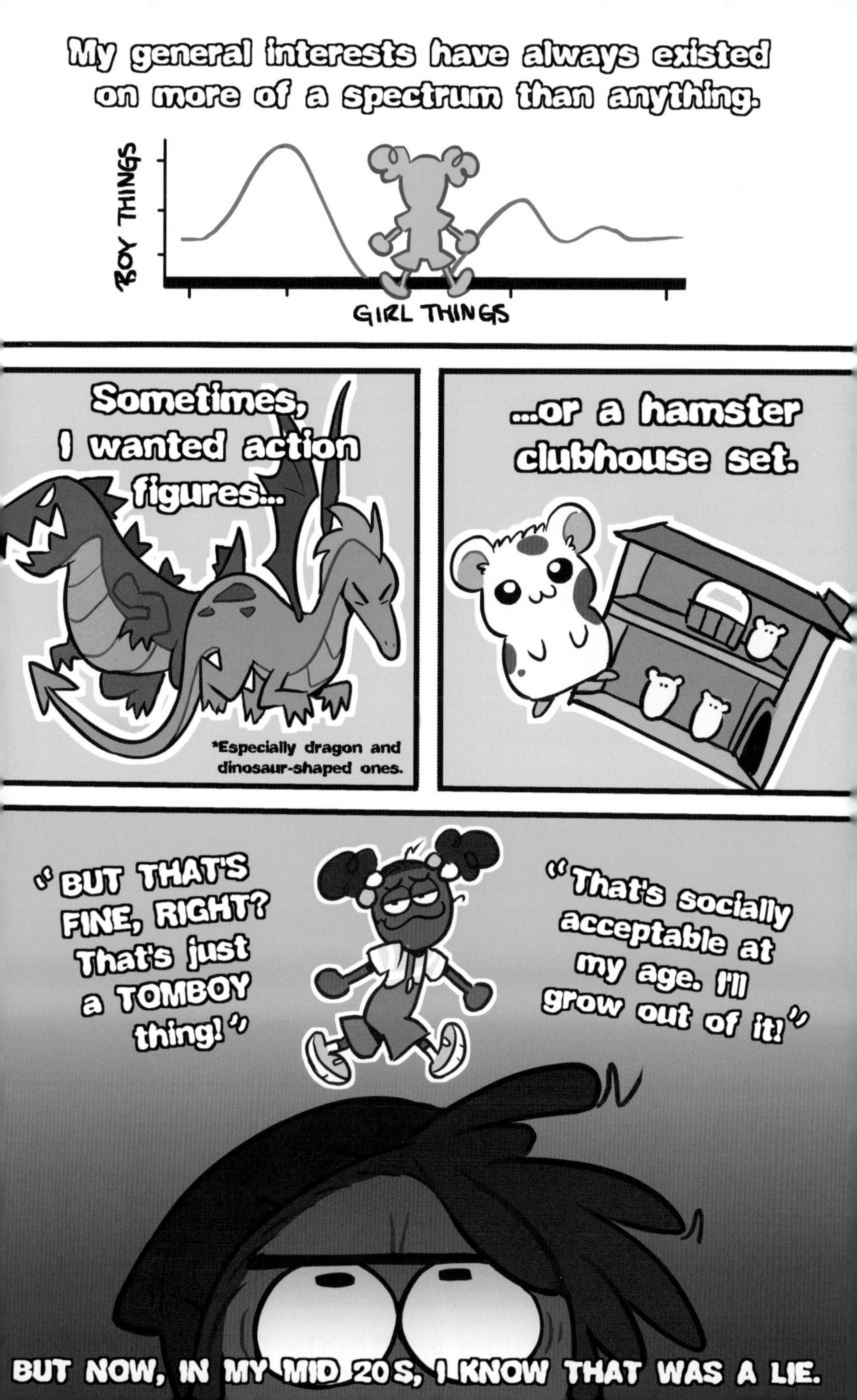

My general interests have always existed on more of a spectrum than anything.
BOY THINGS
GIRL THINGS
Sometimes, I wanted action figures...
*Especially dragon and dinosaur-shaped ones.
...or a hamster clubhouse set.
"BUT THAT'S FINE, RIGHT? That's just a TOMBOY thing!"
"That's socially acceptable at my age. I'll grow out of it!"
BUT NOW, IN MY MID 20S, I KNOW THAT WAS A LIE.

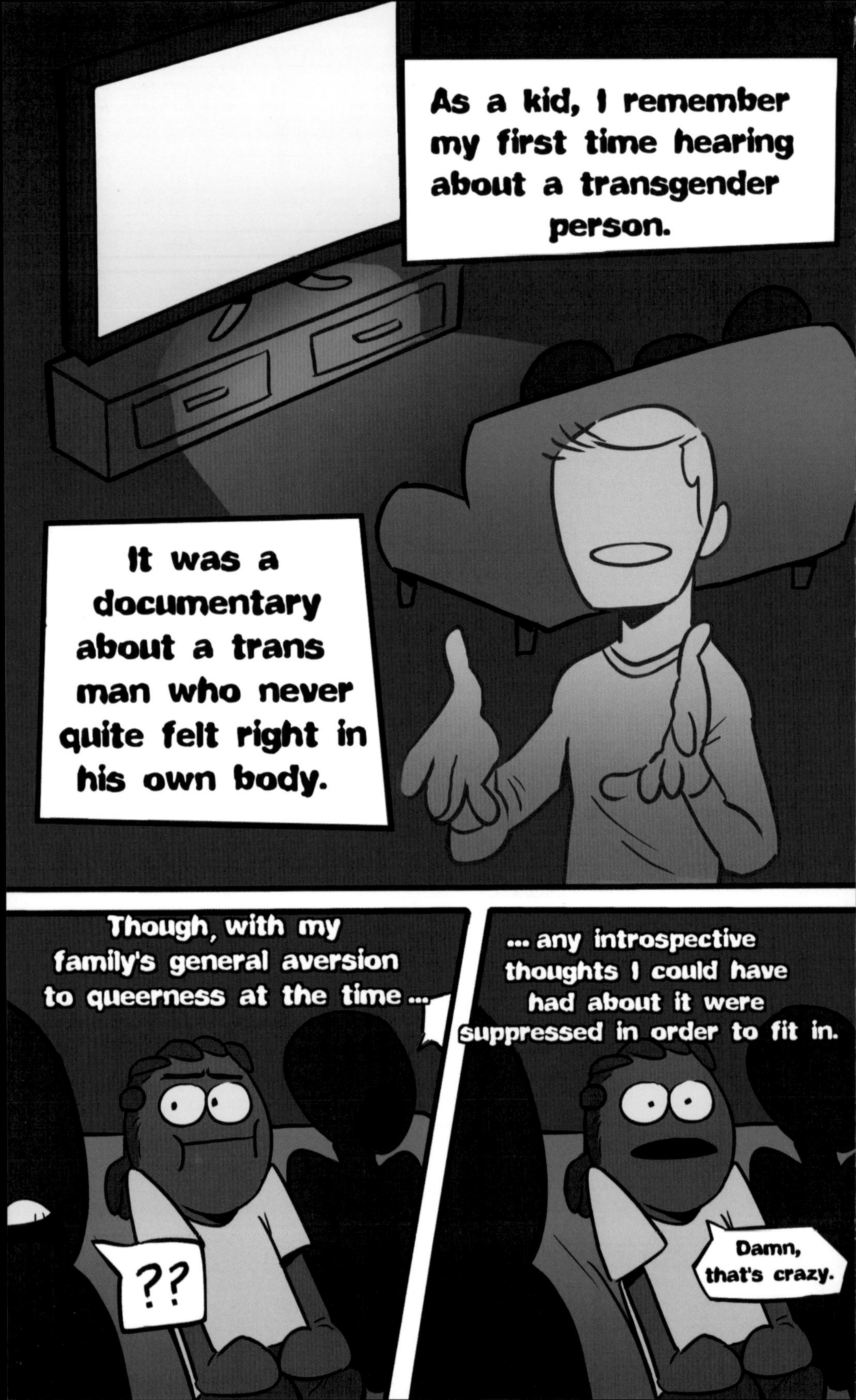
As a kid, I remember my first time hearing about a transgender person.
It was a documentary about a trans man who never quite felt right in his own body.
Though, with my family's general aversion to queerness at the time...
??
... any introspective thoughts I could have had about it were suppressed in order to fit in.
Damn, that's crazy.

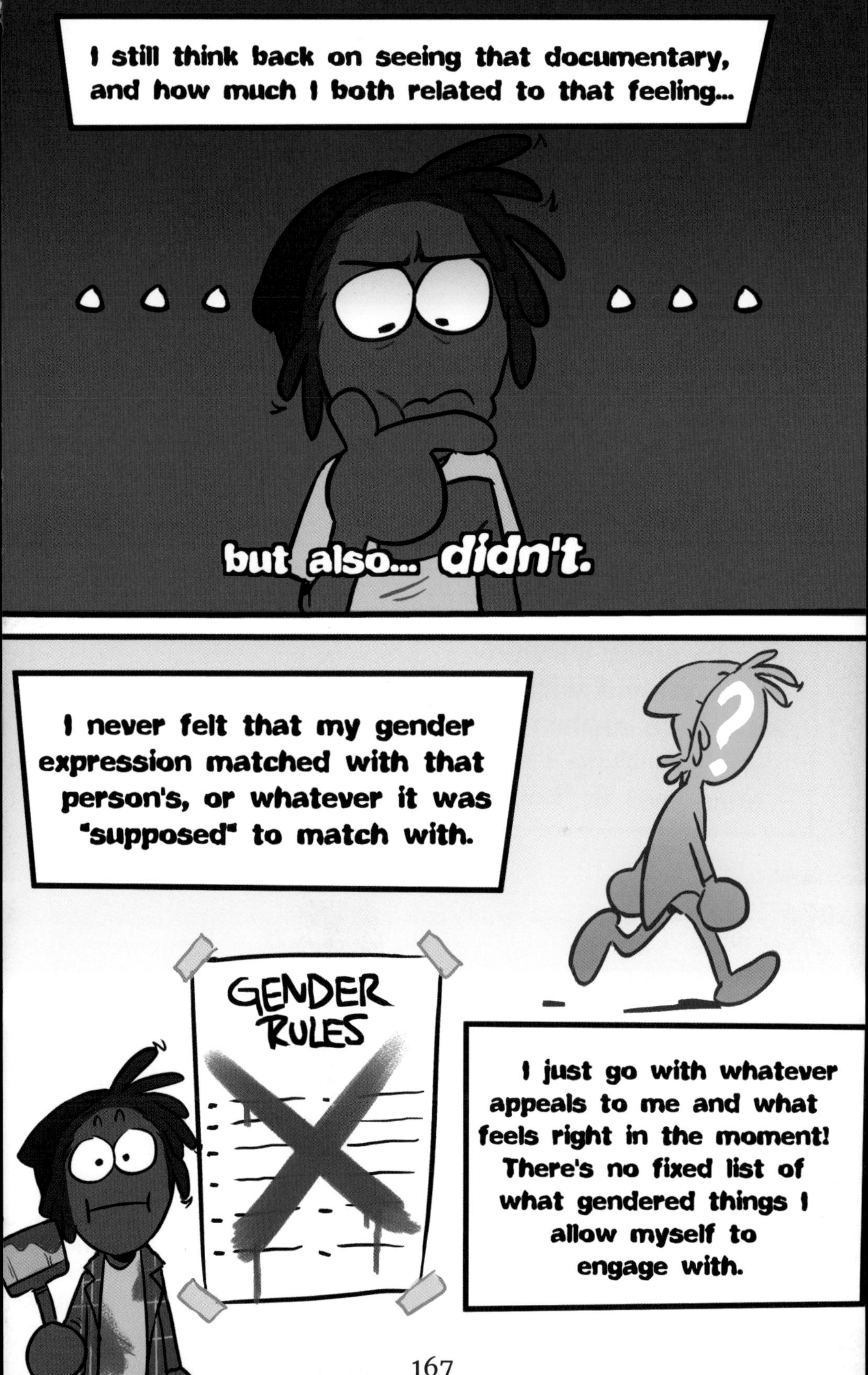
I still think back on seeing that documentary, and how much I both related to that feeling...
but also... didn't.
I never felt that my gender expression matched with that person's, or whatever it was "supposed" to match with.
GENDER RULES
I just go with whatever appeals to me and what feels right in the moment! There's no fixed list of what gendered things I allow myself to engage with.

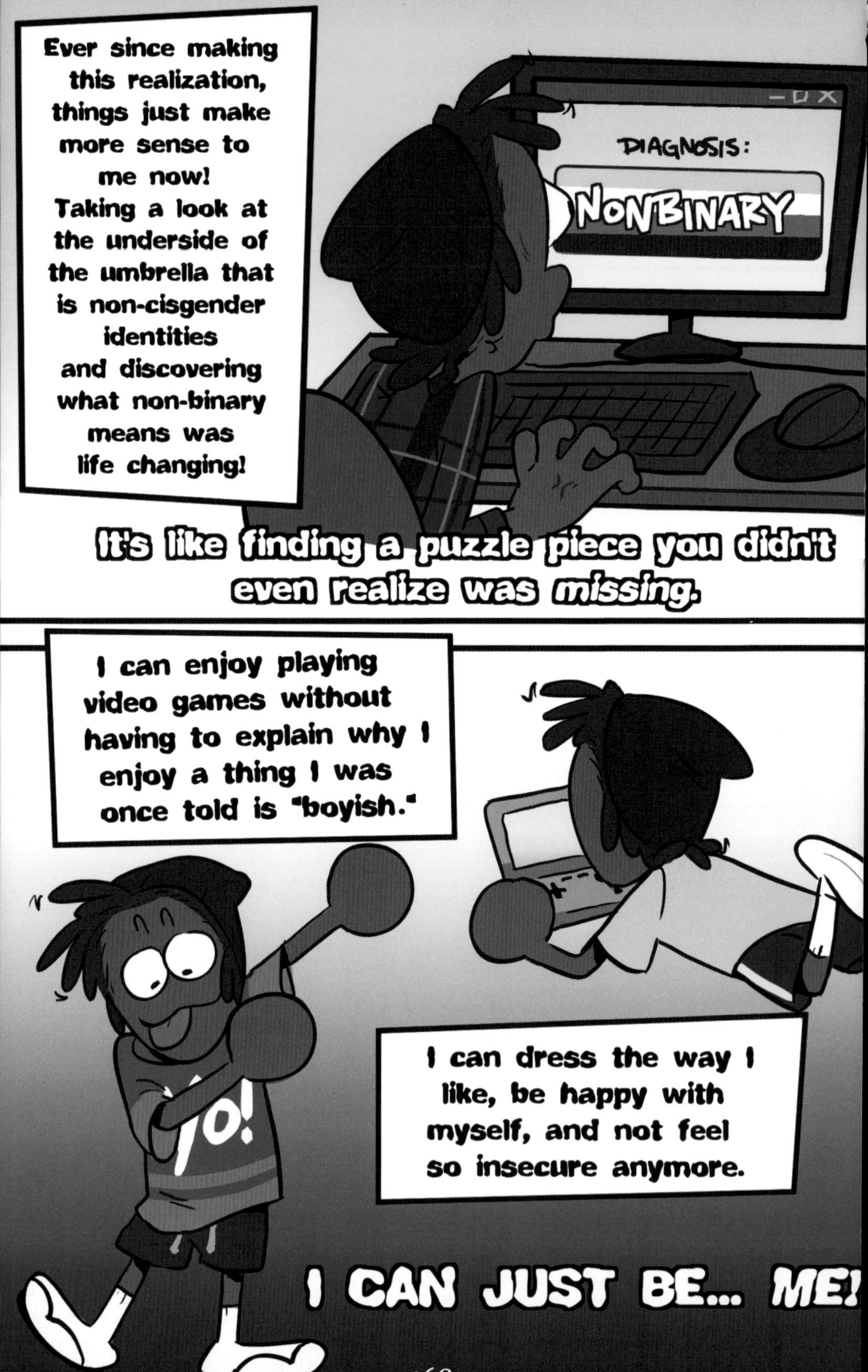
Ever since making this realization, things just make more sense to me now! Taking a look at the underside of the umbrella that is non-cisgender identities and discovering what non-binary means was life changing!
DIAGNOSIS:
NONBINARY
It's like finding a puzzle piece you didn't even realize was missing.
I can enjoy playing video games without having to explain why I enjoy a thing I was once told is "boyish."
I can dress the way I like, be happy with myself, and not feel so insecure anymore.
I CAN JUST BE... ME!

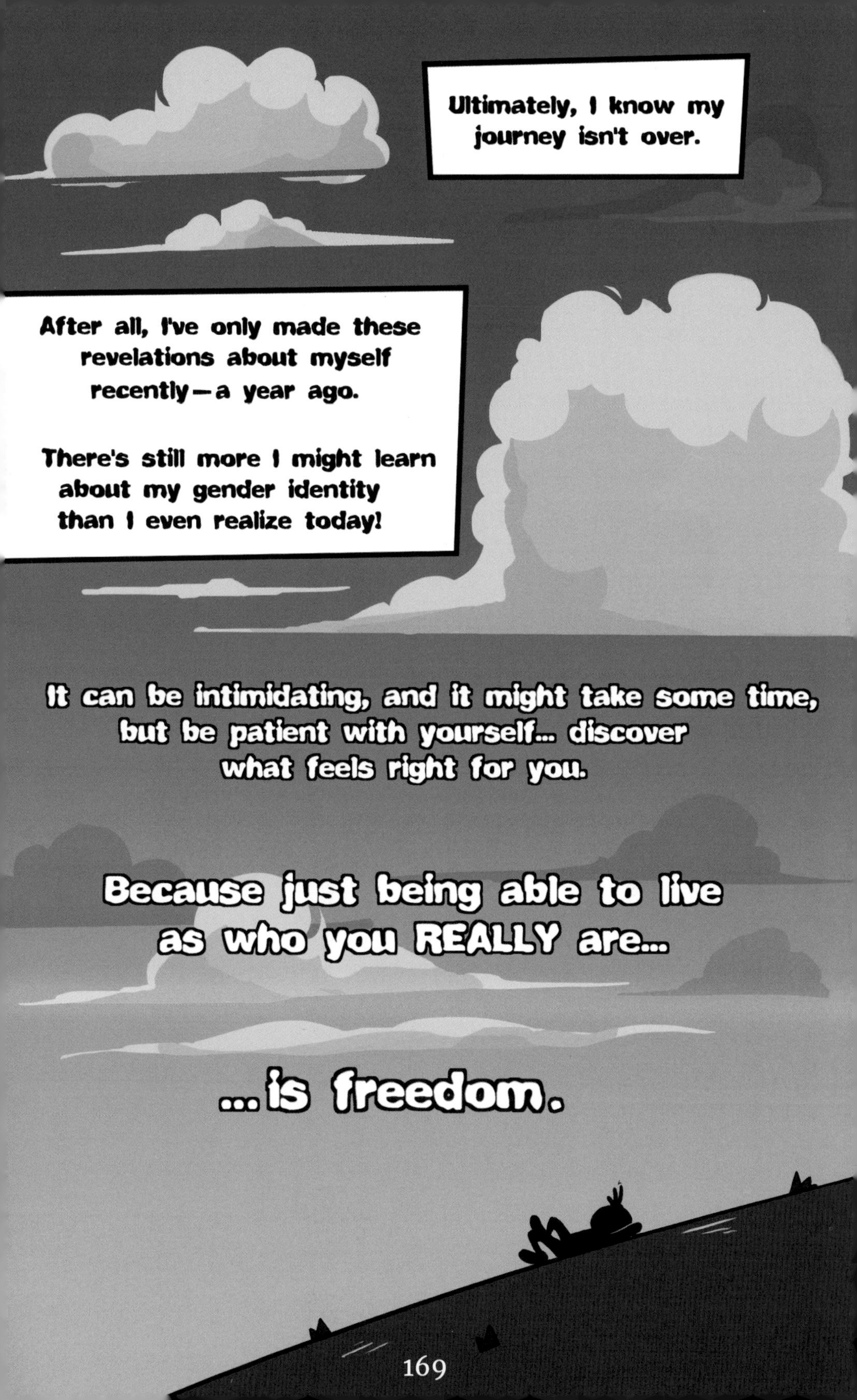
Ultimately, I know my journey isn't over.
After all, I've only made these revelations about myself recently—a year ago.
There's still more I might learn about my gender identity than I even realize today!
It can be intimidating, and it might take some time, but be patient with yourself... discover what feels right for you.
Because just being able to live as who you REALLY are...
...is freedom.

KYLA AIKO
(SHE/THEY)

Kyla is an Asian-American writer and artist who lives in a town with an ocean view. Their debut middle grade graphic novel, *Foxes, Fire, and Other Magic*, releases in Spring 2024 from Feiwel and Friends/Macmillan. In addition, they're also an assistant on the Webtoon Original *Everything is Fine*. In their spare time, you can find them making handmade noodles or listening to Mitski and Mao Buyi.

Visit their website:
aikosmith.com

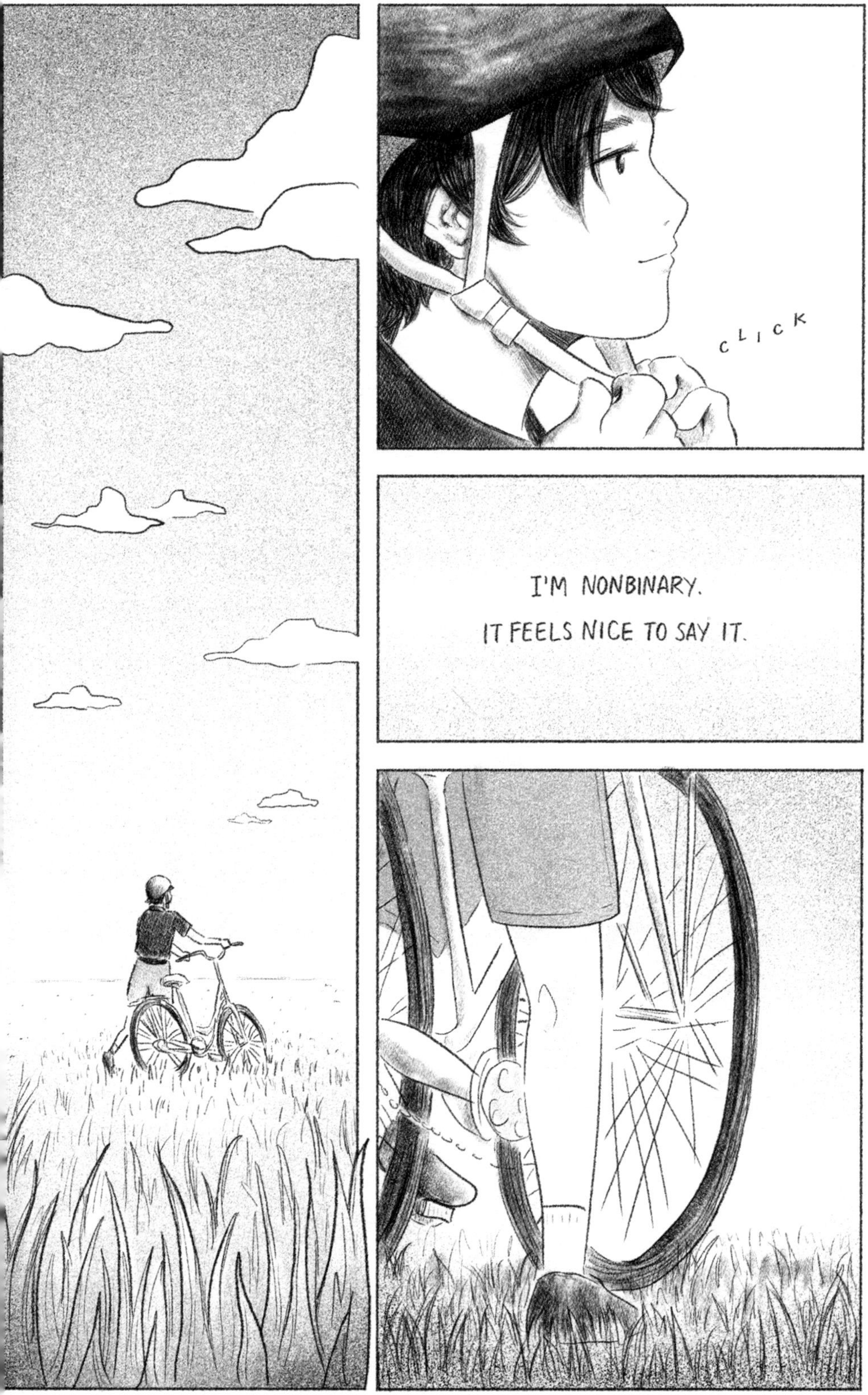
CLICK
I'M NONBINARY.
IT FEELS NICE TO SAY IT.

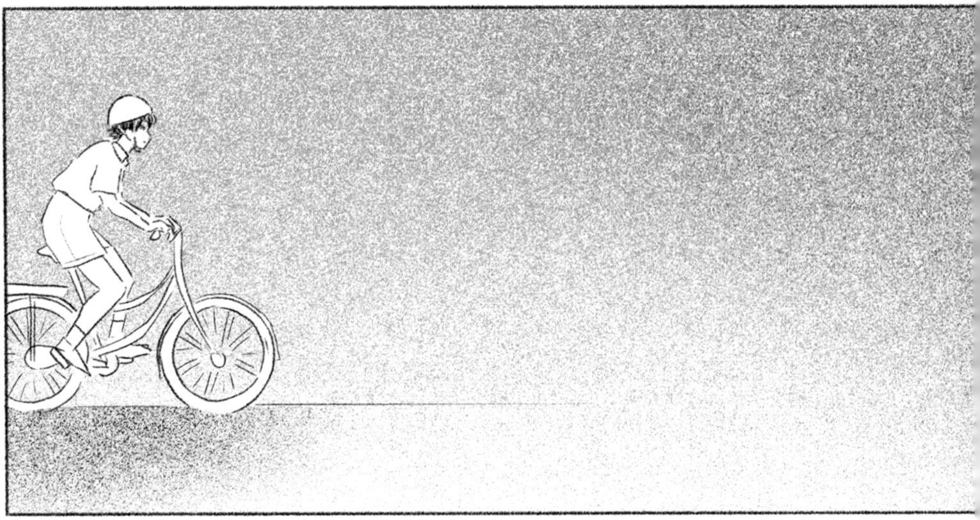

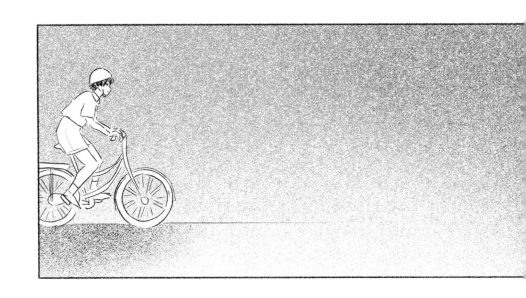

FOR A WHILE, I DIDN'T HAVE
WORDS FOR WHAT I FELT.

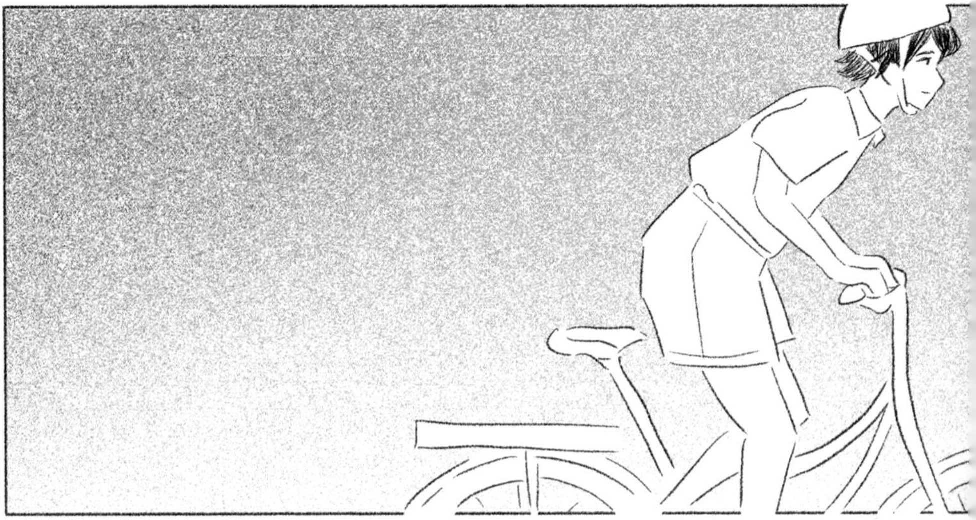

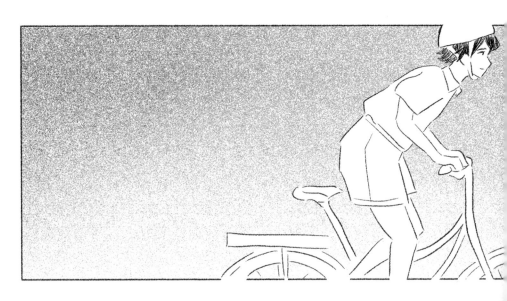

AND THAT WAS OKAY TOO.

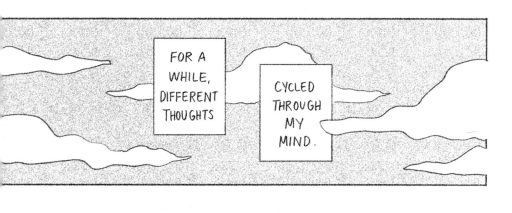

FOR A WHILE, DIFFERENT THOUGHTS CYCLED THROUGH MY MIND.

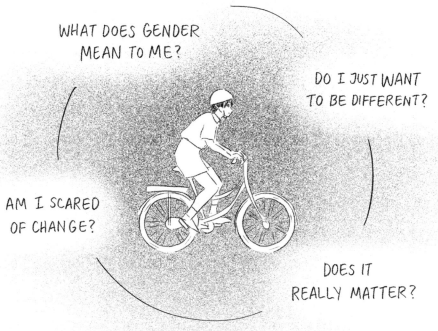

WHAT DOES GENDER MEAN TO ME?

DO I JUST WANT TO BE DIFFERENT?

AM I SCARED OF CHANGE?

DOES IT REALLY MATTER?

I HAD DOUBTS.

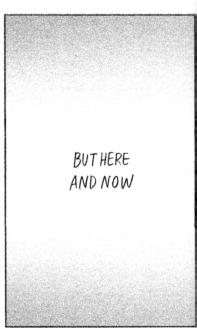

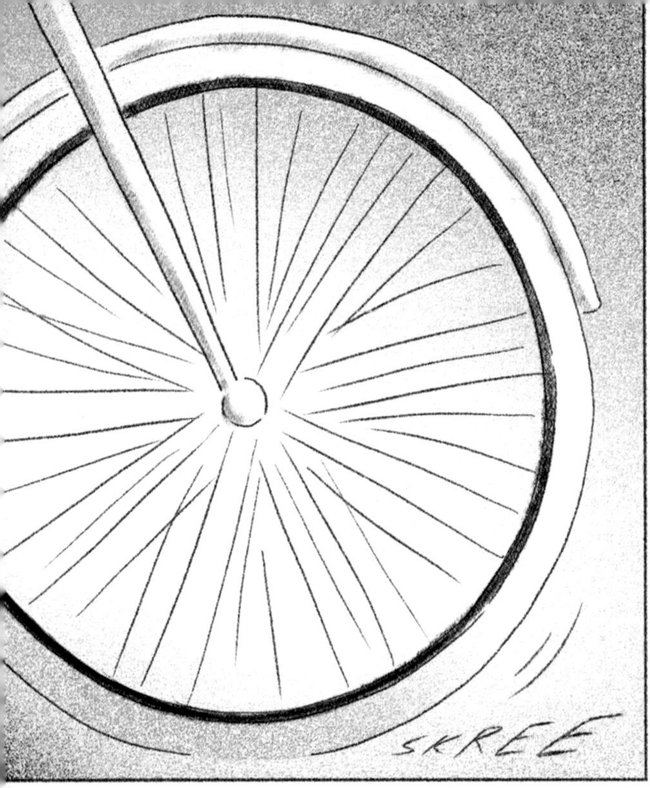
SKREE

BUT HERE
AND NOW

I KNOW HOW I FEEL.

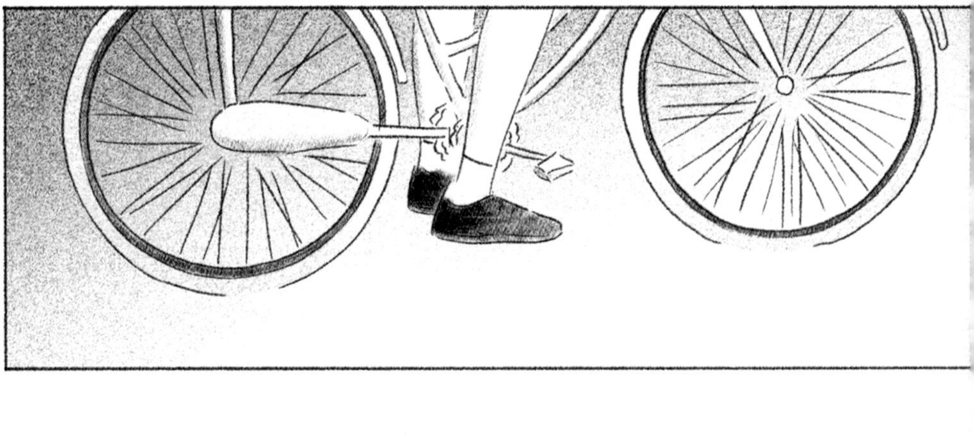

AND I KNOW WHO I AM.

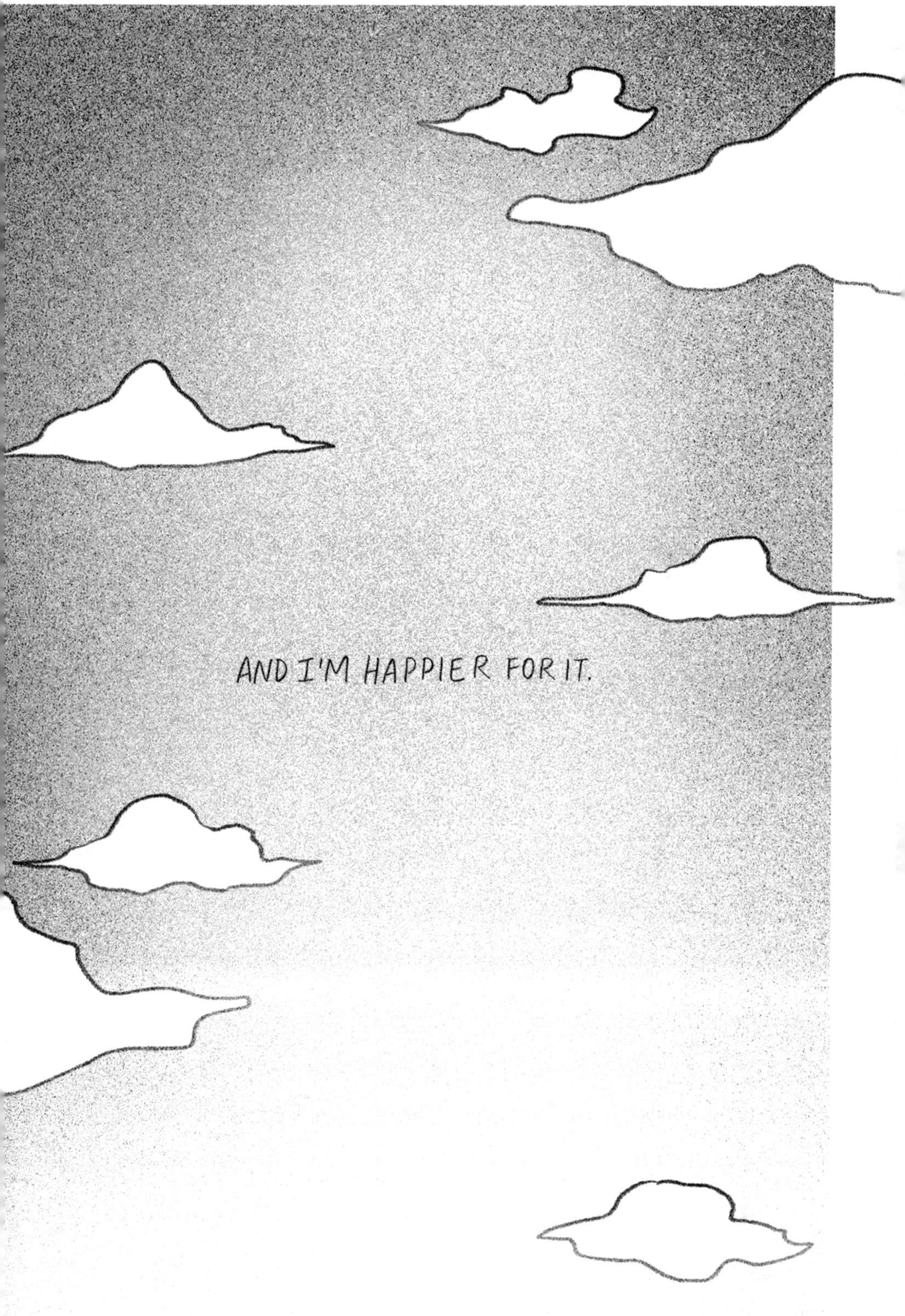
AND I'M HAPPIER FOR IT.

RESOURCES

CENTERLINK

An international non-profit organization with over 290 member LGBTQ centers worldwide that provides essential services and promotes growth, wellness, and connectivity in their communities.

lgbtcenters.org/LgbtCenters

GENDER SPECTRUM

An organization committed to the health and well-being of gender-diverse children and teens through education and support for families. They also offer training and guidance for educators, medical and mental health providers, and other professionals.

genderspectrum.org

PRISM COMICS

A non-profit organization and website where LGBTQ and LGBTQ-friendly comic creators network and share their comics and readers find works that speak directly to their experiences and lives.

prismcomics.org

TRANSGENDER TEEN SURVIVAL GUIDE

A blog that answers a variety of questions about gender identity and expressions.

transgenderteensurvivalguide.com

THE TREVOR PROJECT

A 24/7 crisis intervention helpline for LGBTQ+ youth.

thetrevorproject.org